D0363113

Introducing English Semantics

Introducing English Semantics is a comprehensive and accessible introduction to semantics, the study of meaning.

Focusing on the English Language, Charles W. Kreidler presents the basic principles of semantics. He explores how languages organize and express meanings through words, parts of words and sentences.

Introducing English Semantics:

- deals with relations of words to other words, and sentences to other sentences
- illustrates the importance of 'tone of voice' and 'body language' in face-to-face exchanges, and the role of context in any communication
- makes random comparisons of features in other languages
- explores the knowledge speakers of a language must have in common to enable them to communicate
- discusses the nature of language; the structure of discourse; the distinction between lexical and grammatical meaning
- examines such relations as synonymy, antonymy, and hyponymy; ambiguity; implication; factivity; aspect; and modality
- has a wealth of exercises
- includes a glossary of terms

Written in a clear, accessible style, *Introducing English Semantics* will be an essential text for any student following an introductory course in semantics.

Charles W. Kreidler is Emeritus Professor of Linguistics at Georgetown University. His previous publications include *The Pronunciation of English* (1989) and *Describing Spoken English* (1997).

C282215

Introducing English Semantics

Charles W. Kreidler

Routledge
Taylor & Francis Group

LONDON AND NEW YORK

ROUTLEDGE

"For Jim and Cynthia, Julie and Mike"

First published 1998
by Routledge
2 Park Square, Milton Park, Abingdon,
Oxon OX14 4RN

Simultaneously published in the USA
and Canada
by Routledge
270 Madison Ave, New York, NY 10016

Reprinted 1999, 2001, 2002, 2003,

2004, 2006

*Routledge is an imprint of the
Taylor & Francis Group*

© 1998 Charles W. Kreidler

Typeset in Times Ten by Keystroke,
Jacaranda Lodge, Wolverhampton

Printed and bound in Great Britain by
TJ International, Padstow, Cornwall

*British Library Cataloguing in
Publication Data*
A catalogue record for this book is
available from the British Library

*Library of Congress Cataloguing in
Publication Data*
Kreidler, Charles W., 1924–
    Introducing English semantics /
Charles W. Kreidler.
    Includes bibliographical references
1. English language – Semantics.
2. English language – Semantics –
Problems, exercises, etc.   I. Title.
PE1585.K69   1998
420.1′43–dc21   97–34090
                                              CIP

ISBN 0–415–18063–5 (hbk).
ISBN 0–415–18064–3 (pbk).

Contents

7 Reference   129

8 Sentences as arguments   155

9 Speech acts   175

13 The semantics of morphological relations   267

Preface

This textbook is intended to introduce principles of linguistic semantics at university level. In writing it I have had two groups of students in mind: I hope it will be useful for imparting a knowledge of semantics to students specializing in linguistics and that it also can be used in a general liberal-arts curriculum, in a course that leads non-specialists to think about the nature of language as they might otherwise not do. Little or no background in linguistics is assumed.

As the title suggests, the book differs from any other text now in print in its special focus on the English language and in the attention it gives to the lexical and grammatical devices that English employs to express meanings. Students should finish the course with a sense of what semantics is about and how semantic analysis is done; they should also have a deeper appreciation of English and of the nature of language in general.

I have avoided extensive formalism or an overly theoretical framework. And, since the field or semantics includes much more than an introductory text can cover, some instructors will want to supplement what is here. I hope the suggested reading lists at the end of each chapter will be of use for that purpose.

Learning linguistics requires a heavy involvement with data – words, phrases, sentences and more extended discourse – and I have tried to provide these both in the presentation of

concepts and in material for practice. The discussion, throughout the book, is carried along through numerous illustrative sentences which serve as points of departure for the concepts and definitions introduced. Technical terms are given in bold when they are first introduced; the most important of these are explained in the Glossary at the end of the book. When an asterisk precedes a phrase or sentence, it indicates that the construction is not acceptable; it is something that speakers of English do not say. Practice exercises in every chapter call on students to participate continually in the development of topics, mainly by leading them to examine their own use of the English language. Some of the exercises have obvious answers; in other instances it will be found that speakers of the language do not entirely agree about some meaning, or are not sure. Here group discussion can be a valuable part of the learning experience.

I am grateful to a number of anonymous readers of the manuscript for helpful suggestions and indeed for making me see my own weaknesses and strengths. The staff of Routledge have been remarkably kind and smoothly efficient in bringing this work to publication. Responsibility for the contents rests with me, of course.

C. W. K.

Chapter 1

The study of meaning

In this chapter we consider different approaches to the investigation of meaning. Linguistic semantics, the approach taken in this book, is concerned with what knowledge individual speakers of a language possess which makes it possible for them to communicate with one another. This leads us to a brief consideration of what language is and how a child acquires it. Finally we demonstrate some of the knowledge that all speakers have about the nature and expression of meaning in their language.

1.1 The systematic study of meaning

We are all necessarily interested in meaning. We wonder about the meaning of a new word. Sometimes we are not sure about the message we should get from something we read or hear, and we are concerned about getting our own messages across to others. We find pleasure in jokes, which often depend for their humor on double meanings of words or ambiguities in sentences. Commercial organizations spend a lot of effort and money on naming products, devising slogans, and creating messages that will be meaningful to the buying public. Legal scholars argue about the interpretation – that is, the meaning – of a law or a judicial decision. Literary scholars quarrel similarly over the meaning of some poem or story.

Three disciplines are concerned with the systematic study of 'meaning' in itself: psychology, philosophy and linguistics. Their particular interests and approaches are different, yet each borrows from and contributes to the others.

Psychologists are interested in how individual humans learn, how they retain, recall, or lose information; how they classify, make judgements and solve problems – in other words, how the human mind seeks meanings and works with them.

Philosophers of language are concerned with how we know, how any particular fact that we know or accept as true is related to other possible facts – what must be antecedent (a presupposition) to that fact and what is a likely consequence, or entailment of it; what statements are mutually contradictory, which sentences express the same meaning in different words, and which are unrelated. (There is more about presupposition and entailment later in this chapter.)

Linguists want to understand how language works. Just what common knowledge do two people possess when they share a language – English, Swahili, Korean or whatever – that makes it possible for them to give and get information, to express their feelings and their intentions to one another, and to be understood with a fair degree of success? Linguistics is concerned with identifying the meaningful elements of specific languages, for example, English words like *paint* and *happy* and affixes like the *-er* of *painter* and the *un-* of *unhappy*. It is concerned with describing how such elements go together to express more complex meanings – in phrases like *the unhappy painter* and sentences like *The painter is unhappy* – and telling how these are related to each other. Linguistics also deals with the meanings expressed by modulations of a speaker's voice and the processes by which hearers and readers relate new information to the information they already have.

Semantics is the systematic study of meaning, and linguistic semantics is the study of how languages organize and express meanings. Linguistic semantics is the topic of this book, but we need to limit ourselves to the expression of meanings in a single language, English. Here and there throughout the book we make comparisons with other languages, but these are meant to be illustrative of language differences, not full accounts of what differences exist.

1.2 The nature of language

All animals have some system for communicating with other members of their species, but only humans have a language which allows them to produce and understand ever-new messages and to do so without any outside stimulus. Bees, birds, dolphins and chimpanzees, among other animals, transmit and interpret a fixed number of messages that signal friendliness or hostility, the presence of food or of danger, or have to do with mating and care of offspring. But human language differs from these animal communication systems in two crucial ways (Hockett 1957: 574–85; Bickerton 1990:

10–16). First, animals can communicate only in response to some particular stimulus. Bees, when they have located a source of nectar in some group of plants, fly back to their hive and report this discovery by doing a dance that indicates the approximate direction and distance to the site, but in general non-human communication takes place on the spot, and is concerned with what is immediately present. No animal can tell another one about past experiences, and still less are they able to communicate their plans for the future. Humans alone are able to talk about vast numbers of things which come from accumulated knowledge, memory and imagination. Human language is **stimulus-free**. Second, while animals have only a fixed repertoire of messages, human language is **creative**: we are always producing new utterances which others understand; we comprehend new sentences which others have produced (as you understand this sentence, though it is not likely you have read it before).

The importance of stimulus-freedom and creativity is often overlooked. Throughout history various thinkers have tried to describe and explain language as if language is only related to the phenomenal world, the objects and events that we can observe through our senses. The simple fact is that the human mind deals easily and frequently with what does not exist, or what does not yet exist. Nobody can explain just how people are able to abstract elements from their sensory world and put these elements together in ways that are partly familiar, partly new. Yet that is just what happens when the architect envisions a building not yet erected, the composer puts together a concerto that is still to be played, a writer devises a story about imaginary people doing imaginary things, or when all of us take delight in nonsense and concoct names for things that might exist or might not.

The productivity of language is due to another feature which distinguishes our communication from that of other animals. While some bird songs are different arrangements of a repertory of elements, generally each signal emitted by a dog or donkey or dolphin is an indivisible unit, different from any other signal that the animal may utter. Human utterances, on the other hand, are composed of interchangeable units on two levels. An utterance consists of words in a particular sequence (at least one word and usually more than one), and a word consists of sound-units, or phonemes, in a particular order. A fairly small number of phonemes, which are meaningless, combine to make a vast number of meaningful words; for example, the English words *pat*, *tap* and *apt* consist of the same three phonemes, differently arranged, and these three phonemes occur over and over in combinations with a relatively small number of other phonemes to make up thousands of combinations that we call words.

This freedom from context is possible only because language is conventional, or has the feature of **arbitrariness**. There is no natural relation between the word *goat*, for instance, and what that word designates. Since ancient times people have been arguing about whether language is 'natural' or not. We can only conclude that it is natural for humans to have language – that a human child has a natural propensity to acquire the language which is used by the members of its family. But the ways in which meanings are communicated through language are not natural, nor is one language more natural than another.

All human societies have language and – contrary to some popular but unfounded opinions – every known language is complex and subtle, capable of expressing whatever its speakers need to express and capable of changing to meet the changing needs of the speakers.

1.3 Language and the individual

Every human child, with a few pathological exceptions, learns the language of the society in which it grows up. A child acquires the fundamentals of that language in the first five or six years of life – perhaps the greatest intellectual feat of its lifetime. How the child does this is one of the most intriguing puzzles in the study of human nature. All we know is that the child follows a general timetable in the process of acquisition. Just as the baby sits up, then crawls, stands and walks according to an innate timetable, so the child, at about the age of twelve months, begins to imitate its parents' ways of naming what is in the environment (*bed*, *bottle*, *doll*, *baby*, *mama*, etc.) and of telling the characteristics and events in which these things can be observed (*wet*, *empty*, *up*, *sit*, *all-gone*). Children who can hear learn speech and deaf children learn sign language, provided they are exposed to a medium which they can perceive. By the age of eighteen months the child is likely to be producing two-word utterances (*Baby up, Daddy byebye, Mama shoes, Dolly sit*). Soon utterances become more and more complex, and these utterances are clearly invented, not just repetitions of what parents may have said. Processes like making questions and negative statements are acquired – processes that go beyond a mere reflection of what is in the environment and make it possible for the child to express himself and interact with others (Lenneberg 1967; Clark and Clark 1977: 295–403).

The child acquires the ability to make use, as speaker and hearer, of the most important communication system of the community. Through this possession the individual enjoys a life of being able to inform, to express feelings and thoughts, perhaps to influence others in smaller or larger ways, and to learn.

Our ability to use language and our ability to think and conceptualize, develop at the same time and these abilities depend on each other. So, while we may retain some memory of learning to read and write, which we began around the age of six, we do not remember learning to understand what was spoken to us in the first four or five years of life and still less our struggles to speak. Thus it happens that the knowledge which each of us has about our native language is partly conscious and explicit but to a large extent un-conscious and implicit. We know the language but we do not fully know what we know. We know in the sense that we successfully communicate our intentions to others and we correctly interpret what others tell us – we know how to use the language. But we are not likely to be cognizant of the multiple meanings that common words can have, of the ways in which words are related to one another, of all the potential ambiguities that are always lurking in language.

Because language is creative, our communication is not restricted to a fixed set of topics; we constantly produce and understand new messages in response to new situations and new experiences. At the same time, language use is subject to very specific rules and constraints. There seems to be an infinite number of things we can say, but a language does not have an infinite number of words nor an infinite number of ways of combining words. If it had, we could not learn it.

What is the knowledge that a speaker of a language has about that language? Quite simply, a vocabulary and the ways to use it. More specifically, speakers have two vocabularies, one that they use in producing utterances and a somewhat larger one that is needed for understanding a variety of people. The vocabulary contains numerous names of people and places, as well as what we might think of as ordinary words. The productive vocabulary grows rapidly in early childhood, and for most people changes somewhat throughout life.

And what knowledge does one have that makes one capable of using the vocabulary, productively and receptively? We have to know how to combine the vocabulary items into utterances that will carry meanings for others and we have to grasp the meanings of complex utterances that others produce. With this goes the knowledge of how to pronounce words and utterances and how to recognize the pronunciation of words and utterances produced by others. So, for every word that speakers know, for production or recognition, they must know the pronunciation, how it fits into various utterances, and what it means.

Because we acquire our native language so early in life, our knowledge is mostly implicit. The linguist's task is to explicate this implicit knowledge. To describe a language the linguist writes a grammar. As Chomsky and Halle (1968: 1) put it, we use the term **grammar** to mean two things: the implicit knowledge that a speaker has and the explicit description and explanation of it by the linguist.

Whether we think of the grammar of a language as the knowledge that every speaker of the language has, or the explicit description made by a linguist, or both, the grammar must contain three parts. One part, of course, is semantics, the knowledge (from the point of view of the individual who speaks and hears others speaking), or the description (from a linguist's point of view), of meaningful units like words and meaningful combinations of words like sentences. This whole book is about semantics; here it is more appropriate to consider the other parts of a grammar.

Phonology is the knowledge, or the description, of how speech sounds are organized in a particular language – there are units called phonemes which combine in various possible ways (but not all possible ways) to express meaningful units such as words. These phonemes contrast with one another to make different units of meaning. Sometimes two words sound the same but have different meanings (homonyms), and sometimes sequences of words with the same pronunciation have different interpretations (ambiguity). We discuss homonyms in Chapter 3 and ambiguity in Chapters 3, 7 and 8. One part of phonology is prosody, the melodies with which utterances are spoken; different melodies can make differences of meaning. There is a section on prosody in Chapter 2.

Syntax is the knowledge, or the description, of the classes of words, sometimes called parts of speech, and of how members of these classes go together to form phrases and sentences. Syntax deals with grammatical categories like tense, number, aspect – categories that differ from language to language and which yet are present somehow in all languages. Another part of grammar is **morphology**, the description or the knowledge of word formation: the account of different forms of the 'same' word (cat, cats; connect, connecting, connected) and the derivation of different words which share a basic meaning (connect, disconnect, connection). It is impossible to explore semantics without also dealing with syntax (and vice versa) because the two are closely interrelated: the meaning of a sentence is more than the meanings of the words it contains, and the meaning of a word often depends partly on the company it keeps – what other words occur in the same sentence.

When we say that speakers of a language know the phonology of their language, we mean that they can accurately produce the sequences of sounds that signal different meanings and can recognize the sequences of sounds produced by other speakers and can connect these sequences to the meanings intended by those speakers. But ordinary speakers do not 'know' in the sense that they can describe the complex manipulations of their vocal organs in pronouncing. Any native speaker of English can pronounce and recognize *beat*, *bit*, *meat* and *meek*, but the ability to explain how *bit* differs from *beat* in articulation, and *beat* from *meat* and *meat* from *meek*, is not part of native-speaker knowledge.

Similarly, a speaker knows how to combine words into complex sentences and to grasp the meanings of complex structures that other speakers produce. Any adolescent or adult speaker can produce and can understand a sentence like *We shouldn't expect whoever took these things to be likely to want to return them*, but few speakers would be able to explain the syntax of it.

1.4 Demonstrating semantic knowledge

How can we explain the speaker's knowledge of meanings? Certainly we cannot expect that speakers can clearly define all the words they know. If that were our criterion, we should also expect speakers to be able to explain the meaning of every utterance they will ever produce or comprehend, which is, for all practical purposes, an infinite number. But the obvious thing is that speakers can make their thoughts and feelings and intentions known to other speakers of the language and can understand what others say. This ability requires possession of a vocabulary and for speakers to know how to pronounce every item in this vocabulary and how to recognize its pronunciation by other speakers. They know how to use the production vocabulary in meaningful sentences and to understand the sentences produced by others. And of course they know meanings – how to choose the items that express what they want to express and how to find the meanings in what other people say.

If it is hard to say what meaning is, it is fairly easy to show what knowledge speakers have about meanings in their language and therefore what things must be included in an account of semantics (Bierwisch 1970: 167–75; Dillon 1977: 1–6). The next ten paragraphs demonstrate ten aspects of any speaker's semantic knowledge.

1 Speakers know, in a general way, whether something is or is not meaningful in their language. For example, speakers of English can tell which of the following are meaningful in English.

1a Henry drew a picture.
1b Henry laughed.
1c The picture laughed.
1d Picture a Henry drew.

It is certainly not too much to assume that 1a and 1b are meaningful to speakers of English, while 1c and 1d are **anomalous** (examples of **anomaly**). Sentence 1c has the appearance of being meaningful and it might attain meaning in some children's story or the like, while 1d is merely a sequence of words.

2 Speakers of a language generally agree as to when two sentences have essentially the same meaning and when they do not.

2a Rebecca got home before Robert.
2b Robert got home before Rebecca.
2c Robert arrived at home after Rebecca.
2d Rebecca got home later than Robert.

Sentences that make equivalent statements about the same entities, like 2a and 2c, or 2b and 2d, are **paraphrases** (of each other).

3 Speakers generally agree when two words have essentially the same meaning – in a given context. In each sentence below one word is underlined. Following the sentence is a group of words, one of which can replace the underlined word without changing the meaning of the sentence.

3a   Where did you <u>purchase</u> these tools?
     use buy release modify take

3b   At the end of the street we saw two <u>enormous</u> statues.
     pink smooth nice huge original

Words that have the same sense in a given context are **synonyms** – they are instances of **synonymy** and are **synonymous** with each other.

4 Speakers recognize when the meaning of one sentence contradicts another sentence. The sentences below are all about the same person, but two of them are related in such a way that if one is true the other must be false.

4a   Edgar is married.
4b   Edgar is fairly rich.
4c   Edgar is no longer young.
4d   Edgar is a bachelor.

Sentences that make opposite statements about the same subject are **contradictory**.

5 Speakers generally agree when two words have opposite meanings in a given context. For example, speakers are able to choose from the group of words following 5a and 5b the word which is contrary to the underlined word in each sentence.

5a   Betty cut a <u>thick</u> slice of cake.
     bright new soft thin wet

5b   The train <u>departs</u> at 12:25.
     arrives leaves waits swerves

Two words that make opposite statements about the same subject are **antonyms**; they are **antonymous**, instances of **antonymy**.

6 Synonyms and antonyms have to have some common element of meaning in order to be, respectively, the same or different. Words can have some element of meaning without being synonymous or

antonymous. For example, we should all agree that in each of the following groups of words, 6a and 6b, all but one of the words have something in common. Which is the word that doesn't belong?

6a   street lane road path house avenue
6b   buy take use steal acquire inherit

The common element of meaning, shared by all but one word in 6a and by all but one item in 6b, is a **semantic feature**.

7 Some sentences have double meanings; they can be interpreted in two ways. Speakers are aware of this fact because they appreciate jokes which depend on two-way interpretation, like the following.

7a   Marjorie doesn't care for her parakeet.
      (doesn't like it; doesn't take care of it)

7b   Marjorie took the sick parakeet to a small animal hospital.
      (small hospital for animals; hospital for small animals)

A sentence that has two meanings is **ambiguous** – an example of **ambiguity**.

8 Speakers know how language is used when people interact. If one person asks a question or makes a remark, there are various possible answers to the question or replies one might make to the remark. Thus for the question in 8a some answers are suggested, of which all but one might be appropriate. Similarly the statement in 8b is followed by several possible rejoinders, all but one of which could be appropriate.

8a   When did you last see my brother?
      Ten minutes ago. Last Tuesday. Very nice.
      Around noon. I think it was on the first of June.

8b   There's a great new comedy at the Oldtown Playhouse.
      So I've heard. What's it called? When did it open?
      So do I. Are you sure it's a comedy?

When a question and an answer, or any two utterances, can go together in a conversation and the second is obviously related to the first, they constitute an **adjacency pair**. The ability to deal with adjacency pairs is part of any speaker's implicit knowledge.

9 Speakers are aware that two statements may be related in such a way that if one is true, the other must also be true.

9a   There are tulips in the garden.
9b   There are flowers in the garden.
9c   The ladder is too short to reach the roof.
9d   The ladder isn't long enough to reach the roof.

These pairs of sentences are examples of **entailment**. Assuming that 9a and 9b are about the same garden, the truth of 9a **entails** the truth of 9b, that is, if 9a is true, 9b must also be true. Likewise, assuming the same ladder and roof, the truth of 9c entails the truth of 9d.

10 Speakers know that the message conveyed in one sentence may presuppose other pieces of knowledge. For instance, if 10a is accepted as true, 10b–10e must also be accepted as true.

10a   Andy Murfee usually drives his Datsun to work.
10b   There is a person named Andy Murfee.
10c   Andy Murfee works.
10d   There is a Datsun that belongs to Andy Murfee.
10e   Andy Murfee knows how to drive an automobile.

The meaning of sentence 10a **presupposes** what is expressed in 10b, c, d and e. The latter are **presuppositions** of 10a. Note that a presupposition does not establish the truth of anything. Sentence 10a is meaningful as it is, but it is true only if there is a person named Andy Murfee, who works and owns a Datsun, etc. The sentence is presented AS IF there is a person named Andy Murfee. (There probably is not since we created the sentence for demonstration, just as the writer of a child's arithmetic textbook turns out problems that begin "Timmy Blake has four apples . . . ")

These ten terms have been introduced to show the latent knowledge that people have about their language. We are not suggesting that the points illustrated make up a test that anyone can deal with successfully. People differ considerably, and circumstances differ considerably, so that the way individuals behave in a given situation is not necessarily an indication of what their deeper competence is. Personality factors, such as willingness to cooperate, memory, attention, recent experience, can greatly affect performance. We only want to indicate the general implicit knowledge that speakers have about meaning in their language.

Summary

The study of meaning can be undertaken in various ways. Linguistic semantics is an attempt to explicate the knowledge of any speaker of a language which allows that speaker to communicate facts, feelings, intentions and products of the imagination to other speakers and to understand what they communicate to him or her. Language differs from the communication systems of other animals in being stimulus-free and creative. Early in life every human acquires the essentials of a language – a vocabulary and the pronunciation, use and meaning of each item in it. The speaker's knowledge is largely implicit. The linguist attempts to construct a grammar, an explicit description of the language, the categories of the language and the rules by which they interact. Semantics is one part of the grammar; phonology, syntax and morphology are other parts.

Speakers of a language have an implicit knowledge about what is meaningful in their language, and it is easy to show this. In our account of what that knowledge is, we introduced ten technical terms: anomaly; paraphrase; synonymy; semantic feature; antonymy; contradiction; ambiguity; adjacency pairs; entailment and presupposition.

PRACTICE 1.1

Below are ten pairs of sentences. In each pair assume that the first sentence is true. Then decide what we know about the second sentence, which has the same topic(s). If the first is true, must the second also be true (T)? Or if the first is true, must the second be false (F)? Or does the truth of the first tell us nothing about the truth of the second (X)?

1a   Rose is married to Tom.
1b   Rose is Tom's wife.
2a   David is an unmarried adult male.
2b   David is a bachelor.
3a   This knife is too dull to cut the rope.
3b   This knife isn't sharp enough to cut the rope.
4a   Victoria likes to sing.
4b   Victoria doesn't sing.

5a   Harold has been here for an hour.
5b   Harold is tired of waiting.
6a   Mr Bond has given up smoking.
6b   Mr Bond used to smoke.
7a   Mr Bond still smokes.
7b   Mr Bond used to smoke.
8a   Oil paintings are more expensive than watercolors.
8b   Watercolors cost more than oil paintings.
9a   The Carlson Hotel is more than a century old.
9b   The Carlson Hotel has operated for more than a century.
10a Alice invited some friends to lunch.
10b Alice has friends.

Suggested reading

1 General introductions to linguistic semantics are far from numerous. The following can be recommended for the beginning student who wants collateral or supplemental reading in the subject:

Allan, Keith (1986). *Linguistic Meaning* (2 vols).
Dillon, George (1977). *Introduction to Contemporary Linguistic Semantics*.
Hofmann, Th. R. (1993). *Realms of Meaning: An Introduction to Semantics*.
Hurford, J.R. and Brendan Heasley (1983). *Semantics: A Coursebook*.
Leech, Geoffrey N. (1981). *Semantics*. 2nd edn.
Lyons, John (1995). *Linguistic Semantics: An Introduction*.
Nilsen, D. L. F. and Nilsen, A. (1975). *Semantic Theory: A Linguistic Perspective*.
Palmer, Frank R. (1981). *Semantics*. 2nd edn.
Saeed, John I. (1997). *Semantics*.

The more advanced student will want to be familiar with:

Chierchia, Gennaro and Sally McConnell-Ginet (1990). *Meaning and Grammar: An Introduction to Semantics*, as well as:
Frawley, William (1992). *Linguistic Semantics*.
Kempson, R. M. (1977). *Semantic Theory*.
Lyons, John (1977). *Semantics* (2 vols).

The logical formulation of semantic statements is well explicated in:

Cann, Ronnie (1993). *Formal Semantics: An Introduction.*

2   A very readable discussion of (non-human) animal communication and of the biological basis for humans' language capacity is Wardhaugh (1993), chapters 2 and 3.

3   Full details of these and all other books cited in Suggested reading lists can be found in the Bibliography at the end of this book.

Language in use

The previous chapter dealt with the general knowledge that people have about the language they speak. However, people apply this knowledge when they speak to one another and understand one another in specific acts of communication. In this chapter we look more at the specific features of communication, beginning with observations about non-linguistic **signs** and how we get meanings from them. We introduce a distinction between a **sentence**, a language construction, and an **utterance**, a particular act of speaking or writing. An utterance is typically part of a larger **discourse**. In spoken discourse meanings are partly communicated by the emphases and melodies that are called **prosody**. Vocal and gestural signs can also be the means of transmitting meanings.

2.1 Pragmatics

Chapter 1 discussed the general knowledge that speakers have about their language, but speakers also know how to use this knowledge when they listen and read, when they speak and write – when they communicate. We need, then, to consider what kind of knowledge a person has to have, and use, in particular acts of communication. For a question like "When did you last see my brother?," there are numerous answers that are linguistically appropriate – "Around noon," "Last Tuesday," "I think it was on June first," and so on – but on a specific occasion only one answer (or its paraphrase) is correct. What is correct in a particular instance is, we may say, pragmatically appropriate.

Pragmatics is another branch of linguistics that is concerned with meaning. Pragmatics and semantics can be viewed as different parts, or different aspects, of the same general study. Both are concerned with people's ability to use language meaningfully. While semantics is mainly concerned with a speaker's competence to use the language system in producing meaningful utterances and processing (comprehending) utterances produced by others, the chief focus of pragmatics is a person's ability to derive meanings from specific kinds of speech situations – to recognize what the speaker is referring to, to relate new information to what has gone before, to interpret what is said from background knowledge about the speaker and the topic of discourse, and to infer or 'fill in' information that the speaker takes for granted and doesn't bother to say. Obviously the boundary between semantics and pragmatics is vague, and at the present time various scholars are apt to disagree about where the boundary is. Some of the contents of this chapter may be considered more 'pragmatics' than 'semantics' by some people.

2.2 Natural and conventional signs

A language is a system of symbols through which people communicate. The symbols may be spoken, written, or signed with the hands.

People who use a language to communicate with one another constitute a society, a language community – the English language community, for instance. Within that community there are differences in the way different people use the language, chiefly of a geographical or social nature. When people who have the same native language can understand one another but still notice consistent differences in each other's speech, we say they speak different **dialects** of that language. It is easy to illustrate dialect differences: vocabulary differences like *petrol* versus *gasoline*, *lift* versus *elevator*; alternative ways of framing certain questions: *Have you a pencil?* versus *Do you have a pencil?* versus *Have you got a pencil?*, for instance. It is extremely difficult to say how many differences there are between dialects or to recognize where one dialect ends and another begins.

Language is only one of the common activities of a society. The totality of common activities, institutions, and beliefs make up the **culture** of that society. Cultural groupings are not necessarily coterminous with language communities. In the modern world it is quite the opposite: cultural features are almost always more widespread than any one language. Native speakers of English belong to the so-called Western culture, which has developed from the Hebrews, Greeks and Romans of the ancient world. If it is hard to specify just what consitutes a 'dialect,' it is equally difficult to specify what is included in one 'culture.' Our culture includes, for example, eating with a fork, wearing neckties, knowing at least some of the same proverbs, using at least some of the same gestures for the same purposes, celebrating the arrival of a new year, believing in law and democracy, and hundreds of other major and minor customs and beliefs. The point is that communication takes place against a large common background.

A language is a complex system of symbols, or signs, that are shared by members of a community. It will be useful to consider other signs that we know and how we react to them.

Robinson Crusoe, according to Defoe's novel, was walking along the beach one morning and suddenly saw a human footprint in the sand – made by the man who was later to be called Friday, as it turned out. This experience, after twenty-seven years of living alone on his island, so frightened poor Crusoe that he ran back to the cave that was his home and would not venture out again that day.

A footprint is a natural sign. It is the natural result of a foot treading on a soft surface, and it can communicate a message – that the owner of the foot was recently there – to anyone who observes it. We are all familiar with other natural signs. We see smoke and know that there is a fire, or a fire has just gone out. A black cloud informs us of the possibility of rain. Treetops moving tell us that the wind is blowing. Our own bodies provide such signs as earaches and hunger pangs. In other people we notice and interpret shivering, perspiration, or a head nodding with drowsiness. All sorts of sights, sounds and smells can be natural signs; they communicate to someone who observes and can interpret but their messages are unintentional, the by-products of various events.

In modern life we are likely to be less concerned with natural signs than with conventional signs, the auditory and visual devices that people have created to send routine messages to one another. Day after day we hear such signals because someone intends for us to hear them: horns, whistles, sirens, buzzers and bells. The pop of a gun starts competitive runners, swimmers and jockeys on their respective races. In various sports a whistle or buzzer marks the beginning and end of each period of play. Visual signs are just as prevalent and as varied. We have conventional ways of indicating a slippery road, a bicycle path, the location of a telephone, of men's and women's lavatories, where there is access for the handicapped, where smoking is prohibited, and much more. Humans produce not only single symbols but systems of symbols. Different bugle calls, different bell tones, different numbers of toots on a whistle or flashes of light can form a repertory of messages. The traffic light found at numerous city street intersections is a good example of a simple system. None of these communications uses language, though of course devising, installing and learning them could not be accomplished by people who had no language.

Unlike natural signs, conventional signs have human senders as well as human receivers; each one has an intention and an interpretation. The message may be personal as when a friend rings your telephone or quite impersonal and general, like the warning siren on a speeding ambulance. We can even use devices like smoke detectors and burglar alarms to send messages to ourselves at a later time, in circumstances that we really do not want to occur.

Observing any such sign and getting information from it seems like a simple matter and can take place in an instant, and yet the process of getting information consists of three steps:

1 Perception

The sign and the observer share a context of place and time in which the sign attracts the observer's attention. Robinson Crusoe, to use our first example, walked where the footprint was, looked in the right direction, when there was sufficient light for visibility, and before the print had been obliterated by rain, wind, tide, or the movement of other creatures.

2 Identification

Every perception is a unique experience. To say that we 'recognize' a phenomenon means that we match it with previous experiences stored in our memory. Almost certainly, if you observe a sign and derive some meaning from it, you must have seen a similar sign before. We identify any new thing either as a phenomenon previously observed or, more often, as something that is 'identical' with phenomena we already know, a new token of a familiar type. The human mind cannot deal with an infinite number of separate things; we classify an entity as a new instance of the class of footprints or bushes or sirens or churches. And to identify what something is requires us to recognize what it is not, to discriminate between signs.

3 Interpretation

Meanings are often personal. The meaning of any sign depends on the space-time context in which we observe it. Crusoe's reaction to the footprint was due to the circumstances of his life, the fact that until this moment it had been impossible for him to see any human footprint other than his own. This is clearly an unusual case, but all the time we interpret differently in different contexts.

Conventional signs can have different meanings in different contexts or different circumstances. The whistle of a policeman directing traffic, the whistle of a hotel doorman summoning a taxi, and the whistle of the referee in a soccer game may all sound exactly the same; their different meanings are due to the difference of **context** in which the signal occurs. They have different intentions and are interpreted differently.

2.3 Linguistic signs

Words are linguistic signs, similar in certain respects to natural and conventional signs. They do not 'have meanings' but rather are capable of conveying meanings to those who can perceive, identify and interpret. Words go together to form sentences which in turn are capable of conveying meanings – the meanings of the individual words and the meaning that comes from the relation of these words to one another.

We can discuss individual linguistic signs – words – but since we are interested in language use, and words are not ordinarily used alone, we should direct our attention to whole utterances and how we perceive, identify and interpret them.

Let's consider the matter of perception, identification and interpretation with respect to language use.

In order to grasp what somebody says, we must first of all perceive the utterance – hear a spoken utterance, see a written one. A number of things can create difficulty in perceiving a spoken message: too much noise in the environment, too great a distance between speaker and hearer, insufficient volume in the speaker's delivery, a poor connection if the message is conveyed by telephone, static in a radio message, or insufficient attention on the part of the hearer. A written message must be clear, sufficiently lighted and have the reader's attention.

But hearing alone is not enough, nor is seeing. We get no message from an utterance in a language we don't know. Identification of the elements in an utterance requires speaker and hearer to share what Clark (1996: 92–121) calls 'common ground.' By and large, speaker and hearer use the same vocabulary: they attach the same meanings to the same words and sentences; they have similar pronunciations; and they have, in general, the same ways of putting words together in sentences. Of course there can be different degrees of commonality in the common ground. Speaker and hearer may speak different dialects of the same language, so that their pronunciations differ to some degree and there is some divergence in the ways they express themselves. One – or both – may be a foreigner with only partial mastery of the language they are using. Markedly different pronunciations, use of vocabulary items that the other doesn't know, meanings not shared, syntactic constructions not familiar to both – these disturb the process of identification.

Suppose we hear an utterance, know the language, know the meanings of the words and the sentences formed with the words. We may still not fully comprehend what is said because we don't know what the utterance is about. We don't grasp the speaker's intention, largely because we don't know what is being referred to. On the other hand, when communication is successful, we, as hearers, interpret correctly because we derive some information from what has been said previously (the discourse context) and from knowledge of the speaker and from a grasp of conditions and circumstances in the environment (the physical-social context).

When we listen to someone talking, we first take in a sequence of sounds, a phonetic event, but our understanding is not a matter of grasping one sound after another, nor even one word after another. We organize the message into sense-groups (Clark and Clark 1977: 43–57). Possibly the speaker helps by speaking in sense-groups, making the pauses that are needed for breathing between sense-groups; for example, at some of the places marked '(pause)' in this utterance:

23

> "I'll let you know the answer (pause)
> as soon as I get the information (pause)
> from a friend of mine (pause)
> who lives in Winchester."

(What we call a 'pause' may be an instant of silence or it may be simply the lengthening of a final sound, for example, *information-n-n.*) But conversational speech is not usually so neatly organized. As speakers we typically hesitate as we figure out what we intend to say; we put in 'fillers' (" Well"; "As a matter of fact . . . "); we repeat; we correct ourselves ("I mean"), we appeal to the addressee's understanding ("you know"). So even a short utterance like the one above may come out this way:

> "Well, I'll uh let you know (pause) the answer (pause)
> as soon – as soon as I get the information (pause)
> from a friend of mine (pause) um you know (pause) who
> lives in Winchester."

This may *look* strange on the printed page because in written English we are used to seeing the result of careful planning and polishing, but conversational speech is scarcely ever planned or polished.

As listeners we 'edit' what we hear, separating the pauses, fillers and repetitions from the 'gist' of the message. Thus, although we can't grasp a spoken message without hearing it (perception), our knowledge of the language enables us to distinguish between what communicates and what does not. Listeners – and readers – use their implicit knowledge of the language to grasp the message they are dealing with. For instance, if we encounter the verb *put* in an utterance, we are prepared to find three expressions telling us who puts, what is put, and where it is put. With the verb *travel* we unconsciously recognize that there will be information about the person(s) traveling and perhaps about the starting point, the goal, the route taken, and the duration of time. The verb *buy* must be accompanied by an expression that names the buyer and item(s) bought and there is likely to be information about seller and price, as well. One part of semantic analysis, therefore, is concerned with describing the kinds of expressions which usually accompany various verbs – what roles these expressions play with respect to the verb and to each other – the who, what, where and when. Our study of such roles begins in Chapter 5.

Although we, as listeners, begin with a phonetic message, once we have grasped the semantic content we retain only the sense of the message (Clark and Clark 1977: 49). People frequently give an accurate account of something that has been said but almost always they re-tell it in words that are different from the original message. The account is not an exact repetition of what was said unless the message is fairly short. Thus, as listeners, we begin by identifying the phonetic message and through the phonetic message identify the semantic message.

So much for perception and identification. Now consider interpretation. Comprehension is not just taking in words or even sense-groups. As listeners we use our background information to interpret the message. As Fillmore (1979: 78) puts it, we need to know not only what the speaker says but also what he is talking about, why he bothers to say it, and why he says it the way he does. We have to relate what is being said to what was said previously – relate new information that is coming at us to the information that preceded it. The utterance in our illustration, above, must be part of a larger discourse, and the listener grasps the meaning of 'the answer (to what?)' and 'the information (about what?)' by relating these to what has been said before. The listener has to decide, from the conversation or from knowledge of the speaker, whether the place of residence of the speaker's friend is relevant. The listener has to decide if the speaker is joking, being sarcastic, or is entirely serious, and such judgements and interpretations have to be made within a brief span of time. When we are reading, our interpretation of what the author wants to tell us depends on our background knowledge of the topic, and we probably will be more successful in comprehending if we find the author's style somewhat familiar and to our liking. From the other side, speakers who make themselves understood have to have some notion of what their addressees already know and what the addressees can infer and fill in. Writers have to decide for what potential audience they are writing and how much these potential readers can contribute to the process of comprehending.

Sometimes we can interpret what the speaker intends from clues in the physical context even though we don't understand completely what he or she has said (interpretation without identification) and even without having heard everything said (interpretation without perception). Can you recall an instance in which you did not fully understand what someone said but figured out from the context what he or she meant – what the speaker was trying to do, what the circumstances seemed to require, etc.? If you can't remember such an event, perhaps you can imagine one.

Can you recall an instance in which you understood quite well what somebody said but still could not interpret it, because you did not have background information, didn't grasp what the message was about? If not, maybe you can invent a possible situation.

2.4 Utterance and sentence

Just as conventional signals like the blowing of a whistle can have different meanings in different situations, so different pieces of language can have different meanings in different contexts. Let's illustrate with three fictitious events: A beggar who has not eaten all day says "I'm hungry"; a child who hopes to put off going to bed announces "I'm hungry"; a young man who hopes to get better acquainted with one of his co-workers and intends to ask her to have dinner with him begins with the statement "I'm hungry." The three events obviously have something in common and yet, just as obviously, they are different: they indicate different intentions and are liable to be interpreted differently because the situations and the participants are different.

Each of the three speech events illustrated above is a different **utterance**, and we write an utterance with quotation marks: "I'm hungry." Each utterance contains the same **sentence**, which we write with italics: *I'm hungry*. An utterance is an act of speech or writing; it is a specific event, at a particular time and place and involving at least one person, the one who produces the utterance, but usually more than one person. An utterance happens just once; a spoken utterance happens and then, unless it is recorded electronically, it ceases to exist; a written utterance is intended to last – for a short time in the case of a shopping list, for instance, or much longer, as in the case of a book.

A sentence, on the other hand, is not an event; it is a construction of words (in English or whatever language) in a particular sequence which is meaningful (in that language). In our illustration each of the three utterances contains the meaning of the sentence, and each utterance has an extra meaning or meanings because of the circumstances in which it occurs. The meaning of a sentence is determined by the language, something known to all people who have learned to use that language. It is the meanings of the individual words and the meaning of the syntactic construction in which they occur.

The meaning of an utterance is the meaning of the sentence plus the meanings of the circumstances: the time and place, the people involved, their backgrounds, their relationship to one another, and what they know about one another. All these circumstances we can call the physical-social context of an utterance.

Why distinguish between sentence and utterance? Because it is important to recognize what meanings are communicated to us in language and which meanings we derive from the contexts in which language is used. Because it is important to distinguish between **linguistic meaning**, what is communicated by particular pieces of language, and **utterance meaning**, what a certain individual meant by saying such-and-such in a particular place, at a particular time, and to certain other individuals. The utterance "Our visit to the factory was a wonderful experience" may be spoken as a joke, or sarcastically, or as a straightforward report, among other possibilities. The sentence *Our visit to the factory was a wonderful experience* has none of these meanings in itself – or, to put it differently, it has potentially any of these meanings.

An utterance is often part of a larger **discourse** – a conversation, a formal lecture, a poem, a short story, a business letter, or a love letter, among other possibilities. A spoken discourse is any act of speech that occurs in a given place and during a given period of time. A written discourse may be the record of something that has been spoken, or it may originate for the purpose of being performed aloud, like a play or speech, or it may exist without ever having been spoken or intended to be spoken, like most articles and books. The linguistic context of an utterance can make a difference of meaning, as well as the social context.

PRACTICE 2.2 Context and meaning

> The meaning of any language symbol depends to an extent on the context in which it occurs. Here are two 'narratives' that are rather vague because a lot of details are missing, but in each group the mere collocation of the words that are here tells a sort of story.
>
> (a) . . . pain . . . clinic . . . doctor . . . examine . . . surgery . . . hospital . . . nurses . . . preparation . . . surgeon . . . successful operation . . . quick recovery
>
> (b) . . . rocket . . . preparation . . . countdown . . . blastoff . . . orbit . . . splashdown . . . quick recovery . . . successful operation
>
> The term *successful operation* occurs in both stories. Does it seem to have the same meaning in both of them?
>
> The phrase *quick recovery* also occurs in both stories. Does it have the same meaning in both?

Listeners – and to a lesser extent readers – often have to fill in information that the speaker or writer takes for granted. For example, suppose that A and B are standing somewhere and A says to B, "This was the site of the old Stanwick Theater. The stage was over here on the right and the lobby over there on the left." B will probably understand well enough, but his understanding is due to the fact that he inserts, between the two utterances, the information that the Stanwick Theater had a stage and a lobby – A has not told him so, or has not exactly told him so. The English definite article *the* is used in some proper names like 'the Stanwick Theater', 'the Hudson River', 'the Alps' and it is used with ordinary nouns like *stage* and *lobby* when these have already been introduced into the discourse. Since they are just now entering the discourse, B must relate the new information to what has been said, and he will probably do so without even recognizing that his comprehension is due to his own contribution. A bit of information inserted in such a context is called an **implicature** – a conversational implicature, to be precise. An implicature is a bridge constructed by the hearer (or reader) to relate one utterance to some previous utterance, and often the hearer or reader makes this connection unconsciously. In this case the bridge is easy to construct; our knowledge of the world lets us take for granted the fact that a theater has a stage and a lobby. If the speaker were to say "This was the site of the old Stanwick Theater. It had a stage and a lobby. The stage was over here . . . ," he would seem quite pedantic.

PRACTICE 2.3 Implicatures

In the following short discourses what is the implicature that connects the second utterance to the first?

(a) Is there a garage near here? Our engine is making strange noises.
(b) Barbara: How did you do on the examination?
    Barry: I think I'll just drop this course.
(c) Jim: Would you like to go dancing tomorrow night?
    Laura: We have guests coming from out of town.

Has Laura answered Jim's question? If so, what is her answer? Has she answered a question that he didn't ask? If so, what is the question?

Going back to A's first utterances to B near the site of the Stanwick Theater, what, precisely, are the meanings of 'over here on the right' and 'over there on the left'? Without being present at the scene we don't know the places that these terms designate, but since we know the English language we know that their meanings are contrary to each other and that the speaker is closer to whatever is 'on the right.' Deictic elements like these, which derive their meaning from the place and time of utterance, are examined in more detail in Chapter 6.

2.5 Prosody

We enclose spoken utterances in double quotation marks to distinguish them from sentences, which we print in italics. However, a spoken utterance consists of more than words. In speech meanings are communicated not merely by what is said but also by the way it is said. Read these four brief dialogues.

1   A: Has the Winston Street bus come yet?
       B: Sorry. I didn't understand. What did you say?
2   C: I'm afraid Fred didn't like the remark I made.
       D: Oh? What did you say?
3   E: Some of my partners said they wouldn't accept these terms.
       F: And you? What did you say?
4   G: You're misquoting me. I didn't say anything like that.
       H: Oh? What did you say?

The sequence of words "What did you say?" occurs in all four dialogues but it is pronounced differently in each. Individual speakers may vary somewhat in just what they pronounce, but the four renditions can be represented as follows, where the most prominent syllable is indicated with capital letters and the rising or falling of the voice is indicated by letters going up or down.

```
1           T did you say?
        A
      H
    W


2                    S
    What did you   A
                      Y ?


              Y
3    What did    O
                  U say?


           D
4    What   I
             D you say?
```

We produce all our spoken utterances with a melody, or **intonation**: by changing the speed with which the vocal bands in the throat vibrate we produce rising or falling pitch or combinations of rise and fall. By making one syllable in a sense-group especially loud and long, usually where the change of pitch occurs, we endow that word with a special prominence called **accent**. Intonation and accent together constitute **prosody**, the meaningful elements of speech apart from the words that are uttered.

Within each sense-group one word (more accurately, the stressed syllable of one word) is more prominent than the rest of the group, giving special attention or **focus** to that word. Thus, the more numerous the divisions made, the more points of emphasis there are. Compare "I'd never say THAT" with one focus and "I / would NEVer / say THAT" with three.

Typically, when speech is represented in print, italics are sometimes used to indicate the accent, but this is done only sporadically and unevenly; our writing system largely neglects this important element of spoken communication. A written transcript of a speech can be highly misleading because it is only a partial rendition of that speech. In speech there is always an accent in some part of an utterance, and placement of accent in different parts of an utterance creates differences of meaning.

In the English language accent is mobile, enabling us to communicate different meanings by putting the emphasis in different places. The usual place is on the last important word, for instance:

> My cousin is an ARchitect.

If the utterance is broken into two or more sense groups, each group has its own accent. The last accent is ordinarily the most prominent of all because the pitch changes on that syllable.

> My COUsin is an ARchitect.
> My cousin EDward, who lives in FULton, is an ARchitect.

Thus the speaker can highlight one word or several words in an utterance and give special focus to that word or those words.

The placement of accent on different words ties the utterance to what has been said previously. For example, in reply to the question "What does your cousin do?," one might say

> My cousin
> Edward   } 's an ARchitect.
> He

Here the word *architect* is **new information**, something not previously mentioned, and *Edward* or *my cousin* is old, or **given information**, reference to what was already in the discourse. Suppose, instead, that nothing had been said about anybody's cousin but the discussion had somehow turned to architects. One might then volunteer this information:

My cousin EDward's an architect.

Here *my cousin Edward* is new information and the stressed syllable of the name *Edward* is accented. The phrase *an architect* now represents given information and is de-accented.

Accent, by giving special focus to one word, can create contrast with other words that might have been used in the same place. Moving the accent to different words creates different meanings in what would otherwise be a single utterance.

PRACTICE 2.4 The role of accent

The utterance "Alex phoned Louise last SUNday" may not have any special emphasis, or it may emphasize Sunday as opposed to any other day. Each of the following utterances has an emphasis that makes a contrast. What is the contrast, in each case?

Alex phoned Edna LAST Sunday.
Alex phoned EDna last Sunday.
Alex PHONED Edna last Sunday.
ALex phoned Edna last Sunday.

Thus what effect prosody has in an utterance – what meanings it carries – depends on the total context in which the utterance occurs.

Now let's turn back to intonation, the set of tunes that can differentiate meanings of utterances with the same verbal content. In a tone language such as Chinese or Thai differences of relative pitch or differences in the change of pitch have a lexical function; words with different meanings are distinguished only by the difference of pitch. Intonation does not have the function of differentiating lexical meanings. Intonation applies to a whole utterance or at least to a whole tone unit, though of course a tone unit or an utterance can consist of a single word.

Intonation is achieved by different vibrations of the vocal cords. Greater frequency of vibration results in what we call higher pitch. Intonational changes of pitch may occur at various places in an utterance, but observation shows that changes at or near the end of the utterance have more prominence and are more likely to be meaningful than utterance-internal changes. Physiologically, it is natural that vocal cord vibration should slow to a halt as the speaker reaches the end of an utterance – in other words, that a falling pitch is more 'normal' and, correspondingly, a rising pitch at the end of an utterance is the indication of something special.

In general, as Allan (1986: Chapter 5) points out, a **falling tune** suggests that the speaker is confident of what he or she is saying and the utterance is delivered with finality; it shows speaker dominance. A **rising tune** is more oriented toward the addressee. Naturally, individual speakers differ: some are more assertive in their speech, others more attuned to the feelings of the addressee. And there are dialect differences; it is a common observation that some speakers have a rise where others would end an utterance with a falling tune.

Leaving aside the individual and dialectal differences, we can say that a rise is customary when the speaker is asking the addressee to repeat; it is likely to suggest interest in what the addressee may have to say but it is also used to contradict what has just been said. Thus "↓ Yes", spoken with a fall which we designate with ↓, is what one says in reply to another's query; "↑ Yes", with a rise (indicated here with ↑), is likely to be itself a question. The same word uttered with a fall and then a rise, "↓ ↑ Yes", is likely to suggest the speaker agrees partially – but only partially – with something that has been said, a meaning which might be paraphrased as 'That's true but . . . .'

The description of intonation can be quite complex, with distinctions between short falls and long falls, short rises and long rises, illustrated in different contours – different sequences of such falls and rises. On the other hand, just limiting ourselves to simple contrasts between fall and rise it is easy to show that intonation plays an important part in the way people communicate with one another. Here are some common distinctions made with intonation in utterances that have the same verbal material. Other uses of intonation will come up in later chapters.

1 Statement vs question (fall vs rise)

↓ Yes. ↑ Yes? ↓ This is the place. ↑ This is the place?

With a falling tone "Yes" is an answer to some question and "This is the place" is a statement. With rising tones the speaker seeks confirmation or information from the addressee.

2 Information sought vs repetition requested (fall vs rise)

↑ When? ↑ Where? ↓ When? ↓ Where?

With "When?," "Where?" rising, the speaker is asking for repetition of something that was said; the speaker has understood enough of the previous utterance to know that some time or place was mentioned. The falling intonation in such utterances is a request for information that has not yet been given.

3 Parallel structure vs antithesis (fall vs fall and rise)

This is my sister, ↓ Ellen.
This is my ↓ sister, ↑ Ellen.

If *sister* and *Ellen* have the same tune, a fall on *sister* and a long fall on *Ellen*, the parallel structure indicates a correlation of the two – specifically here, equivalence: that Ellen is the name of the speaker's sister. Fall on *sister* – typically a long fall – and a short rise on *Ellen* denotes lack of correlation, so that Ellen can only be the name of the addressee, a short vocative attached to an utterance.

4 Open question vs alternative question (rise vs rise, fall)

Do you have a ↑ pencil or a pen?
Do you have a ↑ pencil or a ↓ pen?

The distinction here reflects the speaker's attitude, perhaps about what seems appropriate in what the addressee can answer. A yes-no question will have a rise. The alternative question has a rise on the first of the alternatives and a fall on the second.

5 Full statement vs reservation (fall vs fall-rise)

↓ That's true. (or That's ↓ true.)
That's ↓↑ true.

This difference reflects the speaker's attitude. A fall expresses agreement with what has been said; a fall and short rise expresses only partial agreement, agreement with reservations.

PRACTICE 2.5 Intonation

How would you say "Yes, it is" in these two discourses?

(a) Is this your pen?
    Yes, it is. (answering the question)
(b) This isn't your pen.
    Yes, it is.   (contradicting)

In summary, intonation may have a role in distinguishing one meaning (that is, speaker's intention) from another, but it seldom has the sole burden of communicating a meaning. We interpret an utterance according to its position in a discourse, our knowledge of the speaker, our recognition of how things are in our world (Couper-Kuhlen 1986: 209).

2.6 Non-verbal communication

Aside from what we say to one another through the verbal content and the prosody of spoken utterances, we can, in face-to-face communication, transmit less systematic messages to one another by means of audible and visible signs that are not part of language. In addition, our voice or our appearance may have an effect on other participants in a conversation and therefore have an effect on the way our verbal messages are interpreted.

Consider first the standardized noises we make, which are written this way (not very accurately):

ps-st   sh-sh   huh?   unh-huh   m-m-m   b-r-r   tsk-tsk

These count as signs. On the whole they are known to all (or at least large portions) of a language community and indeed may be used by speakers of several different languages. In general, the maker of the sign and those who hear it attach the same meaning to that sign; communication occurs. These seven audible signs indicate, respectively, a request for attention; a call for silence; a request for repetition or clarification; a signal of agreement; an expression of pleasure or enjoyment; an indication of coldness; and an expression of shame or shock.

Then there are other ways of using the voice, as part of the spoken utterance, which cannot be considered either signs or part of language. These include laughing, giggling, crying (which need not accompany an utterance); whisper, falsetto, a quavering or 'breaking' voice; and other elements that are vocal but not verbal: the relative loudness or softness of the voice, high or low pitch, the modulations of pitch from a near monotone to an exaggerated rising and falling, a nasal quality, a rasping sound, the tempo of speech – the speed at which a whole utterance is delivered or the relative timing of syllables, ranging from clipping to drawling. These ways of using the voice cannot be considered signs – they do not signify – but they may be expressive, communicative in a secondary sense. Speakers may want to create a particular effect with their ways of using the voice; listeners may interpret what they hear in particular ways because of vocal features; but if intentions and interpretations coincide, the coincidence is fortuitous. All these ways of using the voice are together called **paralanguage**. The failure to use language – silence – at a particular juncture can likewise be expressive.

Similarly, there are visible signs, **gestures**, which have a standard, shared meaning, and there are elements of appearance – 'body language' – which possibly create an effect on the observer and therefore on the interpretation of a spoken message. The former, the visible signs, have the capacity to communicate in much the way a word communicates; the latter could only be said to communicate in a secondary sense.

Consider these visual signs:

nodding the head in response to an utterance
crossing one's fingers
pretending to yawn, with finger tips in front of mouth
holding up a thumb from a closed fist
pinching one's nostrils closed with thumb and forefinger

Like the audible signs mentioned above, these gestures have recognized, though somewhat vague, shared meanings. The first suggests agreement or affirmation; the second, a hope for success when circumstances are uncertain; the third, boredom; the fourth, determination to make one's cause successful; the fifth, disgust or displeasure with something ('It stinks').

Other physical postures and movements – for instance, gestures with hand or whole body, such as pounding on a table with a finger or a fist, and facial gestures like pursing one's lips, arching the eyebrows, opening the eyes wide, squinting, or fluttering the eyelids – are not conventional signals and do not have meanings in themselves; they may lead an observer to form some particular impression of the speaker, which in turn may have an effect on how the hearer interprets, but they are not in themselves semantic. It is possible that a wink or a broad grin on the speaker's face may communicate to the addressee a visual message that the verbal message is meant facetiously, not to be taken seriously, but there is never any certainty that such is the intended message.

Combinations of paralanguage and gestures can communicate something about the mood of the speaker – anger, boredom, nervousness, elation, for instance – and actors work hard to achieve such effects in interpreting the characters they play. But each actor strives to do so differently. We are not impressed by a budding starlet who uses the same inventory of mannerisms as a seasoned actress.

Other facets of appearance – clothing, hair style, jewelry, cosmetics, facial hair and what is done with it – have an effect on others, intentional or not. The distance between interlocutors and whether they touch each other or not depends on tacit standards that each of us learns from the culture in which we grow up. Whether we sit on the floor or on chairs, cross our legs at the ankles, over the knees, or not at all – these 'say' something about a person's cultural background but they do not communicate semantically.

Just as we learn a language early in life and largely take it for granted, so we also learn these more peripheral elements of communication and, unless we move into a different society, we assume that they are 'just natural.' But gestures, interpersonal distances, the ways the voice is used can be quite different in different societies and thus any of these can have different effects on people of different backgrounds. What is meaningless or mild in one culture may be rude, obscene, or otherwise over-effective in another.

Thus a face-to-face communication event contains linguistic and non-linguistic elements like these:

Linguistic:
vocal and verbal – words put together to form utterances (representing sentences)
vocal and non-verbal – prosody, the intonation and accenting with which utterances are spoken

Non-linguistic:
vocal – paralanguage, the "tone of voice"
non-vocal – distances maintained; appearance; gestures; silence

PRACTICE 2.6 Gestures

Here are ten stylized gestures that are used by speakers of English. Write down what each one 'means' – that is, how you would interpret it in one or more speech situations. Then compare your interpretations with those made by other members of your class.

(a) The index finger of one hand points at someone and the hand is moved up and down three or four times with deliberate motion ('shaking a finger at someone').

(b) The fist, with knuckles down, moves up and down in short movements knocking on something or as if knocking on something ('knocking on wood').

(c) Shoulders are moved upward and down again, possibly repeated ('shrugging shoulders').

(d) Hands are clasped across each other, palm against palm, and forearms move back and forth; this gesture can be executed in front of oneself or over one's head ('shaking hands with oneself').

(e) Hand is held on the stomach, palm inward, and the hand makes a circular movement.

(f) The tongue moves back and forth over the lips ('licking one's lips').

(g) The palm of one hand is brought up and slaps smartly against the forehead.

(h) The hand, slightly cupped, is pulled across the forehead as if wiping something away.

(i) The index finger is pulled across the throat; the gesture may be accompanied by a noise that is made with movement of air (and saliva) on one side of the mouth while the lips are slightly open on that side.

(j) The fingers of the two hands are interlocked and the thumbs move in circles around each other ('twiddling one's thumbs').

In a class composed of students from different countries it will be interesting to compare the signals made in the following situations:

(a) Two people who are acquainted see each other at some distance and greet each other with a gesture.

(b) Two people who have been together move apart and give each other a farewell signal.

(c) One person signals to another one to come forward.

(d) One hand is used to indicate the height of a child or of some object.

(e) The gesture-maker wants to indicate himself/herself.

(f) A movement to signal agreement or an affirmative answer.

(g) A movement to signal a negative answer.

(h) A way of indicating one's opinion that some other person is 'crazy.'

Summary

While linguistic semantics is concerned with the language system that people have in common that makes them able to communicate with one another, pragmatics is the study (and description) of how people actually use language in communicating.

The elements of language are similar to natural signs and, more especially, to conventional signals. A sign is meaningful to us only if we perceive it, identify it and interpret it.

Speakers do not merely have certain abstract knowledge; they use that knowledge in various social contexts. Pieces of language, like other signs, depend on context for what they signify. We recognize social context and linguistic context. We distinguish between sentence, a language formation and utterance, what is produced in a particular social context. The meaning that speakers extract from an utterance is often more than the linguistic message itself; knowledge of reality, the situation, and the participants in the communication event enables the individual to fill in. A conversational implicature is the information that is not spoken but is understood in tying one utterance meaningfully to a previous utterance.

Prosody is an important carrier of meaning in spoken utterances and consists of two parts, accent and intonation. Accent is the comparatively greater force and higher pitch that makes one part of the utterance more prominent than other parts. It has a syntagmatic function, giving focus to the accented word and indicating that other parts of the utterance, especially those that follow, are given information. Paradigmatic focus is an emphasis on one word as opposed to other words that might have been used. Intonation is the set of tunes that can differentiate meanings of utterances with the same verbal content. Intonation patterns are falls and rises in pitch and combinations of falls and rises. Generally a fall indicates speaker dominance or termination. A rise is hearer oriented and suggests continuance.

In speech situations some meanings are conveyed by non-linguistic matters. These include paralanguage, appearance, gestures and silence.

Suggested reading

1 Clark (1996, Chapters 1–4: 3–121), develops the notion of language use as joint action and joint activity by people who possess a common ground.

2 For more discussion of discourse see Schiffrin (1994, Chapter 2: 20–43).

3 For a more extensive, but relatively brief, account of intonation in English see Kreidler (1997, Chapter 11: 180–94). A more thorough description is Cruttenden (1986, Chapter 4: 75–130) which provides descriptions of tunes and their semantic functions; Chapter 5 (134–74) surveys dialect differences in the use of tunes.

The dimensions
of meaning

Anything meaningful in a language is a linguistic expression. Linguistic expressions may be of various length. We recognize three units of meaning: morphemes (which may be less than a word), lexemes (roughly, words and idioms), and sentences. In this chapter we introduce a distinction between **lexemes**, which have semantic relations outside of language, and **function words**, which contribute grammatical meanings to utterances. A lexeme may consist of one or more meaningful units, called **morphemes**, and we discuss different kinds of morphemes. Every lexeme is a combination of form and meaning. Generally we can recognize three aspects of meaning in lexemes: the relation to phenomena outside language, the relation to people's attitudes and feelings and the relation to other lexemes. Two lexemes that have the same form (pronunciation, spelling) are homonyms; a single lexeme with a wide range of meanings is **polysemous**; but it is not always easy to decide if apparently different meanings for one form represent a range of meanings belonging to a single lexeme or meanings of different lexemes, which are homonyms.

3.1 Reference and denotation

In every language there are words like *tree* and *run* and *red* which seem to have an obvious relation to objects and events and descriptions of things in the world around us. Children learning their native language first learn words in association with observable items and situations and events. This simple fact can give rise to an overly simple idea about what 'meaning' is. We are likely to think that a language consists of a large number of words and each of these words has a direct correlation with something outside of language, which is its meaning. And since, if we communicate with one another through language, it must be that we all have the same 'idea' or 'concept' associated with each word. The best known elaboration of this view was made by Ogden and Richards (1923), who developed a mentalistic theory about meaning, an attempt to explain meaning in terms of what is in people's minds. Their explanation centers around this scheme:

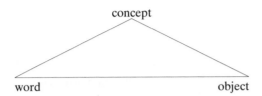

concept

word   object

Ogden and Richards called the bond between word and concept an 'association,' the bond between concept and object 'reference,' and the bond between object and word 'meaning.'

When we hear or read a word, we often form a mental picture of what the word represents, and so we are apt to equate 'concept' with a mental picture. To be sure, it is easier to form a mental picture for some words – DOOR and DOG, for example – than for others such as ORDINARY or PROBLEM or PRETEND. But the idea of a mental picture is misleading. What mental image do you form for DOOR? A revolving door? A folding door? A sliding door, moving horizontally? An overhead door which moves vertically? A door turning on hinges? Is it in a wall, or on a cabinet, or part of a car? Is your image associated with DOG that of a St Bernard or a Pekingese, a mongrel or an Irish Setter? You can picture all of these in sequence but not simultaneously. Clearly the meaning of *door* or *dog* is more than what is included in a single image, and your knowledge of these words is much more than the ability to relate them to single objects. You can use these words successfully in a large number of situations because you have the knowledge that makes this possible.

Just as we distinguished between 'utterance' and 'sentence,' we need to draw a distinction betweeen **reference** and **denotation**. Reference is the relation between a language expression such as *this door*, *both doors*, *the dog*, *another dog* and whatever the expression pertains to in a particular situation of language use, including what a speaker may imagine. Denotation is the potential of a word like *door* or *dog* to enter into such language expressions. Reference is the way speakers and hearers use an expression successfully; denotation is the knowledge they have that makes their use successful.

The trouble with a mentalistic theory of meaning is, first, that not all words can be associated with mental images and some words have a range of meaning greater than any single association. The bigger problem with a mentalistic theory is that we have no access to other people's minds. How can we ever know that we all have the same mental images? If semantics is a science, it cannot operate scientifically by starting with things that are not observable and not comparable.

Furthermore, words are not the only semantic units. Meanings are expressed by units that may be smaller than words – **morphemes** (see below, section **3.4**) – and meanings are expressed in units – sentences – that are larger than words. The sentences *The dog bit a man* and *The man bit a dog*, to use a trite example, contain the same words but they don't express the same meanings.

Furthermore, meaning is more than denotation. People not only talk and write to describe things and events and characteristics; they also express their opinions, favorable and unfavorable. Language furnishes the means for expressing a wide range of attitudes; this aspect of meaning is called **connotation**. Another aspect is **sense relations**: the meaning of any expression varies with context, what other expressions it occurs with and what expressions it contrasts with.

3.2 Connotation

The word *dog* has a certain denotation, the possibility of entering into numerous referring expressions such as the underlined expressions in the following.

1 This dog is a Dalmatian.
2 My children have just acquired a dog.
3 Several dogs were fighting over a bone.

But how do you feel about dogs? How does a particular society value dogs? Hjelmslev (1971: 109–10) pointed out that among the Eskimos a dog is an animal that is used for pulling a sled, the Parsees regard dogs as nearly sacred, Hindus consider them a great pest and in Western Europe and America some members of the species still perform the original chores of hunting and guarding while others are merely 'pets.' Hjelmslev might have added that in certain societies the flesh of dogs is part of the human diet and in other societies it is not. The meaning of *dog* includes the attitudes of a society and of individuals, the pragmatic aspect. It would be wrong to think that a purely biological definition of the lexeme *dog* is a sufficient account of its meaning. Part of its meaning is its **connotation**, the affective or emotional associations it elicits, which clearly need not be the same for all people who know and use the word.

A denotation identifies the central aspect of word meaning, which everybody generally agrees about. Connotation refers to the personal aspect of meaning, the emotional associations that the word arouses. Connotations vary according to the experience of individuals but, because people do have common experiences, some words have shared connotations.

Languages provide means of expressing different attitudes. The referring expressions *that violin* and *that fiddle* can have the same referent – can refer to the same object on a particular occasion – but they do not have the same meaning. They differ in connotation. *Violin* is the usual term, the neutral one; *fiddle* is used for humor or to express affection or lack of esteem. Somewhat similar relations are seen with *automobile* and *car*, *building* and *edifice*, *fire* and *conflagration* and other sets, the members of which have, or can have, the same denotation but differ in the situations in which they are used and therefore have differences in the degree of formality, the style or 'flavor' – the connotation. (We also need to note here that *car*, *building*, and *fire* have larger denotations than *automobile*, *edifice* and *conflagration* respectively.)

The expression of attitudes can be quite subtle. We choose to use one word rather than another. We might, for example, say that Linda is *thin*, or *slender*, or *svelte*, or *skinny*.

PRACTICE 3.1 Connotation

1 How do the following words in each pair differ in connotation?

politician, statesman	cautious, timid
lawyer, shyster	inquisitive, nosey
bargain, haggle	sensitive, touchy

2 It might seem that any name would be appropriate as a label for a commercial product as long as it is easy to remember.

45

However, companies with products to sell make great expenditures of time, talent and money to select brand names which will project the preferred 'image' for cars, cosmetics, detergents *et al.*, but names are often chosen for their connotation rather than for what they denote.

Why is Caterpillar a good name for an earth-moving tractor but not for a sports car? How would you rank the following as possible names for a sports car?

Butterfly   Cheetah   Dolphin   Owl   Rattler   XL4

Would you care to suggest others?

Give an example of a possible name for a men's cologne (which of course is never called perfume) and an example of a name which is very unlikely.

3.3 Sense relations

Meaning is more than denotation and connotation. What a word means depends in part on its associations with other words, the relational aspect. Lexemes do not merely 'have' meanings; they contribute meanings to the utterances in which they occur, and what meanings they contribute depends on what other lexemes they are associated with in these utterances. The meaning that a lexeme has because of these relationships is the **sense** of that lexeme. Part of this relationship is seen in the way words do, or do not, go together meaningfully. It makes sense to say *John walked* and it makes sense to say *An hour elapsed*. It doesn't make sense to say *John elapsed* or *An hour walked*. Part of the meaning of *elapse* is that it goes with *hour, second, minute, day* but not with *John*, and part of the meaning of *hour, second* and so forth is that these words can co-occur with *elapse*.

Part of the relationship is seen in the way word meanings vary with context. A *library* is a collection of books (*Professor Jones has a rather large library*) and is also a building that houses a collection of books (*The library is at the corner of Wilson and Adams Streets*). A number of English verbs can be used in two different ways

– different grammatical association – and then have slightly different meanings. We can say:

4   A window broke.
5   Tom broke a window.

Here what happened to the window is the same, but in the first sentence *broke* is equivalent to 'became broken' and in the second it is equivalent to 'caused to be broken.' (More about this in the next chapter.) Adjectives, too, can have different senses. If you come across some object which you have never seen before, and you wonder about its origin and its purpose, we can say that you are *curious* about it. But we can also call the object a *curious* kind of thing. The same term is used for your subjective feelings and for the supposedly objective properties of this item – a curious person, a curious object. A judge makes decisions; if he is guided by personal whim or choice, the judge is arbitrary (dictionary definition: 'inclined to make decisions based on personal whim') but we also say that the decision is arbitrary (dictionary definition: 'based on personal choice rather than reason'). A lexeme does not merely 'have' meaning; it contributes to the meaning of a larger unit, a phrase or sentence. Take these phrases with the adjective *happy*:

a happy child, a happy family
a happy accident, a happy experience
a happy story, a happy report

When happy combines with a word that has the feature [human], like *child* and *family* in the first line, it is roughly equivalent to 'who enjoy(s) happiness' – a happy child is a child who has or enjoys happiness. In combination with words that have the feature [event] such as *accident* and *experience*, its contribution is roughly 'that produces happiness.' In combination with words that have the feature [discourse] – *story, report* – its meaning is roughly 'containing a happy event or events.' Each of these words has a range of meanings; each meaning is determined by its linguistic context, just as the meaning of *door* on any specific occasion is determined by the physical context in which it occurs.

The meaning of a lexeme is, in part, its relation to other lexemes of the language. Each lexeme is linked in some way to numerous other lexemes of the language. We can notice two kinds of linkage, especially. First, there is the relation of the lexeme with other lexemes with which it occurs in the same phrases or sentences, in the way that *arbitrary* can co-occur with *judge*, *happy* with *child* or with *accident*, *sit* with *chair*, *read* with *book* or *newspaper*. These are **syntagmatic** relations, the mutual association of two or more words in a sequence (not necessarily right next to one another) so that the meaning of each is affected by the other(s) and together their meanings contribute to the meaning of the larger unit, the phrase or sentence.

Another kind of relation is contrastive. Instead of saying *The judge was arbitrary*, for instance, we can say *The judge was cautious* or *careless* or *busy* or *irritable*, and so on with numerous other possible descriptors. This is a **paradigmatic** relation, a relation of choice. We choose from among a number of possible words that can fill the same blank: the words may be similar in meaning or have little in common but each is different from the others.

Since we are used to a writing system that goes from left to right, we may think of syntagmatic relations as horizontal and paradigmatic relations as vertical. A compound expression, such as *book and newspaper*, *cautious but arbitrary*, *read or write* puts two lexemes that are paradigmatically related into a syntagmatic relationship.

As children, we learn vocabulary first through specific associations with specific things, actions, and characteristics (reference) and as we learn to recognize different instances of the 'same' thing, the 'same' event, and so on, we generalize (denotation). Slowly we learn from other members of our speech community and from our personal experiences what associations are favorable and which are not (connotation). And we acquire an implicit knowledge of how lexemes are associated with other lexemes (sense relations). Our implicit knowledge of syntagmatic relations facilitates our perception and identification of what we hear and read, enabling us to correct automatically what we hear and see, or what we think we hear and see, when correction is needed: we must have heard *five o'clock* because **fine o'clock* is not a familiar collocation. (An asterisk inserted before a phrase or sentence in the text indicates that that this is not an acceptable English construction.)

PRACTICE 3.2 Syntagmatic relations

The verb *bake* is typically followed by a noun phrase that refers to some item of food (*bread, beans, ham*, etc.) or of clay (*bricks, pottery*, etc.). Each verb below is fairly limited as to the kind of referring expression that can occur as object. Name one or two nouns that can occur in the object.

bounce _____
brandish _____
brew _____
coil _____
flash _____
furl _____
shrug _____
untangle _____

PRACTICE 3.3 Paradigmatic relations

What a lexeme means depends on what it occurs with and also what it contrasts with. What colors does *red* contrast with in these collocations?

a red apple
red hair
a red traffic light
red wine

3.4 Lexical and grammatical meanings

A dog barked.

The above is a meaningful sentence which is composed of smaller meaningful parts. One of the smaller parts is the phrase *a dog* which refers to a certain animal. We call this phrase a **referring expression**. A referring expression is a piece of language that is used AS IF it is linked to something outside language, some living or dead entity or concept or group of entities or concepts. Most of the next chapter is about referring expressions. The entity to which the referring expression is linked is its **referent**.

Another meaningful part is the verb *bark*, which is also linked to something outside of language, an activity associated, here, with the referring expression *a dog*. We call this meaningful part a **predicate**. The use of language generally involves naming or referring to some entity and saying, or predicating, something about that entity.

The sentence also has several kinds of **grammatical meanings**. Every language has a grammatical system and different languages have somewhat different grammatical systems. We can best explain what grammatical meanings are by showing how the sentence *A dog barked* differs from other sentences that have the same, or a similar, referring expression and the same predicate. The grammatical system of English makes possible the expression of meanings like these:

statement vs question:
    A dog barked.   Did a dog bark?

affirmative vs negative:
    A dog barked.   A dog did not bark.   No dog barked.

past vs present:
    A dog barked.   A dog barks.

singular vs plural:
    A dog barked.   Some dogs barked.

indefinite vs definite:
    A dog barked.   The dog barked.

Grammatical meanings, then, are expressed in various ways: the arrangement of words (referring expression before the predicate, for instance), by grammatical affixes like the *-s* attached to the noun *dog* and the *-ed* attached to the verb *bark*, and by grammatical words, or **function words**, like the ones illustrated in these sentences: *do* (in the form *did*), *not*, *a*, *some*, and *the*.

Now let's return to *dog* and *bark*. Their meanings are not grammatical but **lexical**, with associations outside language. They are **lexemes**. A lexeme is a minimal unit that can take part in referring or predicating. All the lexemes of a language constitute the **lexicon** of the language, and all the lexemes that you know make up your personal lexicon.

The term 'lexeme' was proposed by Lyons (1977: 18–25) to avoid complexities associated with the vague word 'word.' Consider these forms:

(a)   go, going, went, gone
(b)   put up with, kick the bucket, dog in the manger

How many words are there in group (a)? Four or one? There are four forms and the forms have four different meanings, but they have a shared meaning, which is lexical, and other meanings of a grammatical nature added to the lexical meaning. We say that these four forms constitute one lexeme – which, for convenience we designate as *go*.

Group (b) presents a different sort of problem. The expression *put up with* combines the forms of *put* and *up* and *with*, but its meaning is not the combination of their separate meanings. Therefore *put up with*, in the sense of 'endure,' 'tolerate,' is a single lexeme. The same must be true of *kick the bucket* meaning 'die' and *dog in the manger* when it refers to a person who will not let others share what he has, even though he does not use it himself.

3.5 Morphemes

A lexeme may consist of just one meaningful part like these:

> arm chair happy guitar lemon shoe

or of more than one meaningful part like these

> armchair unhappy guitarist lemonade shoehorn

The technical term for a minimal meaningful part is **morpheme**. *Arm, chair, happy, guitar, lemon, shoe* and *horn* are all morphemes; none of them can be divided into something smaller that is meaningful. They are free morphemes because they occur by themselves. The elements *un-, -ist* and *-ade* in *unhappy, guitarist* and *lemonade* respectively, are also morphemes; they are bound morphemes which are always attached to something else, as in these examples.

51

3.6 Homonymy and polysemy

A lexeme is a conjunction of form and meaning. The form is fairly easy to determine: in writing it is a sequence of letters, in speech a sequence of phonemes. But meaning is more difficult to determine. In **homonyms**, such as *bank* 'a financial institution' and *bank* 'the edge of a stream,' pronunciation and spelling are identical but meanings are unrelated. In other pairs, numerous in English, such as *steak* and *stake*, pronunciation is identical but spelling is different, reflecting the fact that the words were once different in their phonological form. English also has pairs of **homographs**, two words that have different pronunciations but the same spelling; for example, *bow*, rhyming with *go* and referring to an instrument for shooting arrows, and *bow*, rhyming with *cow* and indicating a bending of the body as a form of respectful greeting.

Lexicographers and semanticists sometimes have to decide whether a form with a wide range of meanings is an instance of polysemy or of homonymy. A **polysemous** lexeme has several (apparently) related meanings. The noun *head*, for instance, seems to have related meanings when we speak of the head of a person, the head of a company, head of a table or bed, a head of lettuce or cabbage. If we take the anatomical referent as the basic one, the other meanings can be seen as derived from the basic one, either reflecting the general shape of the human head or, more abstractly, the relation of the head to the rest of the body.

Dictionaries recognize the distinction between polysemy and homonymy by making a polysemous item a single dictionary entry and making homophonous lexemes two or more separate entries. Thus *head* is one entry and *bank* is entered twice. Producers of dictionaries often make a decision in this regard on the basis of etymology, which is not necessarily relevant, and in fact separate entries are necessary in some instances when two lexemes have a common origin. The form *pupil*, for example, has two different senses, 'part of the eye' and 'school child.' Historically these have a common origin but at present they are semantically unrelated. Similarly, *flower* and *flour* were originally 'the same word,' and so were the verbs *to poach* (a way of cooking in water) and *to poach* ('to hunt [animals] on another person's land'), but the meanings are now far apart and all dictionaries treat them as homonyms, with separate listing. The distinction between homonymy and polysemy is not an easy one to make. Two lexemes are either identical in form or not, but relatedness of meaning is not a matter of yes or no; it is a matter of more or less.

Examine the different occurrences of the verb *ask* in the following sentences:

6   Fred asked Betty where his golf clubs were.
7   Fred asked Donna if she had seen his clubs.
8   Fred asked Charles to help him find his clubs.

Sentences 6 and 7 are about questions, requests for information. The utterances behind sentences 6 and 7 would be something like "Where are my golf clubs, Betty?" and "Have you seen my clubs, Donna?" respectively. Sentence 8 is not a request for information but a request for a kind of action. The utterance behind sentence 8 might be something like "Help me to find my clubs, Charles." To use a term that we explore further in Chapter 9, a request for action is **prospective**: the asking naturally precedes whatever action the other person takes. A request for information has no such relation to the information sought; it is about what the addressee may know at the time of asking.

Now, do we have two homonymous verbs *ask*, or is there just one verb which happens to have two meanings? (We'll leave aside the possibility of more than two meanings.) Before deciding, it may be useful to look at the correspondences in six languages related to English, three Germanic and three Romance.

English	ask (for information)	ask (for action)
Swedish	fråga	bedja
Dutch	vragen	vragen
German	fragen	bitten
French	demander	demander
Spanish	preguntar	pedir
Italian	domandare	chiedere

If this display shows anything, we can conclude that English *ask* is a polysemous verb that corresponds to two different verbs in some other languages. The context in which *ask* occurs determines whether information or a favor is being requested. Therefore, there is no lexical ambiguity.

PRACTICE 3.4 Homonymy

Dictionaries have a single entry for the common noun *needle* but list various 'meanings,' including the eleven below. Is this a single lexeme? If you think it should be considered as more than one lexeme, how would you divide? (Don't be influenced by the order in which the definitions appear here.)

1 the thin, short, pointed leaf of some trees, such as the pine and spruce. 2 a pointed instrument, usually metal, with a sharp point and an eye through which thread is inserted, for sewing. 3 one of a pair of pointed instruments, usually metal, each with a hook at one end, used for crocheting. 4 one of two or more pointed instruments, made of metal, plastic or other material, around which yarn is wrapped, used for knitting. 5 a pointed, hollow instrument connected to a container which is fitted with a plunger, used for injecting medicine, drugs or other liquid substances into the body. 6 a pointed, hollow instrument through which dyes can be inserted into the skin of an individual, creating tattoo designs. 7 a pointed instrument which is heated in some way and used for burning designs in wood. 8 a pointed instrument which is part of a gramophone and which moves in the continuous groove of a record. 9 a pointed piece of metal or other substance, as on a compass, speedometer, thermometer or the like, which moves and indicates some value, numerical or other, from a range of values. 10 the slender, tapered top of a spire. 11 a rock formation which is very narrow in proportion to its height.

PRACTICE 3.5 Homonymy or polysemy?

Several nouns are listed below. Each is followed by two or more illustrations of how the lexeme is used or by two or more short definitions. For each noun try to decide whether the form represents one lexeme with two or more senses (polysemy) or two or more different lexemes that happen to be pronounced (and spelled) alike (homonymy). Don't consult a dictionary before finishing this exercise.

bark	the bark of a dog; the bark of a tree
bit	a tool for drilling into wood; the cutting edge of an axe; the mouthpiece of a bridle; a small quantity of any substance; a small role in a play or film
compound	a substance composed of two or more elements; an enclosure containing land and several buildings
corn	a grain (in North America, maize; in Scotland, rye); a calloused place in the epidermis, especially on the foot
flight	the act of flying; the act of fleeing
foot	the foot of a person or animal; the foot of a hill; the foot of a bed; the foot of a table; the foot of a ladder; the foot of a page; 12 inches
horn	one of two hard, projected growths on the head of certain animals; a wind instrument
junk	any useless material; a type of sailing vessel
pole	a long, comparatively slender piece of wood or metal, more or less rounded; either of the two points, north and south, where the earth's axis of rotation meets the surface; one of the two points on a battery where opposite electrical forces are concentrated
quarry	an animal that is being pursued or hunted; a place from which stone is excavated
school	an educational institution; a group of fish of the same species moving together
tattoo	markings made on the skin by injecting a dye; a signal on a drum or bugle

3.7 Lexical ambiguity

When homonyms can occur in the same position in utterances, the result is **lexical ambiguity**, as in, for example, "I was on my way to the bank." Of course, the ambiguity is not likely to be sustained in a longer discourse. A following utterance, for example, is likely to carry information about depositing or withdrawing money, on the one hand, or, on the other hand, fishing or boating. Quite often homonyms belong to different lexical categories and therefore do not give rise to ambiguity. For instance, *seen* is a form of the verb *see* while *scene* is an unrelated noun; *feet* is a plural noun with concrete reference, *feat* is a singular noun, rather abstract in nature; and so on.

Ambiguity occurs also because a longer linguistic form has a literal sense and a figurative sense.

9   There's a skeleton in our closet.

Skeleton in the closet can mean 'an unfortunate event that is kept a family secret.' With this meaning *skeleton in the closet* is a single lexeme; with its 'literal' meaning it is a phrase composed of several lexemes.

3.8 Sentence meaning

We communicate with utterances, and each utterance is an instance of a sentence. But how can we explain what 'sentence meaning' is? Two points are obvious. First, the meaning of a sentence derives from the meanings of its constituent lexemes and from the grammatical meanings it contains. So if you know all the lexical and grammatical meanings expressed in a sentence, you know the meaning of the sentence, and vice versa. Second, at least if the sentence is a statement, if you know the meaning of the sentence, you know what conditions are necessary in the world for that sentence to be true.

10   Albert Thompson opened the first flour mill in Waterton.

You don't know whether this sentence is true or not, but you know that if it is true, there must exist (at some time) a person named Albert Thompson and a place called Waterton (presuppositions), that Albert Thompson opened a flour mill, and that there was no flour mill in Waterton before Albert Thompson opened his mill (entailments). You know that if this sentence is true, the sentence *Albert Thompson did not open the first flour mill in Waterton* is false (a contradiction).

Truth-conditional semantics is based on the notion that the core meaning of any sentence (any statement) is its truth conditions. Any speaker of the language knows these conditions. If a sentence is true (or false), what other sentences, expressing partly the same, partly different conditions, can be judged by this sentence? If a given sentence is true, does this make another sentence also true, or does it falsify the other sentence, or is there no truth relation? Matters of truth and logic are of more importance in truth-conditional semantics than meanings of lexemes per se. Chapter 5 contains more about truth-conditional semantics.

We are not yet finished with the dimensions of meaning. Often we derive more meaning from what we hear or read than what is actually in the message. Perhaps this is due to an intuition we have or to the fact that the speaker or writer infers something – hints at some further meaning. In semantics we are not interested in intuitions or hints but we are interested in the instances when the language of the message **implicates** some additional meaning that accounts for our inference. Let's look at some examples.

11   One team consisted of six students from Felman College.

Let's say that this sentence represents an utterance that is part of a larger discourse. We understand what it means even though we are unfamiliar with Felman College (if such an entity exists) because we know the lexical and grammatical meanings of the components and we can deduce that *Felman College* names an entity similar to some that we do know. And we can infer more than this. From the phrase *one team* we infer that the larger discourse contains information about at least one other team. Is this in the meaning of the lexeme *team*? Is a team composed of people necessarily in competition with another team or other teams? Does our inference come from the fact that *one team* is paradigmatically related to *a second team, another team*, and so on? Next, compare:

12   One team consisted of the six students from Felman College.

Sentences 11 and 12 tell the same thing about the composition of the team but 12 is more informative – has more meaning – about students from Felman College. From 11 we can infer that there were at least six students from Felman College. Sentence 12 says that there were only six students from Felman College.

We take up implication again in Chapter 11.

Summary

The notion that every word has a single meaning and every meaning is expressed by just one word is utterly wrong and an obstacle to recognizing the complexities in meaningful expressions and in the meanings expressed.

We recognize several kinds of meaning. Some pieces of language refer to something, real or fictitious, outside of language. Any such linguistic form is a referring expression and what it refers to is its referent. Some linguistic forms make comments about referents; these are predicates. In addition there are grammatical meanings, expressed by bound morphemes (affixes), by function words, and by arrangement of forms in a sentence. Referring expressions and predicates have lexical meaning while grammatical morphemes and function words express grammatical meanings. The totality of lexemes in the language constitute the lexicon of the language, and all the lexemes that one individual knows are his or her personal lexicon.

Any meaningful piece of language is a linguistic form. A minimal linguistic form is a morpheme, which may be a free form or a bound form (an affix). In a sentence certain forms have reference and other forms make predications about them. The minimal form that can have reference or can predicate is a lexeme. A set of forms with grammatical affixes is a single lexeme. A non-minimal form with a single meaning is a single lexeme, an idiom.

In general we can note three 'sides' or aspects in the meaning of a lexicon. The denotation is the relation to phenomena outside of language, including imaginary phenomena; the connotation is the cluster of attitudes that the lexeme may evoke; the sense is its various potential relations to other lexemes with which it occurs in utterances.

Two or more forms that are identical in speech but have different meanings are homonyms, different lexemes; forms identical in writing but not in speech nor in meaning are homographs, also different lexemes. Since a lexeme may have a range of meanings, it is not always easy to decide whether two (or more) meanings attached to a single form constitute two (or more) homonyms or a single polysemous lexeme. If two homonyms can occur in the same place in an utterance, the result is lexical ambiguity.

Truth-conditional semantics is the study of meaning through a consideration of the conditions that must exist for a sentence to be true, and how the truth of one sentence relates to the truth or falsity of other sentences.

Suggested reading

1 When lexemes are highly charged with connotations, we call them 'loaded.' Such connotations are the subject of Bolinger (1980), *Language, The Loaded Weapon*. Chapters 7 and 8 (58–88) are especially recommended.

2 Ruhl 1989 argues that, in semantic analysis, lexemes should be presumed initially to be monosemic, to have a single, highly abstract meaning which of course varies somewhat with context. When differences of meaning between two identically pronounced forms are great and cannot be attributed to differences of context, only then should we consider them to be homonyms.

3 A concise explanation of truth-conditional semantics is Saeed (1997, Chapter 4: 79–105).

Semantic roles

A sentence contains certain information, but the same information can be presented in different sentences and in parts of sentences; the information presented, apart from the way it is presented, is called a **proposition**. A proposition can be seen as consisting of a predicate and various noun phrases (referring expressions), each of which has a different role. This chapter explores the structures of propositions and the various roles that the referents of noun phrases can have.

4.1 Sentence and proposition

A traditional way of defining a sentence is 'something that expresses a complete thought.' This definition is a rather strange way of explaining since it assumes that we know what a complete thought is and with this knowledge can determine whether something is or is not a sentence. But surely the procedure must be the reverse. Sentences are more knowable than thoughts. In spite of individual differences speakers of a language generally agree about what is or is not a sentence in their language. Who can say what a complete thought is?

Compare these language expressions:

1a   We walk in the park.
1b   our walk in the park
1c   for us to walk in the park

We call the first a complete sentence, and in writing we begin with a capital letter and end with a period. We say the other two are not complete sentences. But all three expressions have the same semantic content, the same relation to an action or possible action performed in a certain place by two or more people, one of whom is the speaker or writer. The difference is grammatical. The first expression asserts something, makes a statement. The other two expressions can be parts of statements, as for instance:

> We enjoyed our walk in the park.
> It's not too late for us to walk in the park.

but they do not make assertions by themselves. The formal differences among these three expressions – *we*, *our* and *us*, for example – are a matter of grammar, not semantics.

The semantic content shared by the three expressions is a **proposition**. A simple statement like *We walk in the park* expresses a single proposition, something presented as a fact and therefore subject to verification; generally speaking, one can find out if the proposition is true or false. *We don't walk in the park* is the negation of this proposition, and *Do we walk in the park?* is a question about it.

A proposition can be expressed in different sentences.

2a Helen put on a sweater.
2b Helen put a sweater on.

These are different English sentences, but they convey the same message – they express the same proposition.

3a Richard wrote the report.
3b Richard is the one who wrote the report.
3c The report was written by Richard.
3d The report is what Richard wrote.

We may say that these four sentences also express a single proposition but they differ in **focus**: 3b and 3c give a special emphasis to *Richard*, 3d emphasizes *the report*, and 3a has no particular focus. In the approach taken here, a proposition does not have a focus; a sentence may add a focus and may add the focus in different places and in different ways. The four sentences about Richard embody the same proposition. A proposition, then, can be realized as several different sentences.

Now consider this sentence:

4   Richard wrote a report and Helen did, too.

Anyone who knows English recognizes that this sentence tells us two things, that Richard wrote a report and that Helen wrote a report. The sentence does not say this in so many words but any speaker of English implicitly knows this. Sentence 4 contains two propositions, the first expressed in a straightforward way, the second – Helen wrote a report – through the function words *did* and *too*.

A proposition is something abstract but meaningful. It can be expressed in different sentences and in parts of sentences, perhaps with differences of focus but always with the same basic meaning. And, as you recall, any sentence can be expressed in different utterances, produced by different people at different times and in different places. Schematically:

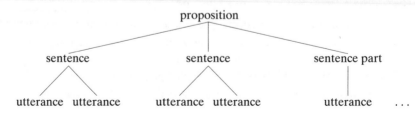

Consider these ways of modifying our original sentence:

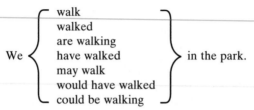

An English sentence has certain kinds of modification that, together, we call **inflection**. Inflection includes **tense** (the distinction between present *walk* and past *walked*, for instance); **aspect** (*are walking, have walked*), and **modality** (*may walk, could walk, should walk*, among other possibilities). Tense, aspect and modality can be combined, as in *were walking, should be walking, would have walked*. These are important semantic elements and are discussed elsewhere in this book, chiefly in chapters 10 and 11, but we consider Inflection separately from the Proposition. A general scheme for a simple sentence, then, has these parts:

Inflection + Proposition (+ Focus)
|
Tense
Aspect
Modality

The description of a sentence is a syntactic analysis. The description of a proposition is a semantic analysis. A syntactic analysis is an account of the lexemes and function words in a sentence, describing how these combine into phrases, and showing the functions that these lexemes and phrases have in the sentence. There are somewhat different ways of doing syntactic analysis, but generally these sentence functions are recognized: **subject**, **predicate**, **object**, **complement** and **adverbial**. Table 4A illustrates some traditional ways of analyzing nine exemplary sentences.

TABLE 4.1 The syntactic analysis of sentences

Subject	Predicate	Object	Adverbial
A window	broke.		
Tom	broke	a window.	
Our dog	is		under the house.
Denise	put	marmalade	on her toast.
Albert	sends	e-mail	to his friends.

Subject	Predicate	Complement	
I	am	thirsty.	
Hector	is	afraid	of the dark.
Mr Whipple	is	a banker.	

Subject	Predicate	Indirect object	Direct object
Albert	sends	his friends	e-mail.

Note that every lexeme and function word is assigned to one of the syntactic functions, subject, predicate, etc., and these functions are listed in the order they have in the sentence. Thus *a window* is subject of the predicate *broke* in the first sentence and object of the same predicate in the second sentence. Note also that the predicate is always a verb. If we change *Albert sends his friends e-mail* to *Albert sent his friends e-mail*, the predicate changes from *sends* to *sent*.

The semantic analysis deals with meaning, the proposition expressed in the sentence, not necessarily with all the function words in the sentence. In semantic analysis we first separate Inflection from Proposition. Then *Albert sends his friends e-mail* and *Albert sent his friends e-mail* have the same proposition, {Albert, send, Albert's friends, e-mail}. The first sentence adds Present Tense to that proposition and the second sentence adds Past Tense.

When Inflection – including Tense – is separated from Proposition, we see that the forms of the verb *be* (*am*, *is*, *are*, *was*, *were*) have no meaning. They are clearly part of the syntactic structure of sentences but not of the semantic structure. In semantic analysis every proposition contains one predicate and a varying number of referring expressions (noun phrases) called **arguments**, like *a window*, *Albert*, *marmalade*, *the house*. The predicate may be a verb, an adjective, a preposition, or a noun phrase. Here are the propositions expressed in the sentences above, with the predicate underlined:

{<u>break</u>, a window}
{<u>break</u>, Tom, a window}
{<u>under</u>, our dog, the house}
{<u>put-on</u>, Denise, marmalade, Denise's toast}
{<u>send</u>, Albert, e-mail, Albert's friends}
{<u>thirsty</u>, I}
{<u>afraid-of</u>, Hector, the dark}
{<u>a banker</u>, Mr Whipple}.

The arguments that accompany the predicate have different semantic functions, or roles, in the proposition. What roles they have depends partly on the nature of the predicate and partly on their own meanings. The semantic structure of a proposition can be represented this way:

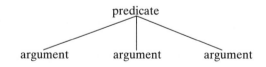

4.2 Semantic roles

5   A window   broke.
6   Tom   broke a window.

Every simple sentence – every proposition – has one predicate and a varying number of referring expressions, or **arguments**. The meaning of a predicate is determined in part by how many arguments it may have and what role those arguments have. For example, the sentences *A window broke*, *A rope broke*, *A plate broke* all contain the verb *break* and a single argument. The breaking of a window, the breaking of a rope and the breaking of a plate are not identical events, of course, and a language might possibly have different verbs to express the coming apart of windows, ropes, plates – and sticks and pieces of ice and other fragile objects. But English *break* can be used with the names of all these things. That is part of its meaning, the scope of its application. What a particular lexeme, such as *break*, can mean depends in part on what lexemes it may co-occur with and what relation it may have with them.

In the sentences *A window broke*, etc. the referring expressions *a window, a rope, a plate* have the same role, the same relation to the verb *break*. Syntactically this function can be called the subject, but that term is too general for semantic analysis. We call this role the affected. A referring expression in the role of affected tells what undergoes the action indicated by the verb, what is changed or affected by this action.

Consider next: *Tom broke a window, Dick broke a rope, Harry broke a plate*. These sentences communicate the same fate for window, rope and plate as the previous sentences. The noun phrases *a window, a rope, a plate* are now syntactically the objects of the verb but in the semantic analysis they still have the role of affected. The referring expressions *Tom, Dick* and *Harry* have the role of agent. The agent role in any sentence is the part played by a referring expression that tells who or what instigates the action of the verb, causes the affect of this action on some other entity, the affected.

Different predicates – verbs, adjectives, prepositions – can be described according to the number of referring expressions, or arguments, that can occur with them and the roles these arguments have. An account of the number of arguments that a predicate has is called the valency of that predicate. Valency theory is a description of the semantic potential of predicates in terms of the number and types of arguments which may co-occur with them. Some predicates, such as *break*, have variable valency: a valency of one in *A window broke* and a valency of two in *Tom broke a window*.

Let's consider the following sentences:

7   It is snowing.
8   My brother snores.
9   Chris is making an omelet.
10 Agnes is writing her mother a letter.

Each of these four sentences is longer than the one before it because it has more arguments. The verbs *snow*, *sleep*, *make* and *write* have different valencies – respectively, valencies of zero, one, two and three – and each of them is typical of a whole group of predicates. In this chapter we discuss valencies of zero, one, and two. Valencies of three or more are taken up in Chapter 6.

4.2.1 Valency zero

7   It is snowing.

(a)   The first sentence in the group above has the verb *snow*, and the subject is *it*, but *it* doesn't name anything. The sentence has a subject because English requires a subject, but this subject does not correspond to anything in the underlying proposition. We say that *snow* is a zero-argument verb. Other zero-argument verbs are seen in the following:

11   It's raining.
12   It sleeted (yesterday).
13   It has been thundering (in the west).

English requires the presence of *it* with **weather verbs** like *rain*, *snow*, *sleet*, *thunder*, but *it* does not refer to anything. These verbs are among the few in the language that do not require some referent to be named in the sentence. Tense and aspect must be expressed (*rains*, *rained*; *is snowing*, *has been snowing*) and indications of time and place can be added (*yesterday*, *in the west*, etc.) but a sentence is complete without anything being named.

Here are similar sentences with **weather adjectives** as predicates:

14   It's windy (today).
15   It was rainy (all last month).

There are not many such adjectives.

We might represent the propositions underlying sentences 7 and 14 this way, keeping in mind that inflection is not part of a proposition:

weather event | weather condition
snow | windy

4.2.2 Valency one

8   My brother snores.

Sentence 8 has the verb *snore* and a subject *my brother*. A lot of verbs are like *snore*: they have a subject but no object. They are intransitive verbs or, in our terminology, one-argument predicates. Other one-argument verbs appear in the sentences below.

16   The dog is sleeping.
17   Larry laughed.
18   The earth rotates (on its axis).

19   Grandfather died (last week).
20   A volcano erupted.
21   The cake fell.

Other examples of one-argument verbs are these:

giggle hum shiver weep whistle work

Now let's consider the role or roles that the arguments have. In the first group, 16–18, the predicates *sleep*, *laugh* and *rotate* express actions; they tell what *the dog*, *Larry* and *the earth* do, respectively. Consequently, each of these arguments names an **actor** that carries out the **action**. These three sentences, then, or the propositions that they express, have this composition, with the arguments indicated in abbreviated form:

Argument | Predicate
actor | action
dog | sleep
Larry | laugh
earth | rotate

Turning to the second group, 19–21, it would be possible to say that Grandfather and a volcano and the cake did something and the respective predicates tell what they did, but these predicates are not like those of the first group. The predicates *die, erupt, fall* tell of an **event**, a change in the condition of the entity named by the argument, and the entity named in the argument undergoes this change, is **affected** by it. The structure of this group of sentences is:

```
     Argument              Predicate
        |                      |
     affected                event
        |                      |
    Grandfather               die
      volcano                erupt
       cake                   fall
```

Table 4.2 gives definitions and illustrations for all the semantic roles introduced in this chapter.

TABLE 4.2 Semantic roles

actor	The role of an argument that performs some action without affecting any other entity. <u>*Sylvia*</u> *left.*
affected	The role of an argument that undergoes a change due to some event or is affected by some other entity. *A <u>window</u> broke. Tom broke <u>a window</u>. <u>Betty</u> likes opera. Opera delights <u>Betty</u>.*
affecting	The role of an argument that, without any action, affects another entity. *Betty likes <u>opera</u>. <u>Opera</u> delights Betty.*
agent	The role of an argument that by its action affects some other entity. <u>*Tom*</u> *broke a window.*
associate	The role of an argument that tells the status or identity of another argument, the **theme**: *Roger is <u>a student</u>.*
effect	The role of an argument that comes into existence through the action of the predicate. *Tillie baked <u>a pie</u>.*
place	The role of an argument that names the location in which the action of the predicate occurs. *The fireman climbed <u>a ladder</u>.*
theme	The role of an argument that is the topic of a predicate that does not express action – a stative predicate. <u>*Audrey*</u> *is a computer expert.*

> For each sentence here decide if it has the semantic structure Actor + Action or Affected + Event. Does the subject name something that is acting or something that is affected?
>
> (a) My head aches.
> (b) All animals breathe.
> (c) Denis is (always) complaining.
> (d) Fanny fainted.
> (e) The pond froze (last night).
> (f) The woman frowned.
> (g) They gossip (a lot).
> (h) Arnold hurried.
> (i) The lock has rusted.
> (j) You were snoring.

One-argument adjectives are numerous. Some of them are used in the sentences that follow.

22   This soup is cold.
23   Terry is impatient.
24   Henrietta was rather reckless.
25   The bottle is empty.

In this group the predicates are adjective phrases which describe the entities named by their subjects. In 24 the label *reckless* may well be an evaluation of Henrietta because of how she acted and, in 25, if the bottle is empty, that is likely to be the result of a change, becoming empty; but none of these predicates express action or change, which are dynamic processes – they simply describe existing states. We might make a distinction here: *cold, empty, tall, heavy, blond* and other adjectives are objective terms; people will generally agree whether any of them is applied accurately to a specific entity at a specific time. *Impatient, careless, clever, thoughtful, pretty, tiresome* and others involve subjective evaluations; they are used when people ascribe qualities or characteristics to entities, and other people may or may not agree. The subject of each sentence is simply the topic or **theme** of what is said. The structure:

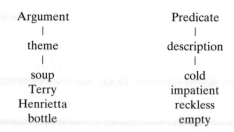

Argument	Predicate
|	|
theme	description
|	|
soup	cold
Terry	impatient
Henrietta	reckless
bottle	empty

Similarly, a referring expression occurring after a form of *be* is a one-argument predicate.

26 This man is a carpenter.
27 Dextrose and fructose are sugars.
28 Eddy Eckstein is the village idiot.
29 Cora and Willis are the class leaders

Each sentence in this group has a referring expression as predicate. The predicate in some way provides an **identity** for the entity named by the subject, as one or more of a kind (a carpenter, sugars) or as the only one or ones of the kind (the village idiot, the class leaders). Structure:

Argument	Predicate
|	|
theme	identity
|	|
man	carpenter
dextrose and fructose	sugars
Eddy Eckstein	village idiot
Cora and Willis	class leaders

Sentences 28 and 29 are **equational** propositions. Theme and identity can be reversed to create sentences that differ only in focus: The village idiot is Eddy Eckstein, The class leaders are Cora and Willis.

In some instances it is difficult to say whether a particular sentence has the structure Agent + Action or Affected + Event, though the distinction is quite clear on the whole. But the difference between the structures Theme + Description and Theme + Identity is not at all clear. How much difference is there, really, between these two?

30a Boris is Russian.
30b Boris is a Russian.

4.2.3 Valency two

9   Chris is making an omelet.

Most verbs take a subject and an object; they are two-argument predicates. One of them is *make*, illustrated in sentence 9 above. Other examples are *need* and *use*. We can't simply say **Chris is making* or **I need* or **Sue used*. A statement with *make* must contain a mention of who makes and what is made, and likewise with *need* and *use*.

31   The cat killed a rat.
32   I broke the window.
33   Bert hit Harry.

34   The cat dug a hole.
35   Chris is making an omelet.
36   Picasso created a masterpiece.

37   Jennie crossed the street.
38   Fiona entered the room.
39   Simon climbed a tree.

The first group of sentences, 31–3, express some action by one entity which affects another entity. The first argument denotes an **agent** and the second argument names the entity affected.

An agent is involved in an action that has some effect on another entity or entities; an actor, on the other hand, is involved in some action (e.g. running) that has no necessary effect on others.

$$
\begin{array}{ccc}
\text{Argument}_1 & \text{– Predicate –} & \text{Argument}_2 \\
| & | & | \\
\text{agent} & \text{action} & \text{affected} \\
| & | & | \\
\text{cat} & \text{kill} & \text{rat} \\
\text{I} & \text{break} & \text{window} \\
\text{Bert} & \text{hit} & \text{Harry}
\end{array}
$$

In sentences 34–6 there is a difference. The cat doesn't just affect a hole nor Chris an omelet nor Picasso a masterpiece. The hole, omelet and masterpiece are the result or **effect** of the action. They come into existence because of the action.

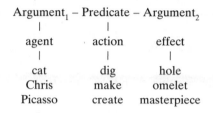

	Argument$_1$	– Predicate –	Argument$_2$
	agent	action	effect
	cat	dig	hole
	Chris	make	omelet
	Picasso	create	masterpiece

The predicates of the third group of sentences, 37–9, also express some action performed by an actor and the action involves movement with respect to a place. To enter, leave, cross or climb entails some location (though the place does not always have to be mentioned; see section **4.4**, below). The second argument in each of these sentences has the role of place.

	Argument$_1$	– Predicate –	Argument$_2$
	actor	action	place
	Jennie	cross	street
	Fiona	enter	room
	Simon	climb	tree

The next groups of sentences do not express any action. They tell how one entity affects – or fails to affect – another entity.

40 The decision surprised us all.
41 You're disturbing everybody.
42 The comedian didn't impress the audience.

43 Oliver was envious of his brother.
44 Oliver envied his brother.
45 Angie was angry with Algernon.

In 40–2 the predicate expresses an **affect**, the first argument names the entity that affects – that has the **affecting** role – and the second argument names the entity that is affected.

	Argument$_1$	– Predicate –	Argument$_2$
	affecting	affect	affected
	decision	surprise	us
	you	disturb	everybody
	comedian	impress	audience

The components of 43–5 have the same semantic roles but the order in which they occur in these English sentences is the reverse. If Oliver envies, or loves, or hates, or admires his brother, it is Oliver who is affected by these emotions. (If the brother is affected by Oliver's envy, a different sentence is needed to communicate this fact.)

$$\text{Argument}_1 - \text{Predicate} - \text{Argument}_2$$

affected	affect	affecting
Oliver	envy	brother

An adjective cannot have a referring expression following directly. There must be a preposition between adjective and noun phrase. We consider the combination of adjective + preposition a compound adjective that takes an object – a two-argument adjective. Some two-argument adjectives appear in the next sentences.

46   I'm afraid of that dog.
47   We were not aware of the accident.
48   Aren't you curious about . . . ?

These also express 'affect' and the affected is in subject position.

$$\text{Argument}_1 - \text{Predicate} - \text{Argument}_2$$

affected	affect	affecting
I	afraid	dog
we	aware	accident
Ella	curious	plans

PRACTICE 4.2

Four structures are represented in the sentences below: 1 agent-action-affected, 2 agent-action-effect, 3 actor-action-place, 4 affecting-affect-affected, the last of these occurring in the order affected-affect-affecting, as well. Read each sentence and tell its structure.

(a) Jenny admired the painting.
(b) Derek bent the tube.
(c) Fabian broke a vase.
(d) The children built a sand castle.
(e) The boys climbed the wall.
(f) I closed the door.
(g) The chef cooked a great meal.
(h) Sandra covered the birdcage.
(i) We crossed the street.
(j) That medicine cured my headache.
(k) A mad bull damaged the fence.
(l) Stout troops defended the castle.
(m) Stout troops destroyed the castle.
(n) We quickly dug a ditch.
(o) Little Audrey drew a picture of two kittens.
(p) (On the way to the post office) I dropped the package.
(q) We enjoyed the concert.
(r) Alan entered the library.
(s) Doris hid the money (in the flowerpot).
(t) Mr Bainbridge (accidentally) killed a bird.
(u) Mother mended the shirt.
(v) The submarine sank a troop ship.

Our next sentences are about neither action nor affecting. The predicate merely acts as a **link** between one argument, a theme, and another argument, its **associate**. The predicate is a linking, or relational, predicate.

49 Sheila is <u>like</u> her mother.
50 This present is <u>for</u> you.
51 Tom is <u>with</u> Ann.
52 The book is <u>about</u> fossils.

$$\text{Argument}_1 - \text{Predicate} - \text{Argument}_2$$

theme	link	associate
Sheila	like	mother
present	for	you
Tom	with	Ann
book	about	fossils

A relational predicate may indicate the relation of a theme and its associate in space.

	Theme		*Link*	*Associate*
53	Canada	is	north of	the United States.
54	The USA	is	south of	Canada.
55	The books	are	in/on	the desk.
56	The bank	is	near/behind	our office.

Some linking predicates locate events in time.

57	The party	will be	on	Saturday.
58	The next game	is	at	three o'clock.
59	The meeting	is	after	class.

So all prepositions which indicate position in space or time are two-argument predicates:

at   in   on   near   beside   under   over

Terms that express kinship and other social relations are linking predicates. You can't be an aunt or a friend or an employee or a mayor without being aunt, etc. of some person or of some entity composed of people.

60	The Browns are neighbors of the Greens.
61	Julie is Carol's daughter.
62	Mr Babcock is my boss.
63	I am an employee of Barton & Dutton.

Theme	*Link*	*Associate*
Browns	neighbors-of	Greens
Julie	daughter-of	Carol
Mr Babcock	boss-of	me
I	employee-of	Barton & Dutton

PRACTICE 4.3

If Mr and Mrs Van Uppington give a sum of money to the Arcadia Arts Association, they are benefactors of the Association. Is there a corresponding term (*benefactee*?) for the Association in relation to the Van Uppingtons? If Uncle Hubert dies and leaves his estate to Fred and Donna, they become his heirs. Is there a common term (not the legalism *legator*) which expresses his relation to them through the bequest? The lexemes *widow(er)* and *orphan* are commonly used as status predicates (*Poor Audrey is an orphan*). Are they used as relational predicates (*Audrey is the orphan of ...*)?

The term associate is intended in a very general way. It includes measurements of size, weight, value, and the like.

	Theme	*Link*	*Associate*
64	This package	weighs	five kilos.
65	It	cost	twenty dollars.

All two-argument predicates, whether verbs, adjectives, prepositions or noun phrases, are transitive predicates in a semantic sense. Syntactically, however, there is a difference: a sentence with a verb, such as *Chris made the omelet* can be turned into a passive sentence, *The omelet was made by Chris*. This passive sentence has the same arguments, but in the passive sentence *an omelet* is the topic, rather than *Chris*. We use passive sentences for two rather different purposes. One purpose is to put emphasis, or focus, on the agent, here *Chris* (*Alison brewed the coffee but the omelet was made by Chris*). The other possible purpose is just the opposite, to avoid mentioning an agent (*Within a few minutes the table was set, coffee was brewed, and an omelet was made*).

4.3 Some changes in valency

We need to take account not only of how many arguments a verb may have but also how many it must have. Instead of the full sentence *Agnes wrote her mother a letter*, for example, it is possible to omit *her mother* or *a letter* or both of them and say just *Agnes wrote a letter*, or *Agnes wrote (to) her mother* or *Agnes wrote*. The sentence is less informative when it has fewer arguments, but it is still a legitimate sentence and the meaning of *write* does not change.

Some predicates can be used in a sentence that has two arguments and in another sentence that has only one argument, as with *Tom broke the window* and *The window broke*. We now look at four different groups of two-argument verbs.

66   The car needs a new battery.

67a   We ate lunch (in the kitchen).
67b   We ate (in the kitchen).

68a   Maureen bathed the baby (in the tub).
68b   Maureen bathed (in the tub).

69a   I rolled the ball (down the street).
69b   The ball rolled (down the street).

Predicates like *need* (66) always have two arguments. While one might possibly think of a context in which an utterance "The car needs" is acceptable, such an occurrence is rare. Certain verbs, *need*, *use*, *want* and others, must have two arguments.

The verb *eat* is different. Comparing 67a and 67b, we see that 67a contains more specific information than 67b, but the meaning of *ate* is the same. The predicate *eat* is inherently two-argument because the action it refers to is two-argument; if you eat, you eat something. But in English we can use the predicate *eat* without mentioning what is eaten.

Consider sentences 68a and 68b: 68b does not simply have less information than 68a; it conveys the information that Maureen bathed herself. Certain predicates, like bathe, are **reflexive**, self-directed, if they occur without an object. Sentence 68a has two obvious arguments: *Maureen*, the actor, and *the baby*, the affected. In sentence 68b the argument *Maureen* could be said to have two roles, actor and affected, since it is Maureen who bathes and Maureen who gets bathed. However, such predicates as *choke*, *drown* and *suffocate* are problematic. Consider, for example:

70a   Harvey drowned his mother-in-law.
70b   Harvey drowned.

In 70a *Harvey* names the agent and *his mother-in-law* clearly tells who was affected by the action of this predicate. In 70b *Harvey* is certainly the affected. Is *Harvey* also the agent? That would depend on whether Harvey committed suicide by drowning or drowned accidentally. Whichever is the case, the information is not in the sentence.

PRACTICE 4.4

The following verbs are like *bathe* and *drown*. Each one can occur with a subject and object, expressing, respectively, agent and affected. And each verb can occur with only a subject, which may express agent and affected, as in the case of *Maureen bathed*, or, as in *Harvey drowned*, the subject tells who is affected but is not clear about agency. Which of the following are like *bathe* and which are like *drown*?

change	scratch	suffocate
choke	shave	undress
dress	show off	wake (up)
fail	stand (up)	wash

Note that with some other predicates we have to use a reflexive pronoun to indicate a reflexive meaning: *I hurt myself, They introduced themselves*. It is possible to say *Maureen bathed herself*, but this sentence conveys no information different from the shorter *Maureen bathed*. In the languages closest to English the use of a reflexive pronoun is more usual. The table on page 82 gives French and German equivalents of some English verbs like *bathe* and *drown*. Reflexive pronouns – *se* in French, *sich* in German as equivalents of English *himself, herself, themselves* – are more usual in those languages than *himself/herself*, etc. in English.

Sentences 69a and 69b are analogous to *Tom broke the window* and *The window broke*. We might say that the predicate *roll* has two different, though related, meanings in the two sentences. First we have a sentence with the structure Agent-Action-Affected; then there is a sentence Affected-Action. What does *roll* 'really' mean? Something that people do to round objects such as balls and hoops and barrels? Or an action that round objects perform? If we take 69a as a sentence that shows the 'real' meaning of roll – something that a person does – then 69b is similar to the passive version of 69a: *The ball was rolled (by me)*.

Or suppose, instead, we say that 69b illustrates the 'true' meaning of roll, an action that balls and other round objects perform. Then the predicate in 69a has a causative meaning: I caused the ball to roll, made the ball roll.

At any rate, the languages which are closest to English –
Germanic, Romance and Slavic – typically use reflexive constructions
in the equivalent of *The ball rolls*, *The window breaks* and the like.

PRACTICE 4.5

Each of the following sentences has a verb and two arguments,
and in each case that verb can also be used in a sentence with
only one argument. Decide which of the three types is represented. Which predicates are like *eat*, which are like *bathe*, and
which are like *roll*? One of them is like *eat* and *roll*.

(a)   Mary woke her husband (at seven o'clock).

(b)   Our team lost the game.

(c)   The boys are flying kites.

(d)   They played tennis (all afternoon).

(e)   The heat melted the paraffin.

(f)   Mr Carson started the car.

(g)   David rang the bell.

(h)   Allen wouldn't help us.

(i)   Yolanda weaves tablecloths (for pleasure).

(j)   Did your barber shave you?

Summary

A sentence is defined as a composite of inflection and proposition,
and a proposition consists of a subject and a predicate. Inflection
includes agreement and tense; agreement is the formal bond between
subject and predicate, a bond that varies considerably from one
language to another. Tense is a system of contrasts that locates the
general meaning of the proposition in the past, present or future,
from the time-perspective of the speaker; and different languages
have quite different tense systems.

TABLE 4.3 An interlingual comparison

English	French	German
abstain (from)	s'abstenir (de)	sich enthalten (von)
develop	se développer	sich entwickeln
dress	s'habiller	sich ankleiden
drown	se noyer	ertrinken
hide	se cacher	sich verbergen
keep away	s'éloigner	sich fernhalten
prepare	se préparer	sich vorbereiten
recover	se rétablir	sich erholen
remember	se souvenir	sich erinnnen
shave	se raser	sich rasieren
spread	s'étendre	sich ausbreiten
stretch	s'allonger	sich erstrecken
surrender	se rendre	sich ergeben
trouble (to do)	se déranger	sich bemühen
undress	se déshabiller	sich entkleiden
withdraw	se retirer	sich zurückziehen

A proposition consists of a predicate and varying numbers of arguments, or referring expressions. The number of arguments that accompany a particular predicate is called its valency. We have examined valencies of zero, one, two and three. The meaning of a predicate is partly determined by the valency and by the semantic roles that these arguments have. In this chapter eight semantic roles have been recognized and given these labels:

> actor affected affecting agent associate
> effect place theme

Two others, source and goal, were mentioned in passing.

Suggested reading

What are called semantic roles here have been called semantic cases, thematic roles, participant roles, or thematic functions by other linguists. Not surprisingly, there are also differences in the number of semantic roles recognized by different writers and in the names given to these roles. A good account, different from the one presented here is Frawley (1992: 201–39).

Fillmore (1968), Anderson (1985), and Allerton (1975) are different introductions to the theory of such semantic roles. Dixon (1991) is an extensive application of such a theory to the description of English grammar. Jackendoff, (1985) and (1990), argues that such semantic roles are unnecessary for semantic analysis, which should, instead, make use of detailed feature analysis of predicates and referring expressions. The argument is continued and more extensively illustrated by Ravin (1990).

Note on the text

In this chapter the semantic role 'agent' has been exemplified only with human referring expressions, as in *Tom broke the window*. However, the cause of a window breaking and similar acts need not be a human. In *A stone broke the window* the phrase *a stone* may be said to have the role of means or instrument (cf. *Tom broke the window with a stone*). In *The storm broke the window* the subject has the role of 'event' (cf. *The window broke during the storm*). Agent, means and event might be regarded as three sub-types of a more general role Cause.

Chapter 5

Lexical relations

One part of knowing the meanings of lexemes in any language is the recognition that two or more lexemes may have some semantic relationship: *father* and *mother*; *father* and *son*; *father* and *paternal*; *employer* and *employee*; *big* and *large*; *big* and *little*; *red, yellow* and *blue*. Each of these sets shows a different relationship. Two of these lexemes, *employer* and *employee*, are related formally as well as semantically; such morphological relations are the topic of Chapter 13. The present chapter deals with semantic relations that have no formal similarity.

We consider two approaches to the description of lexical relations, **semantic field theory** and **truth conditional semantics**. Field theory is an attempt to classify lexemes according to shared and differentiating features. For example, *wasp, hornet, bee* and other items denote 'flying, stinging insects'; *moth* and *housefly*, among others, denote insects that fly but do not sting; *ant* and *termite* are names of insects that neither fly nor sting. (And what differentiates wasp, hornet and bee from one another? What differentiates insects from other living things?) Entomologists develop a careful classification on a scientific basis but semanticists often need to pay more attention to folk taxonomy, the traditional ways in which non-scientists classify the phenomena of their world.

Truth conditional semantics studies lexical relations by comparing predications that can be made about the same referring expression. Its task is to account for the meaning relations between different expressions in a language. Three such relations are **entailment**, **paraphrase** and **contradiction**. Entailment is the relation between two propositions – let's label them 'p' and 'q' – such that if p is true, q must also be true, but if q is true, it does not necessarily follow that p is true. If it is true that my necktie is (entirely) maroon, is it true that my necktie is red? If it is true that my necktie is red, is it true that my necktie is maroon? Paraphrase is the relation between two propositions, p and q, such that if either is true, the other is necessarily true also, and if either is false, the other is false. If it is true that my necktie was cheap, is it true or false that my necktie was inexpensive? If it is true that my necktie was inexpensive, is it true or false that my necktie was cheap? Contradiction is the relation between two propositions such that if either is true, the other is necessarily false. If my necktie was cheap, is it true or false that my necktie was expensive? If it was expensive, was it cheap?

5.1 Lexical fields

To some extent we can 'define' a lexeme by telling what 'set' it belongs to and how it differs from other members of the same set. Some obvious sets of this sort are sports (*tennis, badminton, golf, soccer, basketball* ...), creative writings (*poem, novel, short story, biography, essay* ...), manual occupations (*electrician, plumber, welder, carpenter, painter* ...), colors (*red, blue, black, green, yellow* ...). It is not difficult to say what the members of each set have in common. It may be more troublesome to say just how much is included in the set and to find the truly essential characteristics that differentiate each lexeme in a set from all the others in the same set, to establish the most economical system of features that explains how the members of the set are related to one another.

Some lexical sets involve part-whole relationships (*arm* includes *hand*, which includes *finger* and *thumb*). The set *second-minute-hour-day* is a part-whole relationship that is also hierarchical. Some sets are sequential (numbers *one, two, three* etc.) or cyclical (*January, February*, etc.; *Sunday, Monday*, etc.; *spring, summer, autumn, winter*).

Some sets, mostly small ones, form paradigms. The words *man, woman, boy* and *girl*, all denoting humans, are interrelated this way:

	Male	*Female*
Adult	man	woman
Child	boy	girl

[Human] is the semantic feature shared by all members of the set and through which *tiger, tree* and numerous other lexemes are excluded from the set. Using square brackets to indicate such semantic features, [male/female], and [adult/child] are the features, or components, that differentiate the members of the set from one another.

87

The determination of such features has been called **componential analysis**.

The paradigm provides definitions (*man* = [adult male human], and so on) and analogies (*man* is to *woman* as *boy* is to *girl*, *boy* is to *man* as *girl* is to *woman*); in other words, a paradigm shows that lexemes are systematically related. Definitions can be made somewhat more sophisticated through binary features; instead of [male] and [female] the labels can be [+ male] and [- male] (or [- female] and [+ female]), and instead of [adult] and [child] we may have [+ adult] and [- adult] (or [- child] and [+ child]). But the notion of binarity raises problems: can all contrasts be expressed as pairs, Yes versus No? In this case we may accept that humans are either male or female; sex is a biological distinction and clearly binary. Age, however, is a continuum, and the distinctions we recognize are partly biological and partly social. Being social, they are arbitrary. Note that English has a lexeme *adolescent*, which is [- adult] and [- child], but there are no English terms for male adolescent and female adolescent except *boy* and *girl*.

For a much-used illustration of componential analysis let's consider these nouns:

stool   chair   bench   sofa

These have in common a component [piece of furniture] that is also shared by, for example, *table*, but not by *door*. They also share a component [furniture for sitting], which *table* does not share. How do the four items differ from one another? Clearly, *stool* and *chair* differ from the other two in being [for one person]. Let's say that *chair* differs from *stool* in the feature [having a back]; all chairs have backs while stools do not – but see below. As for the differentiating feature for *bench* and *sofa*, we might be inclined to consider that also to be [having a back]: a sofa must have a back, while a bench may or may not. A better candidate for a differentiating feature is [having upholstery]; a sofa must be [+ upholstery] and a bench is [- upholstery]. Upholstery is not a necessary element, a defining feature, of a chair, nor are arms nor rockers. The important point here is the recognition of two kinds of features, distinctive and non-distinctive. All features that can be recognized in an entity are part of its description, but the definition of a lexeme within a set or field requires us to note what feature or features distinguish it from other members of the set or field and what features are just 'there,' not distinctive. (There is a problem, however, about the lexeme *stool*. A so-called 'bar stool,' with longer legs than most stools, may have a back. Is it then not a stool, or might we say that the distinctive feature for stool is [no back unless long legs]?)

The advantage of componential analysis is that it reflects the system through which lexemes have their respective senses. To tell what something is requires us to tell what it is not, what it contrasts with and what feature or features make the contrast possible. A possible disadvantage of componential analysis, though not a necessary one, is that we may find ourselves unduly concerned with classification of the phenomena represented in language, forgetting that our concern is language itself.

SUGGESTED PROJECTS

Lexical fields that have been studied in English include the following. Choose one (or more) of these articles and report on the content in class:

verbs of cooking	Lehrer (1969)
containers	Lehrer (1970)
verbs of judging	Fillmore (1971)
spatial terms	Clark (1973)
temporal terms	Leech (1969)

Lehrer (1974: 15–43) is a good explanation of the theory of semantic fields.

How many colors are there? It has long been noted that different cultures recognize different numbers of colors and divide the color spectrum in different ways. Berlin and Kay (1969), revised in Kay and McDaniel (1978), showed that there is a hierarchy of eleven basic colors and that different societies choose from this hierarchy in certain possible sequences. This is a good topic for further investigation.

5.2 Kinship

Kinship systems make an interesting area for componential analysis. Kinship is universal since all humans are related to other humans through blood ties and through marriage, but kinship systems differ from society to society. A relationship is a kind of predicate. Sentences such as *Harold is Alice's father* and *Rose is Jerry's sister* have a propositional content that we represent this way:

Theme	Predicate	Associate
Harold	father-of	Alice
Rose	sister-of	Jerry

Some of the predicate relations in all kinship systems can be described with four primitive features: [parent], [offspring], [sibling] and [spouse]. We also need the components [male] and [female], of course, which we will indicate as M and F, respectively. Combining M and F with the four basic features gives definitions of eight predicates: father = M parent, mother = F parent, brother = M sibling, sister = F sibling, son = M offspring, daughter = F offspring, husband = M spouse, wife = F spouse.

Other relations are defined by combinations of features: grandmother = parent's F parent, grandfather = parent's M parent, granddaughter = offspring's F offspring, grandson = offspring's M offspring.

Note that in English, and in European languages generally, the difference between male and female is marked only with regard to the person indicated: both males and females call their female sibling 'sister,' a male sibling 'brother.' In contrast, some kinship systems have 'cross-siblings.' Tok Pisin, the national language of Papua New Guinea, began as a creole form of English and has acquired a substantial part of its vocabulary from English, but the way the vocabulary is used often reflects a different cultural outlook. In Tok Pisin the word *borata*, from English 'brother,' means sibling of the same sex as oneself, and *sesta*, from 'sister,' is a sibling of the opposite sex (Hall 1949: 74). Thus:

	male sibling	*female sibling*
male speaker	borata	sesta
female speaker	sesta	borata

In Tok Pisin, then, [same-sex] and [cross-sex] replace M and F as features combining with [sibling].

Languages of East Asia have another feature in their kinship systems, using terms that distinguish older and younger siblings. Mandarin Chinese, for example, has *gē* for '(one's own) older brother,' *dì* 'younger brother,' *jiě* 'older sister,' *mèi* 'younger sister.'

In English *grandmother* names the mother of one's mother and the mother of one's father, and *grandfather* is similarly the father of either parent; the sex of the person named is distinguished but not the sex of the intermediate relative. Compare the Swedish terms *farfar*, *farmor*, *morfar* and *mormor*, which, rather transparently, distinguish the four grandparents from one another. Similarly, the words used in English for siblings of one's parents and offspring of one's siblings have rather wide application. An *aunt*, in English, is the sister of either parent – or the wife of a brother of either parent – and *uncle* is the brother of either parent or the husband of the sister of either. A nephew and a niece are, respectively, the son and daughter of one's brother or sister, and also, respectively, the husband and wife of a sibling's offspring.

That is,

```
uncle   = parent's M sibling; parent's sibling's M spouse
aunt    = parent's F sibling; parent's sibling's F spouse
nephew  = sibling's M offspring; spouse's sibling's M offspring
niece   = sibling's F offspring; spouse's sibling's F offspring
```

Leaving the sex difference aside for the moment, we can condense the four previous definitions this way:

```
uncle/aunt = parent's sibling('s spouse)
nephew/niece = (spouse's) sibling's offspring
```

The lexeme *cousin* is the only English kinship term that does not distinguish sex (though it was borrowed from French, in which the distinction is made – *cousin*, *cousine*). We restrict the lexeme here to 'first cousin.'

```
cousin = parent's sibling's offspring
```

Relations that exist from birth are **consanguineal** relations. Relationships that are established through marriage are called **affinities**. These are expressed in English with the suffix *-in-law*.

mother-in-law/father-in-law = spouse's F/M parent
daughter-in-law/son-in-law = offspring's F/M spouse
sister-in-law = spouse's F sibling; sibling's F spouse
brother-in-law = spouse's M sibling; sibling's M spouse

Again English has a limited number of lexemes with rather wide application. Compare Russian, in which the vocabulary makes meticulous distinctions in affinity, including the following:

svëkor	husband's father
svekrov	husband's mother
test'	wife's father
tëšča	wife's mother
dever'	husband's brother
zolovka	husband's sister
šurin	wife's brother
svojačenica	wife's sister

To describe kinship in Japanese another pair of features must be introduced, [self] and [other]. Japanese has two lexemes for every relationship, one used in talking about one's own kin and the other for somebody else's relatives. Thus *chichi* can be used only for one's own father, *o-toosan* for someone else's father.

	Related to the speaker	*Related to others*
wife	tsuma, kanai	okusan
husband	shujin	go-shujin
mother	haha	o-kaasan
father	chichi	o-toosan
older sister	ane	o-nee-san
older brother	ani	o-nii-san
younger sister	imooto	imooto-san
younger brother	otooto	otooto-san

5.3 Hyponymy

Turning now to truth conditional semantics, let's consider these pairs of sentences:

1a   Rover is a collie.
1b   Rover is a dog.
2a   There are tulips in the vase.
2b   There are flowers in the vase.

Here we see a kind of relation that is an example of **entailment**. If we know that sentence 1a is true, we know that 1b must also be true; but if we know that 1a is not true, we cannot say anything about the truth of 1b; if we know that 1b is true, we do not know if 1a is true or not; if we know that 1b is not true, we know that 1a is not true. The relationship between 2a and 2b is analogous. The term *collie* is a **hyponym** of *dog* and *tulip* is a hyponym of *flower*; *dog* and *flower* are, respectively, the **superordinates** of *collie* and *tulip*. (Some semanticists use the term 'hyperonym' instead of 'superordinate.')

We can also say 'A collie is a dog' and 'A tulip is a flower.' Any lexeme that can be substituted for a hyponym is also a hyponym. *Chihuahua, Dalmatian* and *Irish setter* are other hyponyms of *dog*, and they are **co-hyponyms** of *collie*. *Daffodil* and *rose* are two co-hyponyms of *tulip*.

Note that the denotation of the hyponym is included in the denotation of the superordinate (the set of all collies is included in the set of all dogs), but the meaning of the superordinate is included in the meaning of the hyponym (the characteristic of being a dog is part of the characteristic of being a collie). A sentence with a hyponym (e.g. *There's a Palomino in that field*) is more informative than a sentence with the corresponding superordinate (*There's a horse in that field*).

The relationship between two sentences [a] and [b] that differ only in that [a] contains a hyponym and [b] contains a superordinate can be summarized this way:

$$a \rightarrow b \quad \sim a \rightarrow ? \quad b \rightarrow ? \quad \sim b \rightarrow \sim a$$

The truth of [a] entails the truth of [b], and the falsity of [b] entails the falsity of [a]; but neither the falsity of [a] nor the truth of [b] can lead to any certain conclusion about the other.

The same information can be presented in tabular form:

a	b	b	a
T	T	T	?
F	?	F	F

If we join two of these sentences with *and*,

3a   Rover is a collie and (Rover is) a dog

we create a redundant sentence called a **tautology**. A tautology is a sentence with two predications, such that one entails the other. If we combine two of these sentences but have them differ in polarity,

3b   Rover is a collie but (Rover is) not a dog

the result is a **contradiction**, a sentence with two predications such that one denies the other.

Hyponym and superordinate may be nouns, as in the examples above. The same relation is found also in adjectives and in verbs.

4a   My necktie is maroon.
4b   My necktie is red.
5a   The weary soldiers trudged forward.
5b   The weary soldiers moved forward.

Let's look back at two sentences from chapter 4:

We ate lunch (in the kitchen).
We ate (in the kitchen).

The relation between these sentences is the same as the hyponym-superordinate relation. The first sentence is more informative than the second. If the first sentence is true, the second must also be true – assuming the same identity for 'we' and occurrence at the same time. If the second is false, the first is false.

The foregoing statements suggest that the hyponym-superordinate relationship is a well-established one. In reality, there are various anomalies in lexical relationships – semantic analysis is often messy. Sometimes we find co-hyponyms without a super-ordinate. The Portuguese set illustrated below contains three co-hyponyms and their superordinate. The corresponding English co-hyponyms have no superordinate.

There is no single word in English that can refer to a knife or a fork or a spoon, but to nothing else – no single word that can take the place of X in *A knife is an X, and a fork is an X, and a spoon is an X*, whereas in Portuguese it is possible to say *Uma faca é un talher, uma garfa é un talher, um colher é um talher*. Similarly, English *trunk, suitcase, handbag* name similar items; all of them are included under the **collective noun** *luggage*, but the only possible superordinate would be *piece of luggage*.

Another instance of a lexical gap is seen in these verbs:

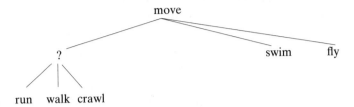

Is there a single term that can be applied to movement over the ground, which is parallel to *swim* and *fly* and which includes *run, walk, crawl* as its hyponyms? English offers only the rare word *ambulate*. The lack of a superordinate for *knife-fork-spoon*, for *trunk-suitcase-handbag*, and for *run-walk-crawl* are instances of lexical gaps.

English possesses separate lexemes for the male and the female of various species of animals that humans have domesticated; one of the two is used when the identification of the sex is not important to the person who is speaking. Thus the specifically female term *duck* and the specifically male term *drake* are included under the general term – the superordinate – which is also *duck*. The relationship of *goose* and *gander* is analogous.

Consider the lexeme *animal* (Palmer 1981: 85–6). It is a co-hyponym of *vegetable* and *mineral*, the three together supposedly encompassing everything that is solid. But the class of animal entities includes birds, fish, reptiles, insects, amphibians and – animals, that is, mammals. And mammals include humans and other organisms such as simians, felines, canines, ungulates, etc., all of which together are distinguished from humans with the name *animals*. So we have:

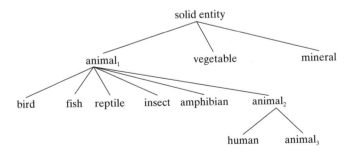

This also illustrates the fact that hyponymy is hierarchical: one term may be a superordinate to various hyponyms and at the same time be a hyponym of some higher superordinate.

We make frequent use of hyponymy in our daily language (Cruse 1986: 91). We say things like "an X and some other Y's" or "Of all the Y's I know, I like X best," where X is the hyponym and Y the superordinate. To define a term often requires giving the super-ordinate for which it is a hyponym. In our early learning of our native language we acquire such general terms as *game, tool, instrument* and *animal* by being told some of the hyponyms included under these terms. In other instances, it seems, we are likely to learn the super-ordinate, like *dog* or *flower*, before learning *collie, dachshund, spaniel* . . . or *nasturtium, delphinium, crocus.* . . . There are also very general lexemes, super-superordinates, as it were: *thing, stuff, place, person*.

5.4 Synonymy

6a   Jack is a seaman.
6b   Jack is a sailor.

Assuming that *Jack* refers to the same person in the two sentences, then if 6a is true, 6b is true; if 6b is true, 6a is true; and if either is false, the other is false. This is our basis for establishing that *seaman* and *sailor* are **synonyms**: when used in predications with the same referring expression, the predications have the same truth value. The lexemes *seaman* and *sailor* are synonyms; sentences 6a and 6b are paraphrases of each other.

Synonyms can be nouns, as in 6a and 6b, or adjectives, adverbs, or verbs.

7a   The rock is large.
7b   The rock is big.
8a   The train traveled fast.
8b   The train traveled rapidly.
9a   The bus left promptly at 10.
9b   The bus departed promptly at 10.

Thus for any two sentences [a] and [b] that differ only in the presence of synonymous terms we can express their truth relationship this way:

$a \rightarrow b \ \& \ b \rightarrow a$ (The truth of [a] entails the truth of [b], and vice versa.)

$\sim a \rightarrow \sim b \ \& \ \sim b \rightarrow \sim a$ (The falsity of [a] entails the falsity of [b], and vice versa.)

In tabular form:

a	b
T	T
F	F

Thus synonymy is an instance of mutual entailment, and synonyms are instances of mutual hyponymy. *Large* is a hyponym of *big*, for example, and *big* is a hyponym of *large*.

If we join two of these sentences with *and*,

10a   The rock is large and (it is) big.

we create a tautology. If we combine two of them but have them differ in polarity,

10b   The train traveled fast but (it did) not (travel) rapidly.

the result is a contradiction.

Two sentences which are paraphrases may differ this way:

11a   Mr Jenkins is our postman.
11b   Mr Jenkins is the person who delivers our mail.

Here the complex term *person who delivers (our) mail* is a paraphrase of the simpler term *(our) postman*, but we do not call it a synonym. Synonyms are typically single lexemes of the same weight. The longer term explains the simpler term, but not the other way around. As we learn a language, we often acquire simple terms like *postman* through some sort of paraphrase.

Dictionaries typically provide a number of synonyms for at least some of the lexemes they define, and in fact there are whole diction-aries of synonyms. But synonymy is not a simple matter, for two lexemes never have the same range of syntactic occurrences, and even where they share occurrences and make predications about the same class of referring expressions, they are likely to differ in what they suggest. It would be wasteful for a language to have two terms that occur in exactly the same contexts and with exactly the same sense.

12a   Mr. Jenkins is our postman.
12b   Mr. Jenkins is our mailman.
13a   Alice is skinny.
13b   Alice is thin.
13c   Alice is slender.
14a   We hid our valuables in the attic.
14b   We concealed our valuables in the attic.
15a   Integral calculus is a hard subject.
15b   Integral calculus is a difficult subject.

While *postman* and *mailman* make equivalent predications, as in 12a and 12b, we consider this a dialect difference rather than an instance of synonymy. Some speakers of English know only one of these terms, but which term it is depends on where the speaker lives, or where the speaker grew up. Some speakers know both lexemes but use one more than the other or use one exclusively but recognize the other. Other synonyms that are dialectally different are *lift* and *elevator, firefly* and *lightning bug, skillet* and *frying pan.* Here too we are dealing with a difference in pragmatic value. If you use one of the lexemes in any of these pairs almost exclusively, you may well associate the other one with some particular person(s) or situation(s) – the term may elicit in you a reaction that is more than just a matter of reference or predication.

With 13a–c we have a slightly different kind of synonymy. The adjectives *skinny, thin, slender* mean 'the same thing,' perhaps, but they differ in connotation, the values that people give to them: *thin* is neutral, *skinny* is somewhat pejorative, and *slender* is flattering. Similar sets of evaluative adjectives are *cheap* and *inexpensive, frugal* and *stingy, fat* and *plump.*

The verbs *hide* and *conceal* (14a, b) also differ in pragmatic value: *hide* is more common than *conceal.* But there is another difference, a subtle matter of potential co-occurrence: it is possible to say *We hid in the attic,* as well as *We hid the treasure in the attic,* but we cannot say **We concealed in the attic. Hide* has a valency of 1 or 2, but *conceal* requires two arguments always.

Sentences 15a and 15b illustrate a similar point. Two (or more) terms can be synonymous only if they are compatible with the same subjects. The terms *hard* and *difficult* are both compatible with *calculus* and with *subject,* but *difficult* is not a synonym of *hard* in *hard chair, hard knock* and the like. *Hard* and *difficult* have different ranges of compatibility; the ranges overlap but they are not co-extensive.

Ranges and their overlap can be illustrated this way:

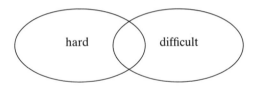

English, because of its double-barreled vocabulary, Germanic and Romance, seems to have numerous pairs and even trios of synonyms. Ten such pairs of nouns are given below. For each pair try to decide what difference the two words have – a context in which one is possible but the other is not, or a difference in the effect created where they share a context. You may also want to say which is of Old English origin and which came from French.

ache, pain	error, mistake
altitude, height	force, strength
center, middle	labor, work
cord, string	pace, step
dale, valley	sight, vision

In the phrase *a funny story* we can replace *funny* with the synonymous adjective *humorous*. In *a funny feeling* a better synonym for *funny* is *peculiar*, but *humorous* and *peculiar* are not synonymous with each other. Each predicate below is illustrated in several contexts. Give a synonym for each context and test to see whether a single term can be synonymous in more than one of the contexts.

a clear sky, a clear stream, a clear speech
a wild party, wild geese, wild rice

5.5 Antonymy

16a   Alvin is watching television now.
16b   Alvin isn't watching television now.

Two sentences that differ in polarity like these are mutually contradictory. If one is true, the other must be false. Two sentences that have the same subject and have predicates which are **antonyms** are also mutually contradictory.

17a   The television is on now.
17b   The television is off now.
18a   Mr Adams is an old man.
18b   Mr Adams is a young man.
19a   The road is wide here.
19b   The road is narrow here.

Lexemes like *on* and *off*, *old* and *young*, *wide* and *narrow* are pairs of antonyms. Antonyms are opposite in meaning, and when they occur as predicates of the same subject the predications are contradictory. Antonyms may be nouns like *Communist* and *non-Communist* or verbs such as *advance* and *retreat*, but antonymous pairs of adjectives are especially numerous.

English has various pairs of measure adjectives:

long	short	tall	short
high	low	wide	narrow
old	young	deep	shallow
old	new	thick	thin

They are measure adjectives because they can be combined with expressions of measurement: *four feet long, two meters high, nineteen years old*, etc. We note, first, that these adjectives, like others relating to size (e.g. *big/little, large/small, heavy/light*) are antonymous, and, second, that their meanings are very much dependent on the topics they are associated with; a big rat is not as big as a small elephant, for instance.

In each of the pairs of measure adjectives above, one member is **marked** and one unmarked. The unmarked member is also the **global member** of the opposition. For example, in the pair *old* and *young, old* is the global, unmarked adjective. It is used with units of time to express age. When we say *The baby is four days old*, we are not saying that the baby is old, and in saying *The box is three inches deep* we are not saying that the box is deep. (Which is the global member of the pair *long/short*? *wide/narrow*?) We sometimes say things like "She is 40 years young" but this is precisely a marked expression. Presumably, *She is 40 years young* is equivalent in truth-value to *She is 40 years old*.

5.6 Binary and non-binary antonyms

There are different kinds of antonymous relationships. *On* and *off* are **binary antonyms**: an electric light or a radio or a television set is either on or off; there is no middle ground. Other binary pairs are *open/shut, dead/alive, asleep/awake*. The terms *old* and *young* are **non-binary antonyms** and so are *wide* and *narrow*. They are opposite ends of a scale that includes various intermediate terms: Mr Adams may be neither old nor young, the road may be something between wide and narrow. (Non-binary antonyms are also called polar antonyms; like the North and South Poles, they are at opposite ends with territory between them. Analogously, binary antonyms might be called hemispheric antonyms; as with the Northern and Southern hemispheres [or the Eastern and Western hemispheres], there is no space in between, only a line of demarcation. Some semanticists use the term 'complementary antonyms' in place of 'binary antonyms' and 'contrary' instead of 'non-binary.')

The difference between binary and non-binary antonyms can be shown this way:

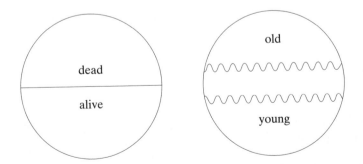

Adjectives that are non-binary antonyms can easily be modified: *very old, rather young, quite wide, extremely narrow*, and the like.

Logically it would seem that binary antonyms do not accept modifiers – an organism is either dead or alive, a door is either open or shut, a floor is either clean or dirty, one is either asleep or awake. But language is not logic. *Quite dead*, *very much alive*, *wide open*, *slightly dirty* are meaningful expressions. Speakers cannot agree as to whether a door which is 'ajar' is open or shut, nor on the precise location of the distinction between clean and dirty. In previous chapters we have noted that language is fluid–flexible. The other side of this flexibility is that language is, in some respects, necessarily vague.

PRACTICE 5.2

Among the following pairs of antonyms, which are binary and which are non-binary? What problems do you find in making this decision?

true, false
tall, short
expensive, cheap
beautiful, ugly
happy, unhappy
pass, fail
hot, cold
deep, shallow
legal, illegal
rich, poor
fast, slow
rude, polite

PRACTICE 5.3

Give an antonym for the adjective in each of the following collocations:

a light package
a light color

a tall building
low prices
low heels
a hard problem
a hard chair
a soft voice
a narrow road
a narrow mind
a thick board
thick soup
a sweet apple
sweet tea
a strong body
strong feelings

What is the antonym of *raw* in the following?

raw fruit, raw materials, raw weather

As we see from the list above, the opposite of *old* is *young* if we are talking about animate beings, but the opposite is *new* with reference to an inanimate object like a newspaper. Adjectives like *old* which participate in two different oppositions are ambiguous. What are the two opposites of *They're old friends of mine? Short* contrasts with *long* with reference to a pencil, a piece of string, or a journey, but the antonym is *tall* when talking about humans and other animals – a difference between horizontal measurement and vertical measurement. (But is a journey necessarily measured on the horizontal dimension in our times?)

Non-binary adjectives are also gradable adjectives. We can say, for instance, *very long, rather short, quite strong, somewhat weak, too old, young enough, extremely rude, utterly happy.* Each such expression constitutes a measurement – a rather imprecise one – against some norm or standard. The standard may or may not be explicit, and indeed in most everyday use of language usually is not. Arguments about whether something is, for instance, really soft are often due to failure to establish a standard. Of course, a standard is more easily established for descriptive adjectives like *long, heavy, expensive* than for evaluative ones such as *pleasant, clever,* or *tiresome.*

From a logical point of view binary adjectives are not gradable. What can it mean to say that some action is very legal, some product is perfect enough, some person is too asleep? But people treat these essentially ungradable adjectives as if they were gradable. Something is either complete or incomplete, but we sometimes say *more complete*.

Some pairs of antonyms are morphologically related; one member of the pair is formed by adding a prefix to the other:

happy, unhappy; proper, improper; trust, distrust; tie, untie;

or by changing a prefix:

exhale, inhale; converge, diverge; progress, regress; inflate, deflate.

More examples of such pairs will be found in Chapter 13.

5.7 A comparison of four relations

Synonyms	*Hyponym and Superordinate*
(p) Jack is a seaman.	(p) Rover is a collie.
(q) Jack is a sailor.	(q) Rover is a dog.

$$p \Leftrightarrow q \quad {\sim}p \Leftrightarrow {\sim}q \qquad\qquad p \Leftrightarrow q \quad {\sim}q \Leftrightarrow {\sim}p$$

(The symbol $\Leftrightarrow$ indicates double entailment: the truth of [p] entails the truth of [q], and the truth of [q] entails the truth of [p].)

Non-binary antonyms	*Binary antonyms*
(p) Luke is rich.	(p) The window is open.
(q) Luke is poor.	(q) The window is closed.

$$p \to {\sim}q \quad q \to {\sim}p \qquad\qquad p \Leftrightarrow {\sim}q \quad {\sim}p \to q$$

We see from this table that synonyms and binary antonyms are mirror images of each other: if one of two sentences containing synonyms is true, the other is true; if one is false, the other is false. Of two sentences with binary antonyms, if one is true, the other is false, and if one is false, the other is true. Non-binaries are like binaries in that the truth of either member of the pair entails the falsity of the other member, but unlike binary antonyms, both members of a non-binary pair can be false. Hyponym and superordinate form a still different pair: the truth of the hyponym entails the truth of the superordinate, and the falsity of the superordinate entails the falsity of the hyponym.

5.8 Converse antonyms

To illustrate synonymy, hyponymy and antonymy in the previous sections we presented pairs of sentences; each sentence of a pair had the same subject and different predicates; each predicate had a valency of one – there was only a subject and no other referring expression. The next paired sentences contain **converse predicates**, which necessarily have a valency of 2 or more.

20a The map is above the chalkboard.
20b The chalkboard is below the map.
21a Sally is Jerry's wife. (Sally is the wife of Jerry)
21b Jerry is Sally's husband. (Jerry is the husband of Sally)

Converseness is a kind of antonymy between two terms. For any two converse relational terms X and Y, if [a] is the X of [b], then [b] is the Y of [a]. In 20a *map* has the role of Theme and *chalkboard* the role of Associate; in 20b the roles are reversed. The same applies to *Sally* and *Jerry* in 21a and 21b.

The features [parent] and [offspring], introduced in section **5.2**, are converse features: if A is the parent of B, B is the offspring of A (represented symbolically: A parent-of B $\rightarrow$ B offspring-of A). Common converse pairs include kinship and social roles (*husband-of/wife-of; employer-of/employee-of*) and directional opposites (*above/below; in front of/behind; left-of/right-of; before/after; north-of/south-of; outside/inside*).

There are a few pairs of converse 3-argument predicates: give-to/receive-from; sell-to/buy-from; lend-to/borrow-from.

22a Dad lent me a little money.
22b I borrowed a little money from Dad.

If A gives X to B, B receives X from A. All three of these pairs of predicates are built around the relationship of **source** and **goal**, which we examine in Chapter 6.

23a Danny broke a window.
23b A window was broken (by Danny).
24a Olga wrote a marvelous essay.
24b A marvelous essay was written (by Olga).
25a Simon climbed the wall.
25b The wall was climbed (by Simon).

26a   This package weighs two kilos.
26b   *Two kilos is/are weighed by this package.

If a predicate consists of a verb and its object and the object has the role of Affected (23), Effect (24), or Theme (25), there is a converse sentence in which the original object becomes subject, the verb is passive, and the agent may be deleted. Of course there is no such passive converse when the object of the verb, or apparent object, has the role of Associate (26a).

Some conjunctions, or clause connectors, like *before* and *after* form converse pairs.

27a   Herbert left the party before Jean (left the party).
27b   Jean left the party after Herbert (left the party).

We see that in all these examples of sentences with converse pairs, [a] and [b] are paraphrases. Since *above* and *below* are converse antonyms, sentences [a] and [b] have the same truth value. Thus,

$$a \Leftrightarrow b \qquad {\sim}a \Leftrightarrow {\sim}b$$

Consider these paraphrastic sentences:

28a   The dictionary is heavier than the novel.
28b   The novel is lighter than the dictionary.

Although *heavy* and *light* are non-binary antonyms, the comparative forms are converse: more heavy = less light; more light = less heavy.

29a   The dictionary is more expensive than the novel.
29b   The novel is less expensive than the dictionary.

These are also equivalent sentences; *more expensive* and *less expensive* are converse terms. Factoring out the common term, *more* and *less* are converse.

In the discussion of simple antonymy we recognized non-binary antonyms like *rich* and *poor*, which are gradable, and binary antonyms, like *asleep* and *awake*, which are not. In converse relations most adjectives allow for gradience – more A and less A, with a scale along which there are various amounts of "more" or "less." Converse relations with other parts of speech are more like binary antonymy: *parent* and *offspring*, *over* and *under*, *give* and *receive* are not relationships that occur on a scale.

There are practical constraints on converseness. Though we can say *A newspaper kiosk is in front of the Grand Hotel*, it would be unusual to speak of the Grand Hotel as being behind a newspaper kiosk. Converseness requires the two arguments, theme and associate, to be of about the same size, rank, or importance. Talmy (1975) uses the terms **figure** and **ground** for entities of unequal rank like these. The figure, here the newpaper kiosk, is located with respect to the ground, here the Grand Hotel, but not the ground with respect to the figure.

5.9 Symmetry and reciprocity

A special kind of converseness is the use of a single term in a **symmetrical** relationship, seen in these examples:

30a Line AB is parallel to Line CD.
30b Line CD is parallel to Line AB.

This relationship can also be expressed as:

30c Line AB and Line CD are parallel to each other.

or simply as:

30d Line AB and Line CD are parallel.

To generalize, if X is a symmetrical predicate, the relationship *a X b* can also be expressed as *b X a* and as *a and b X* (*each other*). Here 'a' and 'b' interchange the roles of Theme and Associate. The features [sibling] and [spouse] are each symmetrical (C sibling-of D → D sibling-of C; E spouse-of F → F spouse-of E).

PRACTICE 5.4

Each sentence below contains a symmetrical predicate preceded by one referring expression and followed by another. Restate them with a compound subject that contains both referring expressions; for example, "Angle BAC is equal to Angle ACB" should be changed to "Angle BAC and Angle ACB are equal (to each other)."

(a)   This box is the same size as that basket.
(b)   Sean is married to Eileen.
(c)   The Greens are neighbors of the Browns.
(d)   Your answer is irreconcilable with my answer.
(e)   Figure A is congruent with Figure B.
(f)   *Sailor* is synonymous with *seaman*.
(g)   The picture your child drew is practically identical with the picture my child made.
(h)   This picture is quite different from that picture, I'd say.
(i)   In fact, this one makes a strong contrast with the other one.
(j)   Janice is related to Josie.
(k)   The bank is adjacent to the pharmacy.
(l)   Pat met Paula at three o'clock.

Other examples of symmetrical predicates appear in these sentences:

31   The truck is similar to the bus.
32   Line AB intersects Line CD.
33   Hampton Road converges with Broad Street.
34   Oil doesn't mix with water.

The following sentences have predicates that appear to be symmetrical but are not.

35a   The truck collided with the bus.
36a   Tom agreed with Ann.
37a   Prescott corresponds with Dudley.
38a   The market research department communicates with the sales department.

If the truck collided with the bus, it is not necessarily true that the bus collided with the truck (35a), and analogous observations can be made about 36a–38a. On the other hand, in

35b   The truck and the bus collided.
36b   Tom and Ann agreed.
37b   Prescott and Dudley correspond.
38b   The market research department and the sales department communicate.

we are informed that the truck collides with the bus and the bus with the truck, and the action is likewise symmetrical in 35b–37b. (34b–37b are ambiguous as they stand, of course, since these sentences may be the result of ellipsis: The truck and the bus collided with a taxi, Tom and Ann agreed with me, and so on.) The verbs in these sentences are **reciprocal predicates**, not symmetrical predicators. If X is a reciprocal predicate, the relationship $a\ X\ b$ does not entail $b\ X\ a$ but $a\ and\ b\ X$ does entail $a\ X\ b$ and $b\ X\ a$ (leaving aside the possible ambiguity).

Reciprocal predicates are mostly verbs like those in sentences 35–8 and the following:

argue-with concur-with conflict-with co-operate-with
correlate-with intersect-with merge-with overlap-with
embrace fight (with) hug

Symmetrical predicates are adjectives combined with a preposition *with*, *from*, or *to*:

1   A and B are congruent (with each other)
     $\equiv$ A is congruent with B and B is congruent with A (where '$\equiv$' is the sign for semantic identity)
     commensurate concentric congruent contemporary identical
     intimate simultaneous synonymous

2   A and B are different (from each other)
     $\equiv$ A is different from B and B is different from A
     different

3   A and B are equivalent (to each other)
     $\equiv$ A is equivalent to B and B is equivalent to A
     equal equivalent related

Symmetrical predicates may also be participles formed from causative verbs: If I connect X and Y, X and Y are connected with each other. Other such causative verbs are:

1   A combines X and Y $\equiv$ A combines X with Y and Y with X
     compare confuse group mix reconcile

2   A disconnects X and Y $\equiv$ A disconnects X from Y and Y from X
     disconnect distinguish separate

3   A connects X and Y ≡ A connects X to Y and Y to X
     connect join relate tie

5.10 Expressions of quantity

Our study of hyponyms and superordinates can throw light on some terms that seem at first to be very far removed from these topics, **quantifiers** like *all, no, some, many, few*. What do these words mean? How did we learn to use them when we were very young? Almost certainly a child acquires the use of these items in connection with noun phrases that have quantifiable referents. Told to put away 'all' his toys, a child learns that this means putting away the doll and the wagon and the toy rabbit and the ball . . . and so on until 'no' toy is still out. The meaning of *no* (or *not any*) is acquired in similar contexts: not the doll and not the wagon and not the toy rabbit. . . . Semanticists may explain these lexemes in a more sophisticated way, like this:

Given a set X that consists of $X_1, X_2, X_3, \ldots X_n$, all $X = X_1$ & X_2 & $X_3 \ldots$ & X_n; no $X = {\sim}X_1$ & ${\sim}X_2$ & ${\sim}X_3 \ldots {\sim}X_n$. More sophisticated, perhaps, but not more illuminating.

The meanings of *some, many* (or *much* in uncountable noun phrases), and *few* (*little* in uncountable NPs) are vague, and the vagueness exists by tacit agreement of the language community. In a group of 10 items, *a few* is 2, 3, or perhaps 4; *many*, or a *lot*, is 9, 8, or maybe 7; and *some* is any number from 2 to 9. A speaker can employ these terms in an acceptable way without necessarily knowing the exact quantity, and an addressee accepts the terms without necessarily expecting to know the exact quantity.

Logically, *all* includes *some, few* and *many*. Thus someone who tells us that he has done some of the assigned exercises, when he has in fact done all of them, is not lying. Pragmatically, however, *some* is in contrast with *all*. If our speaker accents the word – "I've done SOME of the assignments" – the accent gives *some* paradigmatic focus and serves to exclude any quantifier other than *some*.

The study of hyponymy reveals some interesting facts about these quantitative terms, as Barwise and Cooper (1981) and Larson (1990) have shown. Consider, first, a two-argument predicate like *chase* and a subject that includes *all*.

39a   All dogs chase cats → All collies chase cats
39b   All collies chase cats ~ → All dogs chase cats
39c   All dogs chase cats ~ → All dogs chase angoras
39d   All dogs chase angoras → All dogs chase cats

Occurrence of a superordinate term in the subject (here *dogs*) entails the truth of a similar proposition containing any hyponym, illustrated here with *collies*, but a statement about the totality of the hyponym leads to no certain conclusion regarding the superordinate. In contrast, occurrence of a superordinate in the object (here *cats*, meaning 'some cats') yields no conclusion about the hyponym, (some) *angoras*, but occurrence of the hyponym in object position entails the truth of the corresponding proposition with the superordinate.

Note, incidentally, this special case of 39a:

All dogs chase cats → Rover chases cats

and this special case of 39d:

All dogs chase Tabby → All dogs chase some cat.

The quantifier *no* also expresses a totality, but it has a somewhat different role in entailment, as sentences 40a–d show.

40a   No dogs chase cats → No collies chase cats
40b   No collies chase cats ~ → No dogs chase cats
40c   No dogs chase cats → No dogs chase angoras
40d   No dogs chase angoras ~ → No dogs chase cats

SOME
(a)   Some dogs chase cats ~ → Some collies chase cats
(b)   Some collies chase cats → Some dogs chase cats
(c)   Some dogs chase cats ~ → Some dogs chase angoras
(d)   Some dogs chase angoras → Some dogs chase cats

FEW
(a)   Few dogs chase cats ~ → Few collies chase cats
(b)   Few collies chase cats ~ → Few dogs chase cats
(c)   Few dogs chase cats → Few dogs chase angoras
(d)   Few dogs chase angoras ~ → Few dogs chase cats

MANY
(a)   Many dogs chase cats ~ → Many collies chase cats
(b)   Many collies chase cats ~ → Many dogs chase cats

(c)   Many dogs chase cats ~ → Many dogs chase angoras
(d)   Many dogs chase angoras → Many dogs chase cats

The table below summarizes these facts – whether or not, for any of these quantifiers, the superordinate or generic term entails the hyponyms or specific term, as subject (first term) and as object (second term).

| | First term | | Second term | |
	Gen → Spec	Spec → Gen	Gen → Spec	Spec → Gen
ALL	+	−	−	+
NO	+	−	+	−
SOME	−	+	−	+
FEW	−	−	+	−
MANY	−	−	−	+

Summary

Lexemes are related to other lexemes on various semantic criteria. Field theory tries to discover sets of lexemes such that members of a set share some semantic feature(s) and are differentiated from one another by other systematically distributed features. Sets may be hierarchical, part-whole, sequential, cyclical, and may form structural paradigms.

All societies have kinship systems, which can be analyzed in terms of a few semantic features that co-occur. The features parent, offspring, sibling and spouse are universal. Older and younger siblings are named differently in some cultures. Gender figures differently in different systems, so that relations on the mother's side may have different names than those on the father's side, and similarly for the bride's family as distinct from the bridegroom's family. Logical entailments, paraphrases, and contradictions derive from conjunctions, negative 'not,' and quantifier pronouns like 'no one' and 'someone.' Meaning relations of this sort are used to make inferences.

Truth conditional semantics investigates the relations among lexemes that can be predicates for the same referring expression. Two such predicates may be related to each other as synonyms, as hyponym and superordinate, or as antonyms. Among antonyms we distinguish binary and non-binary antonyms; non-binary antonyms are opposite ends of a scale along which intermediate degrees exist; for binary antonyms there are no intermediate degrees. For any pair of sentences in which the predicates are synonymous, antonymous, or related as hyponym-superordinate a truth table can be established, setting out what can be known about one sentence if the other is known to be true or to be false.

Two predicates are converse antonyms if each links noun phrases in the roles of theme and associate, the noun phrases occur in reverse roles with the two predicates, and the resulting sentences have the same truth value. A symmetrical predicate also links noun phrases in the roles of theme and associate; the noun phrases may be reversed without changing the truth of the predication.

Quantifiers such as *all*, *some*, *no* can be understood and explained by comparing sentences in which a superordinate term and a hyponym are contrasted in subject position and in object position.

Suggested reading

For lexical analyses within the framework of field theory see, in addition to the works mentioned in section **5.1**, Nida (1975) and (1979).

Cruse (1986) contains the most extensive exploration of lexical relations published to date. Recommended chapters are: 6, Taxonomies; 7, Meronomies; 9, Opposites I: complementaries and antonyms; 10, Opposites II: directional opposites; 11, Opposites III: general questions; 12, Synonymy.

A more thorough analysis of lexical relations than that presented here is Lyons (1977), Chapter 9.

Transition and transfer predicates

Verbs and other predicates determine what meaning a sentence expresses and, to a large extent, they determine what roles the accompanying arguments have, and even what kinds of noun phrases occur as arguments. In this chapter we explore predicates that have a valency of more than two. Many such predicates express transition, movement from one place to another, respectively the Source and the Goal. Some predicates express transfer, causing the movement of an entity from one place or person to another place or person. Movement through space requires some amount of time, so that a semantic account of some predicates has to include a **time frame**. We will see that some predicates are specialized in meaning and others are quite general. For example *walk*, *drift* and *fly* indicate particular ways of moving while *go* is general. The former are called more **marked**, the latter less marked.

6.1 Transition

Chapter 4 dealt with predicates that have a valency of zero, one or two. This chapter takes up predicates with a valency of three or more. Many of them express the going or coming from one place to another. These are predicates of transition.

1   The bus goes from Greenville to Stratford.
2   Carlo came to this country from Italy.

Others express the moving of something from one place to another.

3   Fenwick drives the bus from Greenville to Stratford.
4   Jane rowed the boat from one side of the river to the other.

These are predicates of transfer. Transfer verbs are the causative equivalent of the transition verbs above: Fenwick causes the bus to go . . . , Jane caused the boat to move. . . .

Transfer includes putting and removing:

5   Squirrels are stashing nuts in that oak tree.
6   Thieves stole some money from the cash box.

and giving and taking away.

7   Ronnie gave Rosie some flowers.
8   The accident deprived Alex of his livelihood.

Communicating something to someone through language is also a form of transfer:

9   Mother told the children a story.
10   Agnes is writing her mother a letter.

Finally, there is a miscellaneous group of predicates with three or more arguments that are not so easily classified: we introduce someone to another person, we suspect somebody of something, and so on. Verbs of communication are an important part of Chapter 9. In this chapter we concentrate on verbs of transition and transfer other than verbs of communication.

Sentence 1 tells of the movement of an inanimate object from one place, the source, to another place, the goal.

Argument$_1$	Predicate	Argument$_2$	Argument$_3$
theme	action	source	goal
bus	go	Greenville	Stratford

Sentence 2 is similar in role structure, except that the entity moving is animate.

Argument$_1$	Predicate	Argument$_2$	Argument$_3$
actor	action	goal	source
Carlo	come	this country	Italy

In English the source is most often indicated by *from* and the goal by *to*, as here, and they occur in either order.

11a He emerged from the dark cellar into the bright sunlight.
11b He plunged from the bright sunlight into the dark cellar.

To is replaced by *into* to express the notion that the goal is not simply a location but an area which contains. As these examples show, the containing area is not necessarily an enclosed space – a speaker is free to treat any area as an enclosed space.

A sentence may express a Path, a place or area between the Source and Goal.

12 The <u>bus</u> goes from <u>Greenville</u> to <u>Stratford</u> by way of <u>Compton</u>.
  theme   source goal   path

13 The <u>boat</u> drifted over the <u>water</u> from <u>one place</u> to <u>another</u>.
   theme   path source goal

The path is indicated by a form that may follow one of several prepositions: *via, by way of, through, across* or *over*. The theme or actor NP is subject of the sentence. To generalize, sentences with transition verbs have this argument structure:

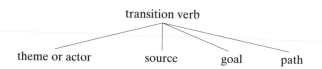

transition verb

theme or actor   source   goal path

Source, goal and path are optional in sentences and may appear in any order among themselves. But they are implicit in the meaning of transition verbs, whereas other verbs of motion like *shake, quiver, tremble* and *vibrate* denote movement that does not necessarily involve change of location.

Movement through space requires time. Sentence 1 informs us that the bus is at Greenville at Time Zero and at Stratford at Time Plus, where Time Plus is later than Time Zero, and at Compton at some time between. The verb *go* in sentence 1 can be represented on a time frame like this:

go   Time 0   Time +
    Theme at Source Theme at Goal

14 The road goes from Greenville to Stratford by way of Compton.
15 The driveway extends from the street to the garage.
16 Curtains hung almost from the ceiling to the floor.

In these sentences *from* and *to* introduce source and goal, respectively, but the road, driveway and curtains do not move from one to the other, and so there is no Time Zero or Time Plus. The driveway is at the street and at the garage simultaneously. The verbs extend, hang, spread and others are verbs of spatial extension. The predicates *go*, *extend*, *hang*, as they are used here, are verbs of pseudo-transition. Whereas the first thirteen sentences have dynamic predicates, these three are stative. Of course, some verbs can be stative or dynamic.

The time frame for a predicate like *extend*, as in sentence 15 is:

> *extend*   Time
>   Theme at Source and Goal

17   Harrison returned to his hometown from the big city.

Here three times are implied: at Time Minus, which is earlier than Time Zero, Harrison was in his hometown, at Time Zero he was in the big city, and at Time Plus he was again in his hometown.

> *return*   Time –   Time 0   Time +
>   Theme at Goal   Theme at Source   Theme at Goal

Of all transition verbs *move* is the least marked, the one that lacks a special focus. *Go* is probably a more common verb, but it carries the semantic feature [away from speaker], contrasting with *come* [toward speaker]. Common transition predicates are the following.

Unmarked: move
Focus on Goal:

> get   [general]
> come [goal is where speaker or addressee is or will be]
> go   [goal is away from speaker]

Focus on Manner:

> creep [animate subject; slow movement over a surface]
> rotate [wheel or globe; turns on an axis]
> gallop [subject is a horse or on a horse, moving at the fastest gait]

Focus on Path:

>   drift [effortless movement in moving water]
>   float [seemingly effortless movement in water or air]
>   fall [source is higher than goal; involuntary movement]

Focus on Cause or Purpose:

>   escape   [source is undesirable place]
>   emigrate [as above; source-oriented]
>   immigrate [as above; goal-oriented]

PRACTICE 6.1

Divide the following verbs of transition into three groups, those whose meaning has a focus on manner, a focus on path, or a focus on cause or purpose.

>   flee
>   jump
>   march
>   migrate
>   run
>   soar
>   trot
>   walk

FOR FURTHER EXPLORATION:

English *come* and *bring* have deictic properties, since in any utterance in which either occurs the goal is the place where the speaker or the addressee is at the time of speaking or where either will be at a later time. See Fillmore (1973) for an account of the verb *come*.

6.2 Transfer

18   Fenwick drives a bus from Greenville to Stratford by way of Compton.

agent	theme	source	goal	path
|	|	|	|	|
Fenwick	bus	Greenville	Stratford	Compton

The verb *drive* is a predicate of transition, and this sentence has a causative meaning corresponding to Sentence 1: Fenwick causes the bus to go from Greenville, etc., and of course he moves with the bus. Compare the next sentence.

19   The King banished the rebels from his realm (to another land).
      agent   affected   source   goal

The role structure in 19 is similar to 18 but of course the King does not move with the rebels. Thus two sorts of transfer verbs can be distinguished, typified by *drive* (as used in 11a), in which the agent moves, and *banish*, in which the agent does not move.

These are shown on the timescales below.

drive	*Time 0*	*Time +*
	Agent and Theme at Source	Agent and Theme at Goal

banish	*Time 0*	*Time +*
	Theme at Source	Theme at Goal

drive

Acts that change location of both Agent and Theme are the following:

Unmarked: move
Focus on Manner:

    drive   [object = vehicle and subject = driver; or object = animal(s) and subject is behind the animal(s)]
    convey [unmarked]
    haul   [transfer in vehicle suggested]
    drag   [subject moves object over a surface, object is inert]

Focus on Goal:

    bring   [goal is location of speaker, not necessarily at time of speaking]
    take   [goal is not location of speaker]

Focus on Aspect (involving some relation of time):

restore [object was previously at goal]

Acts that change location of theme only are expressed in the following verbs:

Focus on Goal:

push [object is moved away from original position of agent]
pull [object is moved toward agent]

Focus on Source:

expel [agent = person of authority in source]
evict [as above; source is dwelling, affected is a tenant]

Focus on Path:

throw [object moves through air]
lift [vertical movement upward]
raise [vertical movement upward or into upright position]
drop [vertical movement down; may be involuntary]
lower [as above; voluntary]

Compare the next sentence with sentence 14.

20 We spread a red carpet from the sidewalk to the door.

To spread something is to cause it to be simultaneously at Place X and Place Y, the Source and the Goal.

21 The court restored the property to its lawful owner (from one who was not the lawful owner).

To restore something is to cause it to be in the same place or possession at Time Plus as it was at Time Minus and as it was not at Time Zero.

restore	Time −	Time 0	Time +
	Theme at Goal	Theme at Source	Theme at Goal

What kind of verb is *carry*? What focus does it have? What kinds of transfer does it include? You may want to consult a dictionary, but consider only the uses that designate real movement of physical objects.

22 The guard admitted us to the museum.
23 Nectar attracts bees to flowers.
24 The judge sentenced the convicted man to jail.

With certain verbs the expression of the goal is all-important and the source is not important or is not specified. These sentences, for instance, tell the addressee that we were first not in the museum and then we were; bees which are not at flowers come to flowers because of the nectar; the convicted man is first not in jail and then he is. These are verbs of accomplishment – more specifically, causing change of location.

25 The team gave a present to Harry [gave Harry a present].
26 Our school awarded the trophy to Millie [awarded Millie the trophy].
27 Mrs Carson bequeathed her fortune to her servants.

With some verbs – *give*, *award* and *bequeath* are examples – *from* is missing because the source appears as subject. In 25, for example, the present comes from the team; the team is both source and agent of the giving. (Some verbs permit two kinds of expression: Theme *to* Goal or Goal Theme, give a present to Harry or give Harry a present.) Verbs like those in 25–7 have this argument structure, illustrated here for *give*:

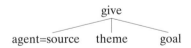

Here is a group of verbs that occur as predicates in sentences with this structure:

give   [most common, least marked]
award   [the object is a prize] *

bequeath	[the source is typically, but not necessarily, deceased; cf. *inherit*, below]
bestow	[the source is a person of higher social position than the goal]
contribute	[the source is one of several donors]
donate	[the transfer is considered a worthy action]
entrust	[the change is temporary]
grant	[the source is a person of authority]
hand	[the act is physical, the object is relatively small]
lend	[the change is temporary; cf. *borrow*, below]
lose	[the change results from competition between source and goal]
sell	[money is involved in the act; cf. *buy*, below]
submit	[the goal is a person of authority; cf. *grant*, above]

28 Harry received a present from the team.
29 Millie accepted the trophy from our school.
30 Mrs Carson's servants will inherit a fortune from her.

These verbs are the converse of those in 25–7; here the word *to* is missing because the subject names the goal: *Harry*, *Millie* and *Mrs Carson's servants*. Both the verbs in 25–7 and those in 28–30 are transfer verbs.

The argument structure of verbs such as those in 28–30 is illustrated here with *receive*:

Time frame: Time 0, theme at source; Time +, theme at goal. Goal NP is subject, theme NP is object of the verb and the source NP is introduced by *from*.

Typical verbs that fit here are:

get	[least marked]
take	[the action may be legitimate or not; that is, *take* can be equivalent to *accept* or to *steal*]
accept	[the action is legitimate]
acquire	[the circumstances of the action are vague]
borrow	[the change is temporary; cf. *lend*]
collect	[the object is plural or non-countable, or the act is habitual – in other words, the act is distributed]
inherit	[the source is typically, but not necessarily, deceased]
obtain	[the action is the result of effort by the goal]

receive　[the act results from the kindness or generosity of the source]

steal　[illegal act]

31　This gift is for you from your fellow team members.

If there is no verb – only forms of be – *for* introduces the goal. In other words, the preposition *for* acts as a sort of transfer predicate.

Predicates like the ones discussed above give information about a change of ownership, a change from one status in which one entity, the source, possesses, to another status in which a different entity, the goal, possesses. The change of possession is accomplished in a short time, no matter how long the giving has been planned or the reception has been awaited. When we discuss the movement of some person or thing from one place to another, the time for transition and path over which the movement takes place becomes important.

PRACTICE 6.2

Tell the role structure for each of these verbs:

　approach attach connect detach disconnect
　eject liberate release withdraw

Does any of them have variable valency – express transition and transfer? What special semantic features do these verbs have?

A few predicates, most notably *march* and *walk*, occur with meanings of transition (32a and 33a) and meanings of transfer (32b and 33b).

32a　The platoon marched to the parade-ground.
32b　The sergeant marched the platoon to the parade-ground.
33a　Laura walked home.
33b　Fred walked Laura home.

Compare these sentences with sentences like 1 and 3 (*The bus goes from Greenville to Stratford, Fenwick drives the bus from Greenville to Stratford*). The structure is the same except that *bus* is inanimate and has the role of 'theme' while animate NPs have the role of 'actor.'

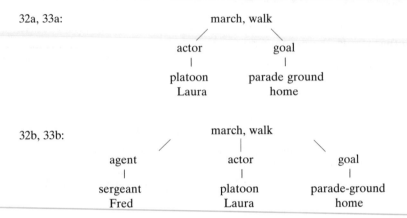

32a, 33a:

	march, walk	
actor		goal
platoon		parade ground
Laura		home

32b, 33b:

	march, walk	
agent	actor	goal
sergeant	platoon	parade-ground
Fred	Laura	home

Some transfer predicates undergo interesting changes in the way the accompanying arguments are presented. Compare *load* and *pack* in the following.

34a We loaded lumber on(to) the truck.
34b We loaded the truck with lumber.
35a I packed some notes in(to) my briefcase.
35b I packed my briefcase with some notes.

Sentences 34a and 35a tell of putting something in a place; that 'something' is affected by the action.

	actor	action	affected	place
34a	we	load	lumber	truck
35a	I	pack	notes	briefcase

Sentences 34b and 35b seem to express the affecting of a place, and the objects in question are the means of affecting.

	actor	action	affected	means
34b	we	load	truck	lumber
35b	I	pack	briefcase	notes

PRACTICE 6.3

1 Some predicates denote, not a change from one physical location to another, but a change from one condition to another, which are the source and goal, respectively. Consider one-argument verbs like these:

change evolve improve deteriorate

and two-argument verbs like these:

promote demote.

What sentence structures do they have? What are the time-scales? What other semantic features are needed to account for the differences among these verbs?

2 What is the difference between the verbs *award* and *reward* – in role structure and in the forms of their sentences?

3 The verbs *teach*, *instruct* and others can be regarded as predicates of transfer – here, the transfer of knowledge or information. What role structure and what special features do they have?

Summary

The thematic structure, or role structure, of a predicate is clearly related to its meaning, and predicates with similar meanings have similar thematic structures. In this chapter we have examined predicates with a valency of three or more. All such predicates describe the movement of some entity, concrete or abstract. The entity from which the movement originates has the semantic function of source and the entity which represents the end of movement has the function of goal. Predicates of transition have arguments in the roles of theme or actor, source, goal and path, though the last three are not necessarily expressed in a sentence. Predicates of transfer have the same argument roles plus an agent. Time frames, including a time zero, a later time, and perhaps an earlier time, display the difference between real transition and pseudo-transition and between transfer that includes movement of the agent and transfer that does not.

Suggested reading

Dixon (1991: 94–102), treats verbs of motion and rest; 113–17 deal with verbs of giving. Talmy (1975) analyzes motion verbs.

Reference

A **referring expression** is a piece of language, a noun phrase, that is used in an utterance and is linked to something outside language, some living or dead or imaginary entity or concept or group of entities or concepts. That 'something' is the **referent**, not necessarily physical nor necessarily 'real.'

We need to distinguish three terms: referring expression, referent, and way of referring. *Uncle Fred* and *that canary* are obviously different referring expressions and have different referents when used in utterances. *Lake Ontario* and *a lake* are different referring expressions with different kinds of referent; one referent, Lake Ontario, is unique and the referring expression, *Lake Ontario*, always refers to that referent; the other referring expression, *a lake*, can have different referents in different utterances. *A canary*, *the canary*, *this canary* and *our canary* are different referring expressions with possibly the same referent but they refer in different ways.

In the sections that follow we discuss three ways in which referents differ from one another: unique like *Lake Ontario* versus non-unique like *a lake*; concrete, such as *an apricot*, versus abstract, such as *an idea*; and countable like *a bottle*, *several bottles* versus non-countable like *milk*. Subsequently, we take up different ways of referring and consider such differences as definite and indefinite, generic and non-generic, specific and non-specific.

We also need to recognize a distinction between primary referring expressions and secondary referring expressions. A primary referring expression is a noun phrase like *a dog*, *your friend*, *George Adams*, *the flowers in that basket*; they refer directly to their referents. Examples of secondary referring expressions are: *he*, *the big ones*, *ours*, *that one*. These expressions are headed by pronouns and they refer indirectly; their referents can only be determined from primary referring expressions in the context in which they are used. Secondary referring expressions are the topic of section **4.5**, Anaphora. As you might expect, most of this chapter is about primary referring expressions.

7.1 Referents and referring expressions

We begin with an attempt to clear up some possible sources of confusion:

1a   Howard is your cousin, isn't he?
1b   <u>Howard</u> is your cousin's name, isn't it?

1 A referring expression is not a referent; the phrase *a carrot* can be a referring expression but it is not a carrot. This may seem obvious, but throughout history people have failed to distinguish between lexemes and what lexemes denote. They have treated words as sacred, beautiful, ugly or horrid depending on how they regard the referent ("Syphilis is an ugly word"). Some jokes and riddles achieve their effect by ignoring the distinction between a lexeme and what it represents ("Where can you always find sympathy?" Answer: "In a dictionary".)

Every lexeme is its own name. When we fail to make the distinction between a lexeme used to name itself and a lexeme used with reference outside language, we can create absurdities like this: "*Washington has three syllables and 600,000 inhabitants.*" If this sort of thing is meant in fun, there is no harm, but it can lead to sloppy thinking. In writing we can distinguish between metalinguistic reference – reference to a lexeme or other language expression – and extralinguistic reference – reference to something outside language – by italicizing or underlining a word when it refers to that expression, as with the name *Howard* in Sentence 1b, above. Similarly, "Where can you always find *sympathy*?" "*Washington* has three syllables"; "Washington has 600,000 inhabitants." Of course, italics and under- lining have no effect in speech.

2 There is no natural connection between referring expression and referent. Some ancient philosophers and ancient and medieval etymologists held the opinion that there is – or once was – a natural relation between symbol and what is symbolized. But this is simply not so.

3 The existence of a referring expression does not guarantee the existence of a referent in the physical-social world that we inhabit. We can easily use language to create expressions with fictitious referents such as *the skyscrapers of Antarctica, the present Emperor*

of Texas, the pain-reliever recommended by 91 percent of all doctors. In fact, we need such expressions in order to deny the existence of any physical referent.

4 Two or more referring expressions may have the same referent, but they do not necessarily have the same meaning.

> Robert Blair
> the husband of Mildred Stone Blair
> the father of Patrick and Robin Blair
> the city editor of the Morgantown *Daily Enquirer*, etc.

All these and no doubt other referring expressions may identify the same individual, but they do not mean the same. Two terms may name the same thing but differ in connotation, like *fiddle* and *violin*, or simply differ in the way they refer. The following example provided by Frege (1980), who first called attention to this fact, is famous among semanticists. In the Northern Hemisphere the planet Venus is visible to the naked eye just before sunrise at certain times of the year and just after sunset at other times. Consequently it is known sometimes as the Morning Star, and sometimes as the Evening Star. These two terms – and also the planet Venus – name the same entity but they do not have the same meaning.

A referring expression is used to identify, but the identification may be valid only temporarily (*the girl in the purple sweater*) and it need not be true: you may know who I mean when I refer to *that stupid clown* but your ability to identify doesn't depend on your agreeing with my way of referring. We often use **metonymy** in referring, identifying some entity, especially a person, by some characteristic associated with the entity, as when we refer to someone as 'the horn-rimmed glasses' or when a waitress asks a group of people seated at one table, "Which of you is the tuna salad?"

7.2 Extension and intension

The **extension** of a lexeme is the set of entities which it denotes. The extension of *dog* includes all collies, dalmatians, dachshunds, mongrels, etc., etc. that have ever lived or will ever live and every fictitious creature that is accepted as being a dog. All the things that can be denoted by the noun *lake* are the extension of that lexeme.

The lexeme *Lake Ontario* has a single item in its extension, and *the Dead Sea Scrolls* has a single collection of items as its extension.

The **intension** of any lexeme is the set of properties shared by all members of the extension. Thus everything that is denoted by *lake* must be a body of water of a certain size surrounded by land, and everything denoted by *island* is a body of land surrounded by water – but see below for discussion of some difficulties in applying these definitions.

Extension has to do with reference, but reference, as we know, is not all of meaning: the lexemes *violin* and *fiddle* have the same extension. Extension can change while intension remains the same. The extension of the referring expression *the capital of Australia* is a single item, the city of Canberra. The intension of the same term is 'city in which the national government of Australia is located.' If the capital should be moved at some future time to another city, the extension changes but the intension remains the same. *The Mayor of Chicago* or *the Prime Minister of Great Britain* always has the same intension but the extension of each of these changes from time to time.

In the discussion of hyponymy in Chapter 5 we noted that the denotation of a hyponym like *collie* is included in the denotation of its superordinate, *dog*, but the meaning of the superordinate is included in the meaning of the hyponym. We can now restate this with the terms 'intension' and 'extension': the extension of the hyponym is included in the extension of the superordinate (all collies are dogs) but the intension of the superordinate is included in the intension of the hyponym (the characteristic of being a dog is part of the characteristic of being a collie).

Language is a way in which people classify the phenomena in their world, their lives. The English language leads us to believe that there is a clear difference between lake and pond, between bush and tree, hill and mountain, between greenish-blue and bluish-green. Actually, extensions have fuzzy boundaries because nature does not consist of items discretely separated and clearly differentiated from one another. Sometimes it is the edges that are fuzzy while from center to center the difference is clear enough.

A **prototype** is an object or referent that is considered typical of the whole set. Thus, if you encounter the lexeme *door* in isolation and immediately think of a door swinging on hinges rather than one that slides or rotates, that kind of door is, for you, the prototype of all doors. But not everybody is likely to have the same prototype for a particular set. People in Belize probably do not have the same prototype for *tree* as people in Scotland.

The extension of *bird* includes robins, eagles, hawks, parrots, ducks, geese, ostriches and penguins. What is the intension? What do all the referents of *bird* have in common and which is not shared by non-birds? Which of these – robins, eagles, etc. – seem to you to be closer to a prototype and which farther away? Will all speakers of English agree about this?

Distinctions that we take for granted often turn out to have fuzzy boundaries when we try to explain the difference. We might say, for example, that the difference between a tree and a bush is a matter of size, but a tall bush can be bigger than a tree, and in any case a bonsai tree and a sapling are smaller than any bushes.

PRACTICE 7.2 Intension and extension

How do the lexemes in these pairs differ in their intension (or extension)?

shoe, slipper	cup, mug
fruit, vegetable	door, gate

7.3 Some different kinds of referents

The entities that we refer to are of different kinds and a language may have ways of recognizing different kinds of referents, different reference classes. Three kinds of differences in referents are: **concrete** and **abstract**; **unique** and **non-unique**; **countable** and **non-countable**. To some extent the differences are in the referents and to some extent in the way English, or any language, treats the referents.

7.3.1 Unique and non-unique referents

2a   We swam in <u>Lake Ontario</u>.
2b   We swam in <u>a lake.</u>

Both of the underlined noun phrases are referring expressions. They might have the same referent, but *a lake* can refer to various bodies of water whereas *Lake Ontario* always refers to the same body of water. A referring expression has **fixed reference** when the referent is a unique entity or unique set of entities, like *Lake Ontario, Japan, Boris Yeltsin, the Dead Sea Scrolls, the Philippine Islands*. A referring expression has **variable reference** if its referent may be different every time it is used: *that dog, my uncle, several people, a lake, the results*. When a referring expression has fixed reference, knowledge of it is part of one's general knowledge; we either know what the Dead Sea Scrolls are or we don't know (though of course we may learn what they are from the context in which *the Dead Sea Scrolls* occurs). Recognizing the referent when the expression has variable reference is a matter of specific knowledge; one has to identify *that dog, my uncle* or *the results* from the physical or linguistic context, including knowledge of the speaker, perhaps.

Again, let's note the fluidity of language. Nouns with fixed reference can be used with variable reference: "Every city has a Greenwich Village"; "This fellow is an Einstein"; "We need a new Magna Carta." The name of a person, for example *Shakespeare*, which necessarily has concrete, fixed reference, acquires variable reference when applied to other people ("No Shakespeare wrote this play") and abstract reference for the works produced by that person ("We're reading Shakespeare").

7.3.2 Concrete and abstract referents

Lexemes such as *dog, door, leaf, stone* denote **concrete** objects, which can be seen or touched; the objects denoted by lexemes like *idea, problem, reason, knowledge* are **abstract**; they cannot be perceived directly through the senses. This is not a linguistic difference in itself; there is nothing in the pronunciation of *raisin* and *reason*, for instance, that indicates which lexeme has an abstract denotation and which has a concrete one. But lexemes with different kinds of denotation generally occur in different kinds of utterances and then may have different effects on other lexemes. Consider these contrasts:

the key to the front door	the key to success
a bright light	a bright future

Here the lexemes *key* and *bright* have **literal meanings** when they occur in concrete contexts and **figurative meanings** in abstract contexts.

Language is fluid, so lexemes which typically have concrete denotations can be given abstract ones, and vice versa. A *character* is, first, a kind of mark or sign, something that appears on paper or other surfaces, and is therefore concrete; *character* is also the totality of qualities that define a person or thing, in other words something abstract. *Likeness* is similarity, the quality of being like something (abstract), such as a picture or other representation – a *likeness* of someone (concrete).

7.3.3 Countable and non-countable referents

Noun phrases in English, as in other European languages, are either **countable** or **non-countable**. Both countable and non-countable noun phrases may be concrete or abstract. Concrete countable expressions refer to items that are separate from one another, like apples, coins, pens and toothbrushes, which can ordinarily be counted one by one. Abstract countable phrases have such nouns as *idea*, *problem*, *suggestion*. Non-countable phrases, if their references are concrete, have three kinds of reference. Some refer to continuous substances, such as apple sauce, ink, mud and toothpaste, which do not consist of natural discrete parts. Others name substances that consist of numerous particles not worth counting, like sand and rice. A few non-countables are like *furniture, jewelry, luggage*, collections whose parts have quite different names. Then there are abstract non-countables such as *advice, information, beauty*, which are treated, in the English language, as indivisible.

Countable noun phrases show a distinction between singular and plural while non-countable noun phrases do not:

an apple, a coin, a pen, a toothbrush
some apples, some coins, some pens, some toothbrushes
some apple sauce, some mud, some ink, some toothpaste

The singular countable noun phrase must have an overt specifier; the plural countable and non-countable may have a zero specifier; the specifier *some* can be replaced by zero in the last two lines above.

We do not say that there are countable and non-countable nouns because, as Allan (1986) has shown, nouns display a range of 'countability.' At one extreme there are nouns that occur almost exclusively in countable expressions: *coin*, *pen* and *toothbrush* are good examples. Then there are nouns which in countable phrases indicate (what are linguistically treated as) items and in non-countable phrases denote (what are treated as) substances.

an apple, some eggs   some apple, some egg on the plate
a hair, a piece of string, hair, string, fire, light
a fire, some lights

Certain animals are named in countable phrases but when considered as food the names appear in non-countable phrases.

(a) chicken, (a) lobster, (a) turkey

In contrast, there are animal names of Anglo-Saxon origin such as *cow*, *calf*, *pig*, *sheep*, *deer* – all countable nouns – matched by food names of Norman-French origin: *beef*, *veal*, *pork*, *mutton*, *venison*, which are non-countable.

Some nouns name substances when they occur in non-countable phrases and in countable phrases designate items originally made from those substances.

glass, iron, paper, straw   a glass, an iron, a paper, a straw

What is regarded as a substance, and therefore generally treated as non-countable, may appear in a countable phrase to indicate a certain quantity or type of the substance.

a coffee   a good wine   several cheeses   various soups

At the non-countable end of the continuum are nouns that name collections of items – *furniture, jewelry, luggage* – which are always non-countable. The specific items included in these collections are indicated by countable nouns – *chair, bed; necklace, ring; trunk, suitcase.* In other instances there are matching nouns: *shrubbery* and *shrub, rain* and *raindrop, snow* and *snowflake,* including some that have no formal relationship: *foliage* and *leaf.*

There are a few nouns which occur only as plurals: *scissors, pliers, tweezers; trousers, shorts, jeans,* etc.; *shavings, filings, earnings, savings.*

This language distinction seems to mirror a distinction found in nature: apples, babies, coins, leaves and pebbles are isolable, while dirt, sand, milk, rice and water appear to be continuous entities or composed of such small particles that we don't consider the particles worth counting. However, note the inconsistency of *suds,* a plural countable, and *foam,* a non-countable; of the plural countable *oats* and the non-countable *wheat, rye, barley, corn.*

These distinctions – concrete/abstract, unique/non-unique, countable/non-countable – seem to reflect differences that exist in nature, but only partly so. All languages have reference classes which may be 'natural' to some degree. We take it for granted that countable nouns should be singular or plural, but nature does not have two categories, a category consisting of one single item and another category that consists of all numbers from two to infinity.

PRACTICE 7.3 Concrete and abstract

The following occur in expressions with concrete reference and in expressions that have abstract reference. For each noun give an example of each kind of reference. Is there also a difference of countability?

beauty	curiosity	kindness
novelty	personality	representation

PRACTICE 7.4 Countable and non-countable

Which of the following are countable nouns and which are non-countable? Do any belong to both categories?

beer	glue
copper	livestock
dust	piano
equipment	wire

7.4 Different ways of referring

There are three kinds of referring expressions: proper names, which have unique reference like *Lake Ontario* or *Barbara Collins*; pronouns such as *she, he, they,* which we discuss below in Section **7.6**, Anaphora; and noun phrases that have nouns with variable reference as the head, preceded by a determiner and possibly followed by one or more complements:

determiner	*head*	*complement*	*complement*
a	cat		
that	broom	in the corner	
your	home		
some	questions	to be answered	
the	plate	that is broken	that you mentioned

Some complements can be reduced and become modifiers in pre-head position.

determiner	*modifier*	*head*	*complement*
the	broken	plate	that you mentioned

Complements and modifiers, if present, provide part of the identity of the referent – they answer the question 'which?,' which broom, which plate. Determiners have a more complex role in identifying referents. In a discussion of reference, complements and modifiers are of little importance, but determiners are all-important. Referring expressions with fixed reference, like *Lake Ontario*, do not require complements, modifiers or determiners since their uniqueness makes the question 'which?' superfluous.

There are various determiners, including zero – that is, no overt determiner, as in *We're counting money*; *We're counting coins*. We can recognize several kinds of determiners, to be discussed below. Demonstrative and possessive determiners are different ways of identifying – answering the question 'which?'. Quantifying determiners answer the question 'how much?' or 'how many?'. Indefinite determiners (*a/an*, *some*, *any* and zero) do not identify. The definite determiner *the* is used when identity can be taken for granted.

The **demonstrative** determiners *this* and *that* (plural *these* and *those*) indicate, respectively, that the referent is near or not near the speaker's location.

3   We'll use this table and those chairs (over there).

They also identify present or future events versus past events.

4a   We're going to see 'Madame Butterfly' tonight. We've been waiting for this performance for a long time.
4b   We saw 'Rigoletto' last month. That was a great performance.

(During the twentieth century *this* has acquired a use, among some speakers of English, which is not demonstrative but essentially equivalent to the indefinite *a/an*, as in *I was driving down the street when suddenly this big, black car pulled out in front of me*. The usage began, no doubt, as an attempt to make the narration more dramatic by putting the referent – here, the car – 'right on the scene.' But extensive use weakens whatever dramatic effects there may have been.)

So-called **possessive** determiners refer to an entity in its relation to another referent, but 'possession' is a term for various kinds of relation: *my necktie* expresses ownership; *my brother*, kinship; *my friend* and *my employer*, other associations; *Vivaldi's 'Four Seasons'* expresses authorship; *Donna's picture* may refer to a picture of Donna or to one drawn or photographed by Donna.

Some determiners, **quantifiers**, express the amount or quantity of the entity denoted by the noun. Cardinal numbers are specific quantifiers: *one day, five people, 76 trombones*. General quantifiers are the ones discussed in Section **5.10**: *some eggs, a little milk, a few problems, much traffic, several accidents*. If a countable noun phrase expresses a total, it may be **collective** (*all donkeys*) or **distributive** (*every donkey*).

Demonstrative, possessive and quantifying determiners can be combined, in which case the possessive word follows the noun: *these four books, that idea of yours, several friends of mine.*

Demonstrative, possessive and quantifying reference intersects with three other kinds of reference, generic, specific and definite. These last three require more extensive discussion and illustration.

7.4.1 Generic and non-generic reference

What seems to be the same referring expression may have quite different kinds of reference, as in the following sentences.

5a   A dog makes a fine pet.
5b   Dogs make fine pets.
6a   A dog is lying in the middle of the street.
6b   Dogs are lying in the middle of the street.

In sentence 5a *a dog* has **generic reference**; the sentence is not about a particular dog but about the class of dogs as a whole, dogs in general. We can express the same meaning with sentence 5b, which is also a generalization. You may agree with these sentences without committing yourself to the belief that all dogs make fine pets. Neither sentence is an answer to a question 'Which dog(s)?', for the question is not relevant. *A dog* in sentence 6a does not have generic reference; it clearly does not refer to the whole class of dogs, and a change to *Dogs are lying in the middle of the street* (6b) produces quite a different message. Sentences 5a and 5b are equivalent; 6a and 6b are not. Sentences 6a and 6b do not answer the question 'Which dog(s)?' but the question is relevant. (Some semanticists would prefer to say that reference can only be specific. Then, rather than 'generic reference,' they would prefer the term 'generic use of referring expressions.')

Generic reference in English can be expressed in several ways which are more or less interchangeable.

7a   The dog was man's first domestic animal. =
7b   Dogs were man's first domestic animal.

We know that these have generic reference because the change from singular to plural, or vice versa, does not make a difference. (Note that *man* also has generic reference here; it is equivalent to 'humans,' a general class.)

7.4.2 Specific and non-specific reference

8a   We have a dog.
8b   We'd like to have a dog.
9a   I'm sure there are answers to all your questions.
9b   I trust we can find answers to all your questions.

In sentence 8a, above, *a dog* refers to a specific dog. The reference is to some particular animal, and we could insert the word *certain* before *dog* without changing the meaning. In sentence 8b *a dog* would ordinarily be interpreted as non-specific in reference – 'some dog, not any particular one' – though of course it could mean 'a certain, particular dog.' Similarly, *answers* has specific reference in 9a but not in 9b. Whether a referring expression has a specific referent or not cannot be determined from the expression itself; it is determined by the larger context.

PRACTICE 7.5 Specific reference

Which of the underlined expressions have specific reference and which do not?

1   Somebody telephoned and left a message for you.
2   I hope somebody will tidy up this file cabinet.
3   The last person to leave the office should lock the door.
4   A stitch in time saves nine.
5   Evans sometimes forgets to keep his eye on the ball.

7.4.3 Definite and indefinite reference

Demonstrative, possessive, and quantitative determiners identify a referent in a fairly precise way. The definite determiner *the* occurs in a referring expression when the speaker assumes that the hearer can identify the referent (*I've got the tickets*) or when identification is made part of the referring expression (*I've got the tickets that you wanted*). Indefinite determiners, *a(n)*, *some* and zero, indicate that the referent is part of a larger entity.

When the referring expression is definite, the speaker assumes that the referent can be identified by the addressee for one of four reasons. If none of these reasons applies, the speaker provides the identification.

1 The speaker assumes that the hearer can identify the referent from the physical–social context – a form of deixis (Section **7.5**).

10   Take <u>the cups</u> off <u>the table</u> and put them in <u>the cabinet</u>.

2 The speaker assumes that the addressee can make the necessary implicature to relate a new reference to a previous one.

11   This was the site of the old Stanwick Theater. <u>The stage</u> was over here and <u>the lobby</u> was over there.

3 The reference is fixed and therefore presumably part of the addressee's general knowledge, like *Lake Ontario*. A referring expression with fixed reference is always definite. (A referring expression with variable reference may be definite or indefinite.) Some fixed-reference expressions contain the determiner *the*, others do not. In a few instances expressions with and without the word *the* are equivalent: *the Argentine* = *Argentina*, *the Ukraine* has become *Ukraine*. More frequently, presence and absence of *the* with a name yields two different referring expressions: *the Mississippi* is not the same as *Mississippi*. Family names used in the plural occur with *the* – *the Johnsons*; other personal names do not.

4 The referent, while not unique in the way that Lake Ontario is unique, has a unique or nearly unique position in the more limited world of the speaker and addressee.

12   Careful! You might wake <u>the baby</u>.
13   Have you received <u>the reports</u> from <u>the doctor</u>?

Referring expressions like these are much the same as names. Names like *Richard* and *Barbara* are definite and specific as referring expressions even though there are numerous people so named, just as there are numerous babies, reports and doctors. Expressions like *the baby* and *Richard* have unique status within a certain group of people during a particular period of time. *The Mayor* has unique status for a larger group of people, presumably, than *the baby*, and *the President* has this status for a still larger group. The uniqueness of these expressions may be temporary: the baby grows older, we change doctors, Richard moves out of our lives.

If none of these conditions obtains, the referent is specified by the speaker through some complement or modifier in the referring expression – with the presumption that the complement or modifier makes the referent clear to the addressee.

14a The salesman who came here yesterday was back again today.
14b I'd like to look at the gold ring with a small ruby on the top shelf of that display case.

When the referring expression is indefinite, the hearer has to make a choice from the extension of the noun – that is, has to decide which of all possible referents – what part of the extension – is intended. Frequently in a discourse a topic is introduced as an indefinite referring expression (new information) and subsequent mention of the topic is made with one or more definite referring expressions (given information).

A definite noun phrase presupposes the existence of its referent and an indefinite noun phrase presupposes the existence of more than its referent, a class of referents to which this one belongs.

7.5 Deixis

The most primitive way of referring to something is to point to it. Of course, this kind of reference can only be accomplished with people and concrete things in one's immediate environment. On a less primitive level, every language has **deictic words** which 'point' to 'things' in the physical-social context of the speaker and addressee(s) and whose referents can only be determined by knowing the context in which they are used. For example, if we should encounter a message like the following, on paper or on an electronic recording

15 I was disappointed that you didn't come this afternoon.
    I hope you'll join us tomorrow.

we wouldn't be able to identify the referents of *I*, *you*, *us*, *this afternoon* or *tomorrow* though we understand how the first three and the last two are related to one another; because we know English, we know, for example, that the referent of *I* is part of the referent of *us* and we know the time sequence of *this afternoon* and *tomorrow*. The meaning of any lexeme depends to some extent on the context in which it occurs, but deictic elements can only be interpreted through their contexts.

English examples of deictic words include (1) pronouns *I*, *you* and *we*, which 'point' to the participants in any speech act; *he*, *she*, *it* and *they*, when they are used to refer to others in the environment; (2) locative expressions *here* and *there*, which designate space close to the speaker or farther away; *this/these* and *that/those*, which respectively indicate entities close to or removed from the speaker; and (3) temporal expressions: *now*, *then*, *yesterday*, *today*, *tomorrow*, *last week*, *next month* and so on. These last are all relative to the time when they are used.

Words which can be deictic are not always so. *Today* and *tomorrow* are deictic in "We can't go today, but tomorrow will be fine." They are not deictic in "Today's costly apartment buildings may be tomorrow's slums." Yet the relation between the two words is analogous. Similarly, *here* and *there* are deictic in "James hasn't been here yet. Is he there with you?" They are not deictic in "The children were running here and there." The pronoun *you* is not deictic when used with the meaning 'one; any person or persons,' as in "You can lead a horse to water but you can't make him drink." Similarly, *they* has a generalized, non-deictic reference to people in general, especially those in charge of some endeavor or other, as in "They say that an ounce of prevention is worth a pound of cure," "They don't make good cider the way they used to."

7.6 Anaphora

Some deictic words can also be used as anaphoric items. **Anaphora** is a kind of secondary reference in which a previous reference is recalled by use of special function words or equivalent lexemes. For example, in

16a Jack and Jill tried to lift the box and push it onto the top shelf.

16b   However,
$$\left\{ \begin{array}{l} he \\ she \\ it \\ they \end{array} \right\}$$
slipped and fell to the floor.

the choice of *he*, *she*, *it* or *they* serves as a link to some referring expression that has occurred recently in the discourse – in this illustration to a referring expression in the previous sentence. Every language has special function words which repeat a reference without actually repeating the referring expression or any part of it. Each of the four **pronouns** illustrated here has a particular scope of reference: *they* is tied to the last plural referring expression, *it* to the last singular non-personal expression, *she* to the last singular feminine expression, and *he* to the last singular masculine expression.

Most speakers of English would assume, in this example, that *he* refers to the same person as *Jack* – that *he* has the same referent as *Jack* (or is **co-referential** with *Jack*) – and that *she* is co-referential with *Jill* and *it* is co-referential with *the box* (linguistically, *it* might be co-referential with *the top shelf* but in practical terms that seems unlikely). As for *they*, it can be co-referential with *Jack and Jill* or with *Jack and Jill and the box* as the primary referring expressions, a difference that could be clarified with the choice of *they both* versus *they all*; but it cannot be co-referential with *Jack and the box* alone or with *Jill and the box* alone.

The difference between deixis and anaphora is fairly plain, even though some function words can be used in both functions. If someone says, for example, "She wants to leave now" and nods in Lucy's direction and/or Lucy is the only person present to whom *she* can refer, *she* is used deictically. On the other hand, in the utterance "Lucy has been here for over an hour and she wants to leave now," the word is used anaphorically.

It is important to see that an anaphoric word refers to the referent of the primary referring expression, not to that expression itself.

17a   I asked the secretary to telephone Mr Letterman.
17b   _____ had Mr Letterman on the line in a few minutes.
18a   We watched the sheep moving slowly across the pasture.
18b   _____ seemed to be in no hurry at all.

Should the blank in 17b be filled with *he* or *she*? We have to know the referent of the secretary in order to decide; that information is not in the referring expression itself. Occupational nouns such as *secretary*, *teacher*, *cashier*, *doctor*, which don't indicate gender, are more common in modern English than pairs like *actor/actress*, *waiter/waitress*, which make a gender distinction.

What pronoun fills the blank in 18b? Sentence 18a doesn't tell us whether it was one sheep or more than one, but the pronoun that fills the following blank has to give this information, so if *the sheep* has plural reference, the anaphoric word is *they*. And if there is only one animal in question, the blank may be filled with *it* or *he* or *she* depending on the sex of the sheep and its importance to the person speaking or writing. Of course, countable nouns like *sheep* which can be singular or plural with no overt indication of number are rather uncommon in English, but the choice among *he*, *she*, and *it* referring to a sheep reflects a common fact of English usage: the pronoun for referring to an animal is the same as the pronoun for referring to a lifeless object, *it*, except that a pet-owner or a farmer, who cares about the animal, can refer to a pet or farm animal with the same distinction as is made in referring to people (Halliday and Hasan 1976: 47). Thus the grammatical system of English makes distinctions that the lexicon often ignores.

English is said to have 'natural' gender, which means principally that we use *he*, *she* or *it* in secondary reference, *he* referring to males, *she* to females and *it* for inanimate entities. But this distinction is not upheld rigidly; *she* can refer to an inanimate object, *it* to a baby or an animal, regardless of sex. In other words, it is the referent and, to some extent, the speaker's attitude toward the referent that determines the choice of pronoun, not the noun that would be used in a referring expression.

On the other hand, numerous languages have 'grammatical gender' so that all nouns belong to one gender class or another and other parts of a noun phrase must 'agree' with the noun. In Spanish, for example, we have

esta pared blanca	this white wall
esta camisa blanca	this white shirt
este papel blanco	this white paper
este sombrero blanco	this white hat

Pared and *camisa* belong to the 'feminine' gender, a class that contains some nouns that denote females; *papel* and *sombrero* belong to the 'masculine' gender, a class which has some nouns that denote males. The words for 'this' (*esta* or *este*) and 'white' (*blanca* or *blanco*) must show gender agreement with the noun that heads the phrase in which they occur. An anaphoric phrase can be created by omitting the noun; thus *esta blanca* and *este blanco* both correspond to English 'this white one' but they are not equivalent. The choice of *esta blanca* or *este blanco* depends, not on the referent itself but on the noun that occurs in the referring expression.

Somewhat similar, in other languages, is the use of classifiers. Nouns in Japanese, for instance, belong to different classes. When a noun is modified by a number, a classifier is required with the number, and different noun classes require different classifiers. Examples:

kippu san-mai	three stamps
tegami san-mai	three letters
enpitsu san-bon	three pencils
sereri san-bon	three stalks of celery

Mai is the classifier that accompanies certain nouns, some of which denote flat, thin objects like stamps and letters. *Hon* (or *bon*) is the classifier for another group of nouns, some of which denote cylindrical objects like pencils and stalks of celery. The sentences *San-mai ga arimasu* and *San-bon ga arimasu* can both be translated "There are three"; the classifier is determined by the noun, even when the noun is not there.

19a   There was <u>a strange painting</u> on the wall.

19b   I wondered where ⎰ <u>the painting</u> / <u>the picture</u> / <u>this work of art</u> / <u>it</u> ⎱ had come from.

The four underlined expressions in 19b are co-referential with the underlined expression in 19a. These four are different kinds of anaphoric expressions. As frequently happens in a discourse, the first referring expression, *a strange painting*, is indefinite and each of the anaphoric expressions is definite. The first three of these are examples of **lexical anaphora**, achieved by repeating the same noun head (*painting*), or by using a noun which, in the context, is equivalent in reference, a **synonym** (*picture*), or by using a term which has a more inclusive reference, a **superordinate** (*work of art*) (Halliday and Hasan 1976: 278). Grammatical anaphora is achieved with a pronoun;

the definite anaphoric pronouns are *he*, *she*, *they* and, in this case, *it*.

20   There was ⎧ a picture ⎫ above the mantelpiece
and   ⎨ a picture ⎬ over the desk.
           ⎩ one   ⎭

21   We need ⎧ (some) balloons ⎫ now and we need
              ⎨ (some) balloons ⎬ tomorrow.
              ⎩ some   ⎭

22   There's ⎧ (some) food ⎫ on the table and
              ⎨ (some) food ⎬ in the fridge.
              ⎩ some   ⎭

In sentence 20 the two occurrences of the indefinite (but specific) noun phrase, *a picture*, constitute two different referring expressions since they have different referents. The same is true for the indefinite noun phrases, (*some*) *balloons* and (*some*) *food*, in the next sentences. The substitute for an indefinite referring expression is *one* for a singular countable noun phrase and *some* for a plural countable or non-countable phrase. These substitutes are anaphoric, not because they are co-referential with the earlier noun phrases but because their interpretation depends on the earlier noun phrases with which they are linked.

23   Are you wearing your blue suit or your brown ⎧ suit ⎫ ?
                                                   ⎨ one ⎬

24   Are you wearing your brown shoes or your black ⎧ shoes ⎫ ?
                                                      ⎨ ones ⎬

25   Do you prefer warm milk or cold ⎧ milk ⎫ ?
                                       ⎨ 0   ⎬

When adjacent noun phrases have the same head and different determiners or modifiers, the anaphoric substitute for the head of the second phrase is *one* for a singular countable noun, *ones* for a plural countable noun, and zero for a non-countable noun.

There and *then* replace place phrases and time phrases, respectively.

26   I expected to meet our guests at the airport at three o'clock, but they weren't there then.

There are also anaphoric items that substitute for verb phrases and for clauses, but such anaphora does not have anything to do with reference.

27   I wanted to <u>ride on the carousel</u> but was unable to <u>do so</u>.
28   Diane feels <u>she has done enough now</u> and I think <u>so</u> too.

7.7 Shifts in ways of referring

Sentences 19a and 19b were partly like this:

There was <u>a strange painting</u> on the wall.
I wondered where $\left\{ \begin{array}{l} \underline{\text{the painting}} \\ \underline{\text{it}} \end{array} \right\}$ had come from.

Here the first referring expression is indefinite but specific. In the next sentence the co-referential expression is definite. If the first referring expression is indefinite and not specific, a following co-referential expression may be definite or indefinite.

29a   If we were going to buy <u>a car</u>, we would buy <u>it</u> at Hudson's.
29b   If we were going to buy <u>a car</u>, we would buy <u>one</u> at Hudson's.

A speaker may shift from specific reference to generic reference.

30a   We didn't buy <u>a new car</u> because <u>they</u> cost too much now.

Note the vagueness here. Does *they* mean 'cars' or 'new cars'? Prosody could make one meaning clear.

30b   We didn't buy <u>a NEW car</u> because <u>they</u> cost too much.

Here *they* must be equivalent to 'new cars.'

31   Every woman who has <u>a husband</u> should treat <u>him</u> with respect.

Does *him* have definite reference here? That depends on how we define 'definite.' The expression *every woman who has a husband* has distributed reference and *him*, we may say, acquires distributed reference by association. Thus it is equivalent to 'the husband that every woman who has a husband has,' which McCawley (1988: 333) calls an 'identity of sense.'

What do the underlined words refer to?

1   Pete promised me a souvenir from Paris but I never got it.
2   Pete promised me a souvenir from Paris but I never got one.
3   Frances asked Shirley to lend her some money.
4   Frances promised Shirley to lend her some money.
5   The police arrested several demonstrators because they were destroying property.
6   The police arrested several demonstrators because they felt the demonstration was getting violent.

7.8 Referential ambiguity

Misunderstandings occur when a speaker has one referent in mind for a definite expression like *George* or *the papers*, and the addressee is thinking of a different George or some other papers. No doubt we have all experienced, and been troubled by, this kind of problem in reference. We can see other instances of referential ambiguity that are due to the nature of referring expressions, the vagueness that pieces of language necessarily have.

Referential ambiguity occurs when

1   an indefinite referring expression may be specific or not;

32   I wanted to buy a newspaper.

Here *a newspaper* may refer to a specific newspaper or some newspaper, any newspaper. The ambiguity disappears if we add, on the one hand, *but I couldn't find it* or, on the other hand, *but I couldn't find one*.

2   anaphora is unclear because a personal pronoun, *he, she, it* or *they*, can be linked to either of two referring expressions:

33   Jack told Ralph that a visitor was waiting for him.

3   the pronoun *you* is used generically or specifically:

34   If you want to get ahead, you have to work hard.

(Is *you* the addressee or is this sentence a general platitude?)

4 a noun phrase with *every* can have distributed reference or collected reference:

35   I'm buying a drink for everybody here.
     (One drink for all or one drink for each?)

Summary

A referring expression is, first of all, a noun phrase that is linked to something outside language, its referent. We recognize different kinds of referents and different ways of referring.

Referents may be concrete or abstract, unique or non-unique, countable or non-countable items. To some extent these differences reflect distinctions in the phenomenal world, but linguistic reflections are no more 'natural' than anything else in language, and a given referring expression may sometimes have one kind of referent and sometimes another kind.

A noun phrase has a noun head, a determiner, and perhaps a complement and/or modifier. The determiner determines the way of referring that a particular referring expression has, though there is no simple correlation between determiner and way of referring. A referring expression with a proper noun as head is definite and specific. A noun phrase with a common noun as head may be generic or not, specific or not, definite or not. Two determiners are demonstrative; others indicate quantity; and others show possession. Quantity may be specific or general and if it is total, it may be collective or distributed.

Certain function words refer to parts of the physical–social–temporal context of the speaker or writer and their referents can only be known to one who knows that context. These are deictic elements.

Certain function words and lexemes are used to avoid repetition of referring expressions that have occurred previously in the discourse – less commonly, referring expressions that will follow. These are anaphoric items. English anaphoric items show the same distinctions found in primary referring expressions and in fact make distinctions that are not made lexically.

Any noun with a unique referent has fixed reference. A noun whose reference is non-unique occurs in numerous referring expressions associated with various referents. These associations, whether unique or numerous, are the extension of that noun. The characteristics that the referents supposedly share are the intension of the noun. Language imposes a classification on nature, but the classes are not neatly separated in nature, so that the boundaries of extensions may be fuzzy. Any referent that seems to be a typical member of the extension is a prototype.

Referential ambiguity occurs when the context does not make clear whether a referring expression is being used specifically or not; when the interpretation of a referring expression can be collective or distributed; and when it is not clear to which of two or more referring expressions an anaphoric item is linked.

Suggested reading

Lyons (1995: 294–312), is a very helpful discussion of reference, including deixis. Saeed (1997: 23–50), covers the basic notions about reference and then moves on to discuss the relation of lexemes and concepts to our thinking.

Gundel, Hedberg and Zacharski (1993) propose that there are six uses of deixis in discourse and illustrate these in several languages.

The verbs come, go, bring and take have deictic qualities since they involve movement to or from a place, which may be identifiable only from the physical context. The deictic nature of come is the topic of Fillmore (1966) and (1973).

Chapter 8

Sentences as arguments

Chapter 5 was concerned with how many, and what kinds of arguments different predicates can have. The arguments were all referring expressions, names for real or potential entities. An argument can also be a predication, a real or potential fact, and such an argument is expressed as a clause – that is, a sentence that is embedded in another sentence. In other words, we can make statements and ask questions about facts. For example, these sentences

They KNOW (that) I opened the letter.
Do you WANT me to open the letter?
She WATCHED me opening the letter.
Are you SURPRISED at my opening the letter?

all refer to a putative fact about the speaker opening a specified letter. There are several different kinds of clauses, underlined in the examples above and examined further in this chapter. To a large extent the form of the clause depends on the predicate (verb or adjective) that it accompanies. Predicates are shown in small capitals, above.

Previous chapters have included something about lexical ambiguity and referential ambiguity, different possible interpretations of lexemes. The structure of sentences may also lead to different possible interpretations, and such syntactic ambiguity is studied in the last section of this chapter.

Predicates that have embedded sentences as a theme include the following, those that express:

(a)   knowledge or ignorance of a possible fact

Ivan KNOWS (that) we are here.
I DOUBT if the game will start on time.

(b)   an attitude or orientation toward a fact or possible fact

Jean is DISAPPOINTED (that) you can't join us.

David's parents are ANXIOUS for <u>him to succeed.</u>
It SURPRISED everybody that <u>Sanders appeared at the party.</u>
<u>Sanders' appearance at the party</u> SURPRISED everybody.
The children PRETENDED (that) <u>they were asleep.</u>
The children PRETENDED <u>to be asleep.</u>

(c)   causing, allowing, or preventing the occurrence of a fact

Jerry HAD <u>the barber trim his mustache.</u>
Mama LET <u>Miriam hold the baby.</u>
Mama KEPT <u>Miriam</u> from <u>holding the baby.</u>

(d)   perception of a fact

I SAW <u>Mr Hall come out of the garage.</u>
Ruth HEARD <u>a baby crying.</u>

(e)   saying something about a fact or possible fact

Lily SAYS (that) <u>she'll be a little late.</u>
Please TELL us if <u>you feel ill.</u>
Edward DENIED <u>opening the letter.</u>

(f)   the beginning, continuing, or termination of a possible event

Marilyn QUIT <u>smoking.</u>
Suddenly it STARTED <u>to rain.</u>

We study the semantic groups of predicates in subsequent chapters (11, 12 and 13 especially). As the exhibit above shows, embedded clauses have several different forms, which are the topic of the present chapter. So much of this chapter is about the syntactic forms in which embedded propositions are expressed.

8.1 Full statement clauses

Compare:

1a   Ivan knows the answer.
1b   Ivan knows (that) we are here.
2a   Sally forgot her appointment.
2b   Sally forgot (that) Sara was waiting for her.
3a   The judges announced their decision to the eager contestants.

3b   The judges announced to the eager contestants that they had reached
       a decision.

In 1a, 2a and 3a a noun phrase is object of the verb. In 1b, 2b and 3b
a clause occurs in the same place and with the same role. In 3b the
direct object and indirect object have been rearranged, the shorter
element placed before the longer one.

If sentence 1a has this structure:

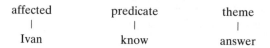

sentence 1b has the same structure except that the theme is a
sentence, symbolized as S-theme:

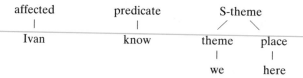

Sentence 2b has an analogous relation to 2a and 3b to 3a.

The S-theme, or clause, is introduced by the meaningless word
that, which may or may not be present. The rest of the clause,
following *that*, is identical with a sentence standing alone: *We are here*,
Sara was waiting for her, *They had reached a decision*. All of these
embedded sentences, or clauses, are statements in which propositions
are presented as facts. Note that the subject of the clause, if a personal
pronoun, must be a subject form, one of the group *I-he-she-we-they*,
not *me-him-her-us-them*, and the verb of the clause can have all the
modifications of the main verb; for example:

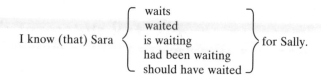

A clause that has these characteristics, subject pronoun as subject and
full possibility of verb modifications, is a full clause. Reduced clauses,
which we examine below, have neither of these characteristics.

Similarly, a combination of adjective and preposition may be followed by an abstract complement: *aware of the problem, disappointed in the results, sorry for the trouble.* The same adjectives may have a clause as complement, in which case the preposition disappears.

4   We weren't aware (that) the meeting had been canceled.
5   Jean is disappointed (that) you can't join us.
6   I'm sorry (that) the election involved so few real issues.

Here are some other adjectives that can be followed by a clause (with the preposition dropping out):

afraid-of   aware-of   (un)certain-about   confident-of
disappointed-in   doubtful-of/about   sure-of

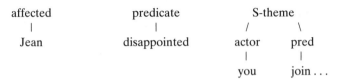

Clauses can also occur in subject position. Let's start again with noun phrases that can be replaced by clauses.

7a   That Jean came to the party surprised everybody.
7b   It surprised everybody that Jean came to the party.
8a   That Mr Goodson remembers so many things is unbelievable.
8b   It is unbelievable that Mr Goodson remembers so many things.

Subject clauses at the beginning of a sentence are unusual. Instead of this order, we more often introduce an empty word *it* and postpone the clause to the end of the sentence (7b, 8b). The predicate of 7a, b has this thematic structure:

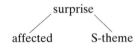

and the predicate of 8a, b has this structure:

8.2 Question clauses

Questions, as well as statements, are embedded in other sentences. They may be information questions, as in the following examples:

9   I wonder when the concert was. (When was the concert?)
10   Robert doesn't know what time it is. (What time is it?)
11   Do you remember where you put the tickets? (Where did you put the tickets?)

```
affected        predicate        Q-theme
   |                |             /      \
   I              wonder       theme      time
                                 |          |
                              concert       ?
```

He asked me when the concert was.

```
actor        predicate        goal         Q-theme
  |              |              |          /      \
  he            ask            me       theme      time
                                          |          |
                                       concert       ?
```

The embedded sentence may be a yes-no question. The word that introduces the embedded clause is *if*, which, unlike *that*, is not deletable.

12   I doubt if George knows the answer. (Does George know the answer?)
13   Please tell us if you feel ill. (Do you feel ill?)

```
                doubt
               /     \
        affected     Q-theme
```

A yes-no question may present two or more alternatives, e.g. *Will your friends stay or leave?* When such an alternative question is embedded, it is introduced with the word *whether*.

14   I wonder whether your friends will stay or leave.

The second alternative need not appear in a sentence.

15   Have you heard whether we get a holiday (or not)? (Do we get a holiday or not?)

8.3 Infinitive clauses

Compare:

16a   I know (that) Sara waits for Sally.
16b   I expect Sara to wait for Sally.

The sentence with *expect* contains one kind of reduced clause, an infinitive clause. The personal pronoun that replaces *Sara* is *her*, not *she*; and the verb *wait* can be expanded only a little; it can be perfect (*I expect Sara to have waited*) or progressive (*I expect Sara to be waiting*), or both (*I expect Sara to have been waiting*); but *to wait* does not distinguish present and past, and it cannot be preceded by a modal verb like *can*, *should*, *must* or *will*.

17a   The Eagles expect the Hawks to win the game.
17b   The Eagles expect to win the game.

The infinitive clause in 17a reflects a sentence or proposition {the Hawks win the game}. What is the embedded proposition of 17b? Obviously, {the Eagles win the game}. We do not say *The Eagles expect the Eagles to win the game* nor *The Eagles expect themselves to win the game*, though the latter is possible. Instead, a rule of English grammar requires an **overt subject** in an infinitive clause when the subject of the infinitive (here, *the Hawks*) is different from the subject of the main verb (here, *the Eagles*), but if the subject of the infinitive is the same as the subject of the main verb, there is a **tacit subject**. In the first sentence above, the infinitive clause has an overt subject, *the Hawks*. In the second sentence the infinitive clause has a tacit subject, *the Eagles*.

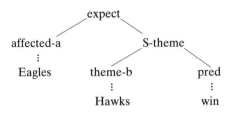

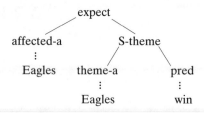

Here are more sentences with infinitive clauses that have tacit subjects:

18   I intend to get a haircut.
19   Martin decided to ask for help.
20   Joyce likes to sing.
21   The children pretended to be asleep.

Certain adjectives also occur with an infinitive clause as complement. One of them is *anxious*:

22   David's parents are anxious for him to succeed, and David, too, is anxious to succeed.

If the clause has an overt subject, it is introduced with the preposition *for*, as illustrated. Other adjectives that take infinitive clauses are these, all of which have human subjects:

afraid content eager glad happy impatient sorry

When an infinitive clause is the object of a certain small group of verbs, the preposition *to* does not appear.

23   Jerry had the barber trim his hair.
24   Mummy let Miriam hold the baby.
25   I helped Ted and Tom (to) change a tire.

The constructions following *had*, *let* and *helped* are infinitive clauses, but infinitive clauses after *have* and *let* do not have the word *to* and infinitive clauses after *help* need not have *to*. (Note that *the barber*, *Miriam* and *Ted and Tom* are replaced by *him*, *her* and *them*, respectively.)

have let (help)

8.4 Gerund clauses

However, there is a group of verbs that can have as object an infinitive clause without *to* or a gerund clause. A gerund clause has a verb with the suffix *-ing*. Note the following paired sentences in which the same verb is followed by infinitive clause and gerund clause.

26a I saw Mr Hall come out of the garage.
26b I saw Mr Hall coming out of the garage.
27a Ruth heard a baby cry.
27b She heard a baby crying.
28a Did you notice a pretty girl walk by?
28b Did you notice a pretty girl walking by?

Verbs that occur in such sentences, 26–8, are **perceptual verbs**, a group studied in detail in Chapter 12.

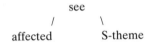

```
                    see
                 /       \
            affected      S-theme
```

see hear smell taste feel watch notice observe

Gerund clauses with tacit subjects are seen in the next group of sentences:

29   I enjoy attending the theater.
30   Edward denied opening the letter.
31   Marilyn has quit smoking.

The subject of the gerund is the same as the subject of the main verb: the sentences are about 'my' attending the concert, Edward's opening the letter, and Marilyn's smoking as well as my enjoying, Edward's denying and Marilyn's quitting.

A small group of adjectives takes gerund clause complements, with a preposition between adjective and gerund.

32   Who is responsible for doing this?
33   I'm grateful for your taking time off.

Other such adjectives are:

ashamed-of aware-of grateful-for thankful-for

All the predicates discussed so far with gerund clauses following are two-argument predicates. There is a subject, a predicate (which may be a verb or an adjective), and then a clause (which may have an overt subject or a tacit subject). How about three-argument predicates with gerund clauses?

34   Deborah advised/allowed/forbade/suggested waiting.

With the verbs shown in sentence 34 the following gerund clause seems to have a tacit subject but the real subject is an unmentioned 'somebody' that is not identical with the main clause subject. There is also an indirect object that is tacit and that is identical with the subject of the clause. Deborah gave advice/permission/encouragement/ a suggestion/ a warning to someone about waiting.

advise allow encourage permit forbid propose suggest warn-against

8.5 Non-factual clauses

We have now considered four kinds of clauses: full statement, full question, infinitive and gerund. The next kind of clause resembles the full statement but is different.
Compare:

35a   I insist that Ronald works very hard.
35b   I insist that Ronald work very hard.
35c   I insist that Ronald should work very hard.

35a is different from 35b and 35c, but 35b and 35c are quite alike in what they say. In 35a the subject ("I") insists that a certain fact is true. In the other two sentences the embedded clause tells what the subject maintains ought to be a fact. In 35a the embedded clause contains information that is presented as true at the time of utterance; in the other two sentences the embedded clause states what someone (someone in authority, it seems) wants to be true at a later time, whether true at the time or not. Some speakers of English prefer the construction with *should*; some prefer the construction without *should* but perhaps use it only in formal communication. The full clause in 35a is a **factual clause**, and we give the name **non-factual clause** to the embedded clause of 35b and 35c, with or without *should*. As long as the subject of the clause names one person (other than *I* or *you*), there is a difference between the factual clause of 35a and the non-factual clause of 35b: the presence or absence of the ending -*s*. With *I*, *you*, or a plural subject this distinction is lost: *I insist that they work very hard* is ambiguous. Of course there is a clear distinction between factual clause and non-factual clause if *should* is used for the latter (but not all speakers make this distinction):

36a I insist that they work hard.
36b I insist that they should work hard.

And there is a clear distinction for any subject if the verb is *be*, whether *should* occurs or not.

37a We insist that your friends are early
37b We insist that your friends (should) be early.

The factual clause can have various modifications for the verb: *We insist that your friends were late/had been late*, etc. The non-factual clause has no such modifications.

8.6 Verbal nouns

You are familiar with gerund clauses as in this sentence:

38 We watched Mark winning the race.

Compare this sentence:

39 We applauded Mark's winning of the race.

The second sentence contains a **verbal noun**, formed like the gerund by adding -*ing*. The difference between gerund and verbal noun is in the kind of constructions they appear in: the subject of the verbal noun is typically possessive and the object of the verbal noun is preceded by *of*. All verbs form a gerund by adding **-ing**. Common verbs of Old English origin, like *win*, form a verbal noun in the same way, so that the only difference is in the syntactic construction. In the French-Latin-Greek part of our vocabulary, however, verbal nouns are formed in a number of different ways but are always distinct from gerunds; for example, *discovery, explanation, improvement, response* versus *discovering, explaining, improving, responding*. The next group of sentences contains clauses in subject and object positions and the clauses contain verbal nouns. As the examples show, when the verb requires a preposition before a following object, the verbal noun keeps the same preposition; if the verb is not followed by a preposition, the verbal noun inserts *of* (Joos 1964: 205–7).

40   I enjoyed our conversation. (We conversed.)
41   Your response to that question was brilliant. (You responded to that question.)
42   The company's employment of a large labor force has added considerably to our local economy. (The company employs a large labor force.)
43   The president will soon announce her selection of a new cabinet officer. (She selects a new cabinet officer.)

If the verb has an overt subject, that subject becomes possessive before the verbal noun, as shown. If the verbal noun has a tacit subject, the verbal noun is preceded by *the*.

44   I enjoyed the conversation. (Somebody conversed.)
45   The employment of a large labor force is beneficial to any local economy. (Somebody employs a large labor force.)
46   The president will soon announce the selection of a new cabinet officer. (Somebody will select . . .)

Here is a summary of the clause structures discussed in this chapter:

Full statement clause (with overt subject):

They know (that) I opened the letter.
It's strange (that) they aren't developing a new product.

Full question clause (with overt subject):

I can't imagine what Marilyn wanted.
Hector didn't tell us if they are developing a new product.

Non-factual clause (with overt subject):

I demand that <u>your bill (should) be paid</u>.

Infinitive clause:

overt subject:	They expect <u>me to open the letter</u>. They made <u>me open the letter</u>. It would be impossible <u>for them to develop a new product</u>.
tacit subject:	I intended <u>to open the letter</u>. They hope <u>to develop a new product</u>.

Gerund clause:

overt subject:	They watched <u>me opening the letter</u>.
tacit subject:	I denied <u>opening the letter</u>. I suggested <u>opening the letter</u>. <u>Developing a new product</u> takes a long time.

Verbal noun:

overt subject:	They excused <u>my opening of the letter</u>. <u>Their development of the product</u> took a long time.
tacit subject:	I defended <u>the opening of the letter</u>. <u>The development of a new product</u> is not easy.

8.7 Comparing types of clauses

Different kinds of clauses can present different kinds of meanings, but this is obvious only when the same predicate can be accompanied by different kinds of clauses. The verb *agree*, for instance, can be followed by an infinitive clause and a full clause.

47a   We agreed to meet again the next day.
47b   We agreed that we would meet again the next day.
47c   We agreed that prices are too high nowadays.

The verb *agree* followed by an infinitive clause indicates a commitment, on the part of the subject, to do something; 47a is about 'our' commitment to meet the next day. That is really all that can be expressed by the infinitive clause after *agree*. A full clause can express all kinds of facts and possible facts, including commitments on the part of the subject. There is not much difference between 47a and 47b; however, 47c is not about a commitment but about knowledge or a belief that 'we' hold in common. (Chapter 9 contains a larger discussion about verbs that express a commitment to do something.)

Some other verbs that can take a full clause or an infinitive clause are:

decide expect hope resolve

48a We convinced Herman to throw away his smelly old pipe.
48b We convinced Herman that he should throw away his smelly old pipe.
48c We convinced Herman that he didn't know what he was talking about.

Unlike *agree*, *convince* is followed by an infinitive clause with overt subject: we convince another person to do something – that is, we use language successfully with another person, causing him or her to do something. We can also use language successfully with somebody, causing him or her to accept the truth or validity of some statement; that is what the full clause expresses (48b, c). Note that 48a implies that Herman threw away his pipe, but 48b goes only as far as his accepting that this is the right action.

The verb *remind* is syntactically like *convince*. If you replace *convinced* with *reminded* in 48a–c, you will find that the infinitive clause and full statement clause have the same senses, the same relation to each other. Of course *remind* is semantically different from *convince* though it shares the sense of using language successfully with another person. How do the two verbs differ? (For more examples see Dixon 1991: 220–31.)

Gerund clause and full clause (Dixon 1991: 218–20):

49a Your son admitted breaking our window.
49b Your son admitted that he broke our window.
49c Your son admitted that this ball is his.

The verb *admit*, as used here, indicates a use of language, generally in response to someone's question or accusation. *Admit* plus an infinitive clause denotes the use of language about an action performed by the subject. The full clause can express the same action – 49b is essentially the same as 49a – but it can express any putative fact, as in 49c. Similar verbs:

confess consider deny imagine regret report

Infinitive and gerund clauses (Dixon 1991: 233–4):

50a The museum wouldn't allow us to photograph the exhibit.
50b The museum wouldn't allow photographing the exhibit.

With *allow* and the verbs listed below the infinitive is used when there is an overt subject for the verb in the included clause, here *photograph*; there must be a subject – it has to be stated who is or is not allowed to photograph. The gerund clause is used to avoid mentioning the specific person(s) allowed or not allowed to photograph the exhibit; the statement applies to all people.

8.8 Syntactic ambiguity

Chapters 4, 6, and 7 have been attempts to show how sentences convey meanings. Sentences may also contain ambiguities, different from the lexical ambiguity and referential ambiguity treated in Chapters 3 and 4. Syntactic ambiguity may be in the surface structure of a sentence: words can cluster together in different possible constructions. Syntactic ambiguity may also be in the deep structure: one sequence of words may have more than one interpretation, generally because the rules of sentence construction allow **ellipsis**, the deletion of what is 'understood.'

Examples of surface ambiguity:

(a) Constructions containing the coordinators *and* and *or*.

51 John and Mary or Pat will go.
52 We'll have bacon or sausage and eggs.
     ([John] and [Mary or Pat], [John and Mary] or [Pat]; [bacon] or [sausage and eggs], [bacon or sausage] and [eggs])

(b) A coordinate head with one modifier:

53 The only people left were old men and women.
54 The postman left a letter and a package for Ellen.
     ([old men] and [women], old [men and women]; [a letter] and [a package for Ellen], [a letter and a package] for Ellen)

(c) A head with a coordinate modifier:

55 Your essay should contain four or five hundred words.
     ([4] or [500], [400] or [500])

(d)   A head with an inner modifier and an outer modifier:

56   The sick pet was taken to a small animal hospital.
([small] [animal hospital], [small animal] [hospital])

(e)   A complement and modifier or two complements:

57   Joe bought the book for Susan.
58   The tourists objected to the guide that they couldn't hear.
([bought] [the book for Susan], [bought the book] [for Susan];
[objected to] [the guide that they couldn't hear], [objected to the guide]
[that they couldn't hear])

(f)   Certain function words, including *not*, have possible differences in scope:

59   The tennis courts are open to members only on Thursdays.
60   I'd like to find ten more interesting articles.
61   They didn't leave because they were angry.
([members only] or [only on Thursdays]; [ten more] [interesting
articles] or [ten] [more interesting articles]; [didn't leave] [because . . .]
or [didn't] [leave because . . .])

Examples of deep structure ambiguity:

(a)   Gerund + object or participle modifying a noun.

62   Overtaking cars on the main road can be dangerous.
('Overtaking cars is dangerous' or 'Cars overtaking are dangerous')

(b)   Adjective + infinitive, tied to subject or to complement:

63   The chicken is too hot to eat.
('Too hot to eat anything' or 'too hot for anybody to eat it')

(c)   Ellipsis in comparative constructions:

64   I like Mary better than Joan.
('Better than I like Joan' or 'better than Joan likes Mary')

There is a worthwhile observation to make regarding ambiguity. A professional student of language can find – or invent – numerous instances of ambiguous discourse, like those just listed. The comedian and joke-writer also discover or create language with double meanings and use it for their purposes. Those who are skilled in preparing commercial propaganda may know quite well how to say one thing and suggest another. And those who prepare contracts and other legal documents are equally concerned with preventing ambiguity. But in our everyday use of language potential ambiguity seldom presents a problem. Occasionally, looking back over something we have written, we recognize the possibility of misinterpretation or, reading somebody else's text, we are not sure what was intended. More often, however, we correctly interpret what our neighbor intends and our neighbor understands what we intend, usually without awareness that a different possible message is lurking in the background. And this fact tells us something about language. There is no exact correlation between pieces of language – words, phrases, sentences – and the phenomena we communicate about. Language fits quite loosely around 'reality.' Any linguistic element has a range of senses; combination of linguistic elements limits the range for each element, creating a total sense that still has a possible range of applications. Our world is always changing – our personal world, our social world, the natural world – and language adapts in whatever way we need it.

PRACTICE 8

The sentence *The ladies were both articulate and amusing* is ambiguous. On the other hand, *The lady was both articulate and amusing* is not ambiguous, and neither is *The ladies were both articulate*. Of course these simpler sentences don't say the same thing as the ambiguous one, but they point out what makes the ambiguous one ambiguous: the word *both* can go with the plural subject or with the compound adjective phrase. Making the subject singular or the adjective phrase simple eliminates ambiguity.

Point out what makes each of the following sentences ambiguous. Can you replace each sentence with two sentences that give (approximately) the same meanings without ambiguity?

(a)   Growing flowers can be very interesting.
(b)   We heard her report.
(c)   I didn't finish that job for lack of time.

> (d)   Susie wanted to try on the dress in the shop window.
> (e)   Terry is the person we wanted to hunt.
> (f)   You didn't help Charlie as much as Chester.
> (g)   Judith is specializing in modern language teaching.
> (h)   Nelson lies to his wife, and so does Nathaniel.
> (i)   We found the new secretary entertaining.
> (j)   I'm going to tell everybody that I know.

Summary

A sentence – representing a proposition – can be an argument in a larger sentence; it then has the status of a clause embedded in the larger sentence. English has several different kinds of structure for embedded clauses, summarized in Section **8.6**. Embedded clauses may incorporate statements or questions and factual or non-factual material; they may have an explicit, overt subject or not. Otherwise, the different clause structures do not differ semantically from one another; rather, the selection of any clause structure is determined by the predicate of the larger sentence. Only when a predicate has two or more embedded clause structures do we see general contrasts of meaning. The full clause can express a wider range of meanings than a reduced clause. Comparing infinitive clause and gerund clause, the latter seems to express more certain involvement of an agent in the action and greater duration of the action.

Languages express an infinite number of things with a limited number of resources – vocabulary resources and grammatical resources. Just as limited vocabulary resources lead sometimes to lexical ambiguity, we have syntactic ambiguity because grammatical resources are limited: the same sequence of lexemes can be grouped into different constructions (surface structure ambiguity) or a sequence of lexemes can result from ellipses in the representation of two different propositions (deep structure ambiguity). We may be aware of ambiguity and then seek to exploit it or to avoid it. Just as often, it seems, we rely on context to interpret utterances and fail to recognize that more than one meaning is there.

Suggested reading

Complement clauses in English have been the subject of investigation by numerous scholars. An illuminating analysis is Quirk *et al.* (1984, Chapter 16). A valuable description, somewhat different from the one presented here, is Dixon (1991, Chapter 7), to which specific page references have already been made above.

Speech acts

We use language for many purposes. We tell others what we know or think we know, we express our feelings, ask questions, make requests, protest, criticize, insult, apologize, promise, thank, say hello and goodbye. Language seems to have as many different functions as there are occasions for using language, but for all the apparent diversity the basic uses of language are rather limited. In this chapter we recognize seven different kinds of utterances, or **speech acts**, classified according to their general purpose – though a single utterance may have overlapping purposes. The description here will apply to written discourse, and therefore to writer and reader, as much as to spoken discourse. Nevertheless, we use the term speaker to include writer and the term addressee to include reader as well as hearer. In addition, although one person may speak or write on behalf of several people and may have a plurality of addressees, whether in writing or speaking, we use singular terms 'speaker' and 'addressee' throughout.

9.1 The form of sentences and the purpose of utterances

Sentences are traditionally designated **declarative** if they tell something, **interrogative** if they ask, or **imperative** if they request action, but this classification is based on the forms of sentences. Actual utterances can have various functions that are independent of form. As we all know, a person can ask a question without truly seeking information ("Did you really like that silly book?") – the so-called rhetorical question – and can make a statement that is intended as a request ("It's very warm in here with that window closed") or produce a command that is not meant to elicit action from the addressee ("Have a good time"). "Did you know it's raining?" can be a way of informing, and the person who says "I suppose you'll be going away for the holiday" may well be soliciting information.

Furthermore, a speaker may, for humor or irony, produce an utterance that is just the opposite of the message he wants to convey. The form of an utterance does not necessarily coincide with the speaker's real intention. Nevertheless, before exploring the different kinds of purposes that speech acts can have, it will be useful to have a look at a syntactic classification of sentences.

Syntactically it is common to recognize three sentence types in English: statement, command and question – or declarative, imperative and interrogatory sentences. Actually on the basis of form there are several different kinds of questions, as we shall examine below.

Statements typically have subject, verb and then perhaps an object, a complement and/or an adverbial phrase, as we saw in Chapter 4.

1a   A window broke.
1b   Tom broke a window.
1c   Denise put marmalade on her toast.

The sequence of elements can be varied somewhat: *On her toast Denise put marmalade*, *Marmalade Denise put on her toast*, but the subject always precedes the verb unless other words are introduced: *What broke was a window*, *The one who broke a window was Tom*, and so on. The verb can be modified for tense, aspect, and modality (Section **4.1**).

Affirmative commands begin with the verb, which does not change; negative commands begin with *do not* plus the verb. The subject, if a subject is present, may be *you* or *everybody, somebody, anybody, nobody*.

2a   Close the door, please.
2b   Don't move.   Don't anybody move.
2c   You be quiet.
2d   Nobody move.   Everybody wait here.

(Compare 2c and 2d with the statements *You are quiet, Nobody moves, Everybody waits here*.)

Questions are of several different kinds. We know that an utterance is a question if it has one or more of these four markers: rising intonation; inverted word order; a question word: *who, what, which, where, when, how, why*; or the word *or*. The different types of questions are distinguished on the basis of the marker(s) present.

1 One kind of question has the word order of a statement but is spoken with a rising tune instead of a falling one.

3a   This is a joke?
3b   You're leaving now?
3c   The Rangers won?

The marker is intonation. These are 'yes-no' questions – the speaker is asking for confirmation or denial of what he understands. Such questions are most likely when the questioner has heard something and wants a repetition.

2 A more common sort of question is made with inversion – putting an operator in first place. An operator (a form of *be* or *have* or one of the modal verbs *can/could*, *will/would*, *shall/should*, *may/might*, *must*, *ought*, *dare* or *need*), which follows the subject in a statement, precedes the statement in a question. If the statement has no such operator, the empty form *do* occurs in the corresponding question.

4a   Is this a joke?
4b   Are you leaving now?
4c   Did the Rangers win?

These are also yes-no questions. The marker is the inverted word order; consequently, intonation is less important and either a rising or a falling tune may be used.

3 A similar but different way of asking the same thing is to make a statement and attach a tag question, as shown below. The tag question has an operator which matches the verb of the statement and a pronoun which matches the subject.

5a   This is a joke, isn't it?
5b   You're leaving now, aren't you?
5c   You aren't leaving now, are you?
5d   The Rangers won, didn't they?

There are two different intonations possible: rising tune is used when the speaker is really seeking information, and a falling tune suggests that the speaker merely wants confirmation of what he or she believes. With the rising tune one might use just *right?* or something similar as a tag. As the examples above show, the tag is typically negative after an affirmative statement and affirmative after a negative statement.

However, there is a less common type of sentence in which an affirmative tag follows an affirmative statement:

6a   This is a joke, is it?
6b   The Rangers won, did they?

These are typically spoken with a falling tune on the tag, and they convey a special meaning of disbelief or detachment.

4   The next type of question has inverted word order but it cannot be answered simply "Yes" or "No." The marker is the word *or*.

7a   Would you like coffee or tea?
7b   Is your son in the Army or the Navy?

The usual intonation is a rise on the first part (here, *coffee*, *Army*) and a fall on the second part (here, *tea*, *Navy*). The questioner gives the addressee two or more alternatives and asks for a choice.

5   The next questions have a question word (or 'WH-word') but are also marked by rising intonation.

8a   You're leaving ↑ when?   ↑ When are you leaving?
8b   She left it ↑ where?   ↑ Where did she leave it?
8c   They couldn't find ↑ what?
8d   ↑ Who couldn't find it?

The question word may appear at the beginning of the question or in the same position in the sentence as the answer would appear. The question word is the place where the voice rises. These ask for a repetition or confirmation of something said previously when the questioner can pinpoint what needs repetition or confirmation. "You're leaving ↑ when?" indicates that the speaker has been told the time of departure but didn't get it or doesn't believe it.

6   Questions that have a question word and do not have a rising intonation (at least not on the question word) ask for new information, not for repetition or confirmation.

9a   Who found the money?
9b   How many people came?
9c   Why are you leaving?

PRACTICE 9.1 Questions

1 A question that begins with a question word carries a certain presupposition. "Who brought the paper in?" presupposes that someone brought the paper in. What do the following questions presuppose?

(a) How many people came to the party?
(b) Why didn't you tell me the truth?
(c) Which one of the programs is better?
(d) When will the film be shown?
(e) Where will the film be shown?

2 Affirmative and negative statements with the same topic and the same predicate are contradictory. If one is true, the other must be false.

Ellen is a brunette. Ellen is not a brunette.

Commands can also be affirmative or negative. Affirmative and negative commands with the same lexical content are contradictory in the sense that no one can obey both such commands at the same time.

Close the window. Don't close the window.

But affirmative and negative questions with the same lexical content cannot be called contradictory. What is the difference between pairs of questions like these?

Did you enjoy the show?   Didn't you enjoy the show?
Why should I believe that?   Why shouldn't I believe that?

9.2 Analysis of speech acts

Truth conditional semantics takes statements as the basic kind of sentence and thus considers that the principal use of language is to state facts, to describe how things are in the world, to present information which, generally, is either true or false. The English philosopher J. L. Austin pointed out, however, that much of our ordinary use of language is just as much asking questions and giving commands as making statements, and even utterances that have the form of declarative sentences, such as "The meeting is called to order," "This court is now in session," "I nominate Patrick P. Pillsbury for secretary-treasurer" are not intended to be statements. Utterances like these are intended to 'make things happen.' We should not ask whether they are true or not but whether they work or not in accomplishing their purpose – in Austin's terms, whether they are **felicitous** or not. And then, to generalize, what are the conditions that make different kinds of utterances felicitous?

Whenever one person speaks to another, the speaker has some intention in producing the utterance, and the addressee interprets the utterance. In spite of occasional misunderstandings the hearer's interpretation often does match the speaker's intention, even when the speaker is joking or being sarcastic. If the form of an utterance does not necessarily coincide with the intended function, how does the hearer correctly know what the speaker's intention is – even recognizing the speaker's humorous utterances and the sarcastic ones? The simple answer is that they know each other. They share a common background, and they are aware of sharing the common background. They may argue, insult each other, use profanity and obscenities, speak with exaggeration or understatement, so long as they are both used to communicating in this fashion. Speakers are less likely to use sarcasm and humor with strangers than with those who know them well, their utterances are more likely to be straight-forward and to follow the norms for politeness, and they are ready to rephrase their messages whenever they see that misunderstanding has occurred. The speaker wants to be understood and the addressee wants to understand.

In every speech act we can distinguish three things, following Austin (1962). What is said, the utterance, can be called the **locution**. What the speaker intends to communicate to the addressee is the **illocution**. The message that the addressee gets, his interpretation of what the speaker says, is the **perlocution**. If communication is successful, the illocution and the perlocution are alike or nearly alike.

Such communication is guided by four factors, which Grice (1975, 1978) called maxims: the maxims of quantity, relevance, manner and quality. As speakers and hearers we are aware of these maxims and of the necessity for them though we do not explicitly recognize their existence.

The maxim of quantity requires the speaker to give as much information as the addressee needs but no more. Accordingly, the speaker must have some sense of what the addressee knows and needs to know. The addressee, being aware of this maxim, assumes that the speaker is not withholding information and is not saying more than necessary – unless there is reason to believe otherwise.

The maxim of relevance requires us, as speakers, to make our utterances relative to the discourse going on and the contexts in which they occur. Correspondingly, as addressees we expect that what we hear has such relevance. If you offer to help in some project and are told, "Do so only at your own risk," you will have to decide whether involvement in the project is really risky or the locution was meant as a joke. If, instead, you are told "Too many cooks spoil the broth," you will probably recognize a proverb (certainly so if the making of broth is not part of the context) and know that the speaker feels the project is already sufficiently staffed. Thus when locutions are apparently irrelevant, they are likely to be successful only when the interlocutors share the same cultural information and/or when they know one another well. Note that in some cultures – Arabic-speaking societies are a good example – the use of proverbs figures large in every conversation: there seems to be a ready-made saying for almost any possible need.

The maxim of manner is to be orderly and clear and to avoid ambiguity. If you ask someone a question and the reply you receive seems strangely obscure, your interlocutor is either a disorganized individual or is deliberately avoiding a straight answer.

The maxim of quality is to say only what one believes to be true. Questions and requests cannot be either true or false, so this maxim applies only to the giving of information, in the kind of speech act that we call assertives (Section **11.3**).

Grice distinguished between violating the maxims and flouting them. If a speaker deliberately lies, expecting the addressee to believe what he says, he is violating the maxim of quality. If he exaggerates, expecting the addressee to recognize the exaggeration, he is flouting the maxim. "Dozens of people came to the party," said when only a few people attended, is either an outright lie or an instance of hyperbole, depending on what the speaker intends the addressee to understand, which in turn depends on the speaker's knowledge of the addressee.

An utterance has a purpose. In order to achieve that purpose – to be appropriate to that purpose – several conditions are necessary: the lexical content of the utterance must be appropriate, the social situation in which it occurs must be appropriate, the speaker must be sincere in what he says, and the hearer(s) accept the utterance as having that purpose.

PRACTICE 9.2 Literal and non-literal meanings

One can acquire a very good knowledge of a foreign language and yet not have a grasp of figurative meanings, hyperbole, understatement and euphemism as native speakers use these. What is the difference between the literal meanings of the following utterances and the way most native speakers would interpret them?

(a) I'm so hungry I could eat a horse.
(b) If I've told you once, I've told you a hundred times . . .
(c) It's rather nice that we get paid for all the work we do.
(d) Willis is not exactly a genius.
(e) I'm sure your little brother likes your teasing him, Allen.

9.3 Seven kinds of speech acts

Speech acts differ in their purposes, whether they deal with real or potential facts, prospective or retrospective, in the role of speaker or addressee in these facts, and of course in felicity conditions.

9.3.1 Assertive utterances

In the assertive function speakers and writers use language to tell what they know or believe; assertive language is concerned with facts. The purpose is to inform.

10a I voted for Aaronson in the last election.
11a Most plastics are made from soy beans.
12a Cape Ann Lighthouse is a mile from the beach.

This is language concerned with knowledge, with cognition. It deals with data, what exists or existed, what is happening or has happened – or not. So assertive utterances are either true or false, and generally they can be verified or falsified – not necessarily at the time of the utterance or by those who hear them, but in a general sense they are subject to empirical investigation.

The above sentences are indirect assertives. Direct assertive utterances start with *I* or *we* and an assertive verb:

10b I say that I voted for Aaronson in the last election.
11b We declare that most plastics are made from soy beans.
12b I can now announce that Cape Ann Lighthouse is ten miles from the beach.

Reported assertive utterances also include assertive verbs: *Jarvis announced that he is voting for Aaronson . . .* , and so on. Assertive verbs are, in English, followed by a full clause. They include *allege, announce, agree, report, remind, predict, protest.* They are independent of time or aspect and are neutral with respect to who is involved in what is reported. They are comments on a state of affairs. We may question whether these really constitute a class of utterances or a class of verbs which introduce information.

Focus on information:

announce	declare	disclose	explain	express	indicate
mention	proclaim	relate	report		

Focus on truth-value of utterance:

affirm	allege	assert	certify	concede
guarantee	swear	attest	bet	claim	contend
maintain				

Focus on speaker's commitment or involvement in what is reported:

confide	deny	profess	protest

Focus on manner of communicating:

emphasize	hint	imply	intimate	stress

Focus on the nature of the message:

> dictate [a spoken message, written by another person]
> narrate recount [the utterance is a unified series of events]
> preach [the utterance has moral or ethical content]

Focus on aspect:

> predict [the utterance is about possible future events]
> recall [the utterance is about previous events]

What makes an assertive utterance appropriate – what are the felicity conditions? What is reported must be feasible, something that can be true or could have been true; the speaker commits himself to the truth of what is reported; and the addressee accepts it as true.

9.3.2 Performative utterances

13   I bid three no-trump.
14   We accept your offer.
15   I declare this meeting adjourned.

Speech acts that bring about the state of affairs they name are called **performative**: bids, blessings, firings, baptisms, arrests, marrying, declaring a mistrial. Performative utterances are valid if spoken by someone whose right to make them is accepted and in circumstances which are accepted as appropriate. The verbs include *bet, declare, baptize, name, nominate, pronounce*.

Naturally there are strong limitations on what can be a performative utterance. First, the subject of the sentence must be *I* or *we*; "He declares this meeting adjourned" is not a performative utterance, as the term is used here. However, we need to distinguish between explicit and implicit performatives. "I declare this meeting adjourned" is an explicit performative; "This meeting is adjourned," if spoken by the same person, is an implicit one. Second, the verb must be in the present tense. And, perhaps most important, the speaker must be recognized as having the authority to make the statement and the circumstances must be appropriate. "I pronounce you man and wife" and "I declare this a mistrial" are valid only if spoken by an appropriate person in socially determined situations.

Thus many performatives take place in formal settings and are concerned with official acts.

A performative is neither true nor false but its purpose is to make a part of the world conform to what is said.

Blessings and curses are performative utterances to the degree that people accept them as having effect. So long as one believes that a particular individual, or anyone at all, can bring down divine favor on another by uttering some formula such as "(May) God bless you," that utterance is a valid performative. And similarly invoking pain or punishment on another person through the performance of a ritual utterance constitutes a curse for those who accept it as performative.

Repeating somewhat, felicity conditions for a performative utterance are the authority of the speaker to make the utterance, the appropriateness of time, place and other circumstances, and the acceptance by the addressee (and others) of this authority and appropriateness.

PRACTICE 9.3 Performative utterances

Each utterance below is a performative. Let's assume that each is made at a place and time that society considers appropriate for it, by a person empowered to produce the utterance, and before other people who accept the purpose and validity of what is said and the authority of the speaker to say it.

(a) This meeting is adjourned. (or "I declare this meeting adjourned.")
(b) I pass.
(c) I sentence you to 90 days in prison.
(d) Michael Arthur, I baptize you in the name of the Father and of the Son and of the Holy Spirit.
(e) I christen this ship the *Bountiful*, and may God bless all who sail in her.

What are the felicity conditions for each utterance? In each case, what is necessary for the utterance to take effect?

9.3.3 Verdictive utterances

16 I accuse you of putting on airs.
17 I congratulate you for performing so well.
18 The Mayor blamed the media for not accurately reporting his accomplishments.

Sentences 16 and 17 are verdictive utterances. Sentence 18 is the report of a verdictive utterance. Verdictives are speech acts in which the speaker makes an assessment or judgement about the acts of another, usually the addressee. These include ranking, assessing, appraising, condoning. Verdictive verbs include *accuse, charge, excuse, thank* in the explicit frame *I _____ you of/for _____-ing*. Since these utterances present the speaker's assessment of the addressee's previous action(s) or of what has befallen the addressee, they are retrospective.

The action is viewed positively:

commend . . . for	compliment . . . on	congratulate . . . for
honor . . . for	praise . . . for	

The action is beneficial to the speaker:

thank . . . for	grateful to . . . for

The action is viewed negatively:

accuse . . . of	charge . . . with
blame . . . for	[presupposes truth of performance]
admonish . . . for	"
criticize . . . for	"
scold . . . for	"

19 The teacher excused/pardoned Henry for missing the meeting.

The verbs *excuse* and *pardon* express speech acts that do more than comment on an alleged previous action, but they presuppose the truth of that action, like *blame, admonish, criticize* and *scold*.

Felicity conditions for verdictive utterances are: the possibility of the act, the ability of the addressee to perform it, the sincerity of the speaker in making the utterance, and the addressee's belief that the speaker is sincere.

PRACTICE 9.4 Verdictive utterances

> Verdictive utterances include accusation, blaming, congratula-
> tion, praise and condolence. In English it is possible to begin a
> verdictive utterance with the words "I accuse . . . " or "I blame
> . . . " or "I congratulate . . . " It is not common to say "I praise you
> . . . ," and as for utterances of condolence, while dictionaries list
> a verb *condole*, it is not in colloquial use. How do we express
> praise and condolence, and when are these appropriate?

A verdictive utterance has this structure:

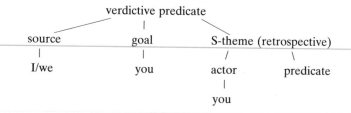

9.3.4 Expressive utterances

20   I acknowledge that I didn't do what I should have done.
21   We admit that we were mistaken.
22   I apologize for having disturbed you.

Whereas a verdictive utterance is about what the addressee has
previously done, an expressive utterance springs from the previous
actions – or failure to act – of the speaker, or perhaps the present
result of those actions or failures. Expressive utterances are thus
retrospective and speaker-involved.

The most common expressive verbs (in this sense of 'expressive') are:

> acknowledge, admit, confess
> deny
> apologize

The structure of expressive utterances can be compared with
that of verdictive ones, above.

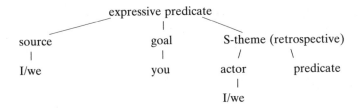

Felicity conditions are similar to those for verdictive utterances: the act was feasible, the speaker was capable of it, the speaker speaks sincerely, and the addressee believes it.

PRACTICE 9.5 Expressive utterances

Another kind of expressive utterance is boasting, but English usage does not have utterances that begin with "I boast that . . ."

How does one recognize that a speaker is boasting?

9.3.5 Directive utterances

Directive utterances are those in which the speaker tries to get the addressee to perform some act or refrain from performing an act. Thus a directive utterance has the pronoun *you* as actor, whether that word is actually present in the utterance or not:

23   (You) wait here.
24   Turn to page 164.
25   Don't (any of you) miss this opportunity to save.

A directive utterance is prospective; one cannot tell other people to do something in the past. Like other kinds of utterances, a directive utterance presupposes certain conditions in the addressee and in the context of situation. The utterance "Lift this 500-pound weight" is not felicitous if spoken to a person incapable of lifting 500 pounds, and "Close the door" is vapid if the only door in the vicinity is already closed. When the utterance can be carried out, the utterance is felicitous, and if not, it is infelicitous.

Three kinds of directive utterances can be recognized: commands, requests and suggestions. A **command** is effective only if the speaker has some degree of control over the actions of the addressee.

26a   I (hereby) order you to appear in court next Monday at 10 a.m.
26b   You must appear in court next Monday at 10 a.m.
27a   I'm telling you not to waste your time on that.
27b   Don't waste your time on that.

Commands can be produced with various degrees of explicitness. Sentences 26a and 27a are more explicit than 26b and 27b but the b utterances are less formal, therefore more usual. They have the form *You must . . .* or they are imperative sentences.

28   Passengers are required to keep seat belts fastened when the sign is lit.
29   Smoking is not permitted in the lavatories.

These utterances are commands, and fairly explicit ones, not because of syntax but because they contain such predicates as *require* and *permit*.

30   The boss demands that these letters (should) go out today.

This sentence, even if it becomes an utterance, is not a command but the report of a command.

The general meaning of a command, then, is:

Speaker, in authority, expresses a wish that Addressee should <not> act as Speaker wants Addressee <not> to act.

(The angle brackets mean, here, that both occurrences of *not* are included in the definition or both are excluded.)

Predicates that can be used in explicit commands (and therefore in reports of commands) are:

(positive)   charge, command, direct, order, tell, demand ("I charge/command/direct/order/tell you to keep silence; I demand that you (should) keep silence.")

(negative)   forbid

A **request** is an expression of what the speaker wants the addressee to do or refrain from doing. A request does not assume the speaker's control over the person addressed. Illustrations appear in sentences 28–30 (the last a reported request).

31   I appeal to you to help as much as you can.
32   We beg you to stay out of the way.
33   The receptionist asked the people in the waiting room not to smoke there.

General meaning:

> Speaker, not in authority, expresses wish that Addressee <not> act as Speaker wants Addressee <not> to act.

Request predicates:

> appeal-to ask beg beseech entreat implore
> petition plead-with request

[*ask* is unmarked; *appeal* suggests that person$_2$ is in authority; *petition* suggests a formal request, very likely in writing; *beseech* is nearly archaic; *request* is followed by the hypothetical clause and therefore rather formal; the others are stronger than *ask*.]

Suggestions are the utterances we make to other persons to give our opinions as to what they should or should not do.

34   I advise you to be prompt; I warn you not to be late.
35   We suggest you (should) pay more attention to what you're doing.

General meaning: Speaker expresses an opinion about Addressee's choice of performance. Addressee is the suggestee, not necessarily the addressee. Presupposition: The suggestee has a choice of performances.

> Positive expressions: advise counsel recommend
> Negative expressions: caution warn

PRACTICE 9.6 Suggestions

What are the features expressed when the following predicates are used in suggestions? Consider the probable wish of the speaker and the probable wish of the addressee.

(a)	I challenge you to ...	I dare you to ...
(b)	I propose that you ...	I suggest that you ...
(c)	I encourage you to ...	
(d)	I would discourage you from ...	
(e)	I (would) remind you to ...	

For all directives the underlying structure can be stated this way:

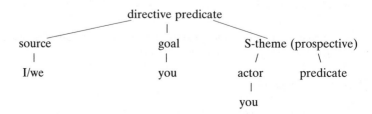

Whether an utterance is or is not a directive, and if so what kind of directive it is, depends in part on syntactic form, in part on choice of predicates (*must*, *demand*, *suggest* ...), and very much on the situation, the participants, and their relative status. Felicity conditions include the feasibility of the act and the ability of the addressee. For a command to be felicitous the addressee must accept the speaker's authority; for a request, the speaker's wishes, and for a suggestion, the speaker's judgement.

9.3.6 Commissive utterances

Speech acts that commit a speaker to a course of action are called **commissive utterances**. These include promises, pledges, threats and vows.

Commissive verbs are illustrated by *agree*, *ask*, *offer*, *refuse*, *swear*, all with following infinitives. They are prospective and concerned with the speaker's commitment to future action.

36   I promise to be on time.
37   We volunteer to put up the decorations for the dance.

A commissive predicate is one that can be used to commit oneself (or refuse to commit oneself) to some future action. The subject of the sentence is therefore most likely to be *I* or *we*, as in 36 and 37.

Further, the verb must be in the present tense and there is some addressee, whether the utterance shows it or not, since the speaker must be making a commitment to somebody. In contrast, 38 and 39 below, with other kinds of subjects or a different tense, are not commitments but reports of commitments.

38   Ernest promised us to be on time.
39   We volunteered to put up the decorations for the dance.

The structure of a sentence with a commissive predicate is this:

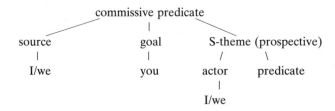

In a commissive utterance the subject is *I* or *we*, as indicated above. Felicity conditions: the speaker is capable of the act and intends to perform it; the addressee has faith in the speaker's ability and intention.

Commissive predicates can be classified this way:

Response to directive

       positive response: agree consent
       [*agree* is more common]
       negative response: refuse decline
       [*refuse* is stronger, *decline* more formal, more polite]

Self-motivated (not response to directive)

       benefactive: offer volunteer
       [*volunteer* suggests a more formal commitment]
       malefactive: threaten

Focus on speech act

       pledge promise swear
       [*promise* is unmarked; a pledge is a solemn promise made in public; to swear is to take a semi-religious oath]

9.3.7 Four speech acts compared

The last four speech acts, and the predicates that occur in them, are alike in being concerned with some action. They differ from one another as to whether the act has purportedly already taken place (retrospective) or is yet to occur (prospective), and whether the speaker or the addressee is the agent of the act.

verdictive	retrospective	addressee-involved
expressive	retrospective	speaker-involved
directive	prospective	addressee-involved
commissive	prospective	speaker-involved

9.3.8 Phatic utterances

No one is likely to think that questions like "How are you?," "How're you doing?" are really meant to get information. We don't assume that statements such as "I'm glad to meet you" or "So nice to see you again" are necessarily expressions of deep feeling on the part of the speaker. The purpose of utterances like these, **phatic utterances**, is to establish rapport between members of the same society. Phatic language has a less obvious function than the six types discussed above but it is no less important. Phatic utterances include greetings, farewells, polite formulas such as "Thank you," "You're welcome," "Excuse me" when these are not really verdictive or expressive. They also include all sorts of comments on the weather, asking about one's health, and whatever is usual, and therefore expected, in a particular society. Stereotyped phrases are common for conveying good wishes to someone starting to eat a meal, beginning a voyage, undertaking a new venture, or celebrating a personal or social holiday.

Felicity conditions are met when speaker and addressee share the same social customs and recognize phatic utterances for what they are.

Summary

Utterances can be classified according to the general purpose of the speaker, which, when communication is successful, is also the addressee's interpretation. Seven kinds of communication have been recognized here.

Phatic conversation is the exchange of greetings and goodbyes, the polite chitchat about weather, one another's health, or whatever is expected in the particular society. Its true purpose is to maintain social bonds. Assertives are utterances that involve the giving and getting of information. Statements, in which information is given, are either true or false and thus subject to empirical validation. Performative utterances make things happen just by being uttered; they include bets and things said in various ceremonies and official acts which affect the people to whom they are said.

The remaining four kinds of utterances form a sort of paradigm. Verdictives are utterances in which the speaker comments on the previous deeds of the addressee or their present result; these include accusing and blaming, congratulating and praising. Expressives occur when speakers tell of their own past deeds and present feelings, conveyed in apologies, boasts and lamentations. Directives and commissives are prospective in orientation. In a directive the speaker tries to influence the actions of the addressee. Directives include commands, requests, and suggestions, a distinction reflecting mainly the degree of influence the speaker has over the addressee. Commissives, finally, are utterances in which the speaker binds himself to perform (or refrain from doing) some act at a later time.

Predicates used in these speech acts and/or in utterances that report them can be further described according to their relative 'strength,' politeness, antecedents and consequences. Direct speech acts contain a first-person pronoun and a predicate that specifies what the utterance is; an indirect speech act lacks these. For each of these kinds of utterance certain conditions must be present in speaker, addressee, and various circumstances for the utterance to be felicitous.

Suggested reading

A good summary of speech act theory is Chapter 3 (49–96) of Schiffrin (1994). A fuller examination is Mey 1993, Chapters 6–8 (109–77).

Note on the text

- The genesis of 'speech act theory' is in Austin (1962), though Austin did not use that term. The account presented here has followed Searle (1976); a somewhat different analysis, derived in part from Searle, is Hancher (1979); another account, completely independent in origin, is Matisoff (1979).

Aspect

We experience events and situations from various points of view and these points of view are often incorporated into our description of the events and situations. We look back on events and situations we have experienced and look forward to events and situations that may exist in the future. Some things that are true seem to be always so, others true just temporarily. We see some events just beginning and situations just coming into existence and other events and situations coming to an end. Some events are viewed as over and done with at some particular time, others as still continuing, and the continuity may be a matter of constant status or constant change. The expression of all these viewpoints is called **aspect**. Aspect is both grammatical and lexical; it is expressed in predicates, especially in verb inflections and collocations of verbs; cf. *It's beginning to break, it's breaking, it broke, it's broken*. However, the expression of aspect may also appear in certain temporal adverbs and in the choice of referring expressions. *He is not here yet* and *He is no longer here* both communicate that he is not here but they incorporate different viewpoints. *Diane arrived* tells of a single event; *People arrived* may relate one event or a number of events.

Along with the viewpoint that we express, aspect also depends on the nature of the predicate used, a lexical matter: differences of aspect are communicated in the semantic features of different predicates; cf. *She learned it* vs. *She knew it*. *She learned it* communicates the change from one status to another, from not-knowing to knowing, presented as a simple event, though of course the process of learning may go on over a period of time and consist of various parts. *She knew it* describes a situation or state without commenting on its boundaries although 'knowing' must have a beginning. Or compare *He threw the ball* and *He bounced the ball*; the latter is likely to be a repetitive action, the former may be a single event or may not. There is no good English name to designate all the intrinsic temporal features of different predicates. The German word **Aktionsart** 'kind of action' is widely used in semantics. At any rate, we cannot divorce the nature of predicates from a discussion of kinds of aspect and how they are expressed in English. As we shall see, one predicate may have more than one way of contributing to the aspect that is expressed.

10.1 Generic and specific predications

Reference and aspect are similar in some ways. Referring expressions are noun phrases, as we saw in Chapter 7, and aspect is expressed primarily in the predicates of sentences, but there are certain similarities. Just as we distinguish between generic and non-generic reference, we can distinguish generic and non-generic aspect. Compare sentences 1a–d with 2a–d below.

1a   Two and two make four.
1b   Rabbits are rodents.
1c   The Atlantic Ocean separates Africa and South America.
1d   A stitch in time saves nine.
2a   Gregory is here.
2b   I have a headache.
2c   The company manufactures silicon chips.
2d   Stella seems happy.

Sentences 1a–d are 'eternal truths,' statements about things that we do not expect to change. They report unbounded situations, or states. Sentences 2a–d, on the other hand, are about temporary states; they are **bounded**. There is nothing in the two groups of sentences, as they are, that indicates this difference, but the difference shows up in the fact that we can add certain **aspectual modifiers**, affirmative and negative, to the second group which would seem out of place in sentences 1a–d.

$2a^1$ Gregory is <u>already</u> here.
$2b^1$ I <u>still</u> have a headache.
$2c^1$ The company does <u>not yet</u> manufacture silicon chips.
$2d^1$ Stella doesn't seem happy <u>any more</u>. / ... <u>no longer</u> seems happy.

Sentences 2a–d state that certain situations exist at the present time. Sentences $2a^1$–d^1 contain the same information but the aspectual modifiers call attention to boundaries, the beginning or the end of these states, changes from one state to another. Let's take one of these sentences, 2a, make it affirmative and negative, and add the four modifications to it.

> <u>Gregory is here</u>.
> Gregory is already here.
> Gregory is still here.
> <u>Gregory isn't here</u>.
> Gregory isn't here yet./ . . . is still not here
> Gregory isn't here any more./ . . . is no longer here.

The modifiers *already* and *not yet* call attention to the beginning of a state, Gregory's being here: *already* indicates that the state has begun; there has been a change from Gregory's not being here to being here; *not yet* (or *still not*) indicates that the state has not begun. *Still* and *not any more* call attention to the end of this state but with a reversal of polarity: *still* informs us that the state – 'being here' – has not ended, and *not any more* (or *no longer*) says that the state of 'being here' has ended. To summarize:

	Previous state	Present state
already	–	+
still	+	+
not yet	–	–
no longer	+	–

Because these aspectual modifiers express something about change from one state to another, they may carry some implication or nuance about a speaker's expectation. "Gregory is already here" may suggest that the speaker did not expect Gregory so soon and "Gregory is still here" that the speaker thought Gregory might have left. The questions "Is Gregory here already?" and "Is Gregory still here?" request the same information about Gregory's presence but differ in the questioner's attitude or expectation.

10.2 Stative predicates and dynamic predicates

The sentences in 1a–d and 2a–d describe states that exist, whether permanent or temporary in nature. The predicates in these sentences are **stative predicates**. Other sentences report activities and have **dynamic predicates**. The change from one state to another is a dynamic event. The following report such changes.

3a   Gregory arrived here.
3b   I recovered from my headache.
3c   The company started manufacturing silicon chips.
3d   Stella lost her tired look.

A stative predicate, according to Comrie (1976: 49), reports a state that requires no expenditure of energy and that continues until energy is expended to change that state; a dynamic predicate reports a situation that will only continue if there is a continual input of energy, but it ceases when energy is no longer expended. Thus <u>the following sentences are stative and have stative predicates</u>:

4a   We waited.
4b   The children were hungry.
4c   Snow lay on the ground.
4d   Ellen needed a dictionary.

The following are activity sentences and have dynamic predicates.

5a   Something moved.
5b   The sun came up.
5c   The boat drifted along.
5d   They discussed the plan.

A stative predicate is typically **durative** in aspect. For each of the sentences 4a–d we can ask 'How long?', 'How long did we wait?' 'How long were the children hungry?,' and so on. And we can add expressions that tell the length of time: *for an hour, all day, from Christmas till New Year's Day, all during the parade, as long as she was studying.*

A stative predication relates a situation that does not change during the time when the predication is valid. Thus, if the sentence *Jesse had a headache all morning* is true, then at every instant during that morning the sentence *Jesse has a headache* was true. To say this in another way, a stative predication relates a situation that consists of homogeneous parts.

Here are other such stative verbs. They suggest a continuing and unchanging state – but some of them, as we will see, can express change of state – can be activity predicates in certain contexts.

Verbs that express feeling: abhor, adore, desire, enjoy, envy, fear, hate, like, long for, mind, prefer, regret, want, wish.

Verbs that express other mental states: believe, doubt, expect, intend, interest, know, suppose, suspect, think, understand.

Verbs that express a relation between two entities: belong, consist, contain, cost, deserve, equal, fit, include, involve, keep, lack, matter, mean, need, owe, own, remain, require, resemble.

Verbs that express a physical stance or position: kneel, lean, lie, sit, stand.

Verbs that express non-action: remain, stay, wait.

Dynamic verbs include those that express some form of physical movement: come, drift, float, go, hop, jump, pound, rotate, run, swim, turn, vibrate, walk.

Verbs of communication: argue, complain, discuss, explain, invite, question, report, say, shout, talk, translate, whisper, write.

Verbs of perception that involve doing something: feel, listen, look at, look for, smell, sniff, taste, watch.

Consider these sentences:

6a   Fred and Ethel argue from morning till night.
6b   The basketball team practiced from September till November.

Does Sentence 6a tell us that Fred and Ethel argue at every moment from morning till night? In Sentence 6b, if it is true that the basketball team practiced from September till November, does that mean that the sentence "The basketball team is practicing" was true at every moment from the first of September until the end of November? Certainly not. 'Duration' is not the same for an activity as for a state. Action is constant but not necessarily continuous.

Some dynamic verbs designate a change occurring over a period of time:

change   deteriorate   dwindle   improve   worsen

In *Grandmother's health deteriorated during the next few months*, the verb indicates a constant change but not necessarily a continuous change nor a constant rate of change.

10.3 Durative and punctual

7   Albert kicked a ball and the ball struck a post.

This sentence contains two verbs that have a **punctual aspect**. Kicking and striking normally designate actions that are momentary. Some other verbs that suggest a momentary action are:

flash hit jump kick leap

These actions have essentially no duration. A sentence like *Albert kicked a ball for ten minutes* has a repetitive, or **iterative**, meaning.

Other punctual verbs, such as *arrive*, tell of a change from one status to another, not likely to be repetitive when only one person is involved, as in *Diane arrived at the office a few minutes after nine.* A number of punctual verbs of this type can be used in the present tense to express an event planned for a future time.

8a   They leave/arrive tomorrow.
8b   The plane lands at 8:40.
8c   The shop opens next week.
8d   Mr Edwards retires in May.

But unplanned acts cannot be expressed this way.

*He falls tomorrow. *She dies next week. *It vanishes soon.

A number of verbs, sometimes referred to as **verbs of mental activity**, occur in both punctual and durative uses:

9a   I (suddenly) remembered that I had an appointment at two.
9b   I remembered (all along) what she had told me.
10a He felt a sharp pain in the shoulder.
10b He felt miserable about what he had seen.
11a Suddenly she knew just what she had to do.
11b She knew the answer yesterday but today she can't think of it.

The 'a' sentences express an event, the act of coming into a state of remembering, feeling, knowing. The 'b' sentences tell of a state in existence. The 'a' sentences express **ingressive aspect** (also called **inchoative** or **inceptive** aspect), the action of entering into a state.

12a Harry reminded me of the appointment.
12b Harry reminded me so much of a fellow I used to know.

This pair of sentences also contrasts a single event that initiates a state (12a) and a state that can continue over a period of time (12b).

But while the verbs in sentences 9–11 are one-argument predicates, *remind* is a two-argument predicate. Here Harry causes me to remember the appointment. The verb *remind* in 12a is **causative**, and *Harry* names the agent that causes the new state.

In English a verb in the past tense can have a punctual or a durative interpretation. "They sat in the last row" can be the equivalent of what is more precisely expressed as *They sat down in the last row* (punctual) or of *They were sitting in the last row* (durative). It can also have a distributed sense, as in *They sat in the last row every time they went to the theatre*. This sentence expresses **habitual aspect**, customary occurrence distributed over various occasions. However, a simple past tense verb can only express habitual aspect if there is some expression of frequency, that is, some expression of how the event is distributed in time (*every time* . . . , *every Saturday*, *twice a month*, *seldom*, *often*, etc.). English has a more specific way of expressing habitual aspect, one which is used only for customary events in the past: *They used to sit in the last row*. With *used to* the predication is specified as 'habitual' whether there is an expression of frequency or not.

Habitual aspect in the present can be expressed with the simple present tense form of a verb.

13 He smokes cigarillos, drinks tea, sleeps eight hours every night, and curses like a trooper.

PRACTICE 10.1

The previous paragraphs have shown verbs of several aspectual types:

durative, unchanging state (e.g. *need*)
durative, continuing activity (e.g. *argue*)
durative, changing activity (e.g. *improve*)
punctual, momentary act (e.g. *flash*)
punctual, change of state (e.g. *arrive*)

How do the following verbs fit these five categories? Are there overlaps or ambiguities?

die, fall, float, hope, jump, knock, mature, possess, wonder

The sentence 'She kept staring out the window' tells of a durative act; 'She kept glancing out the window' is about a repetitive act; 'She kept looking out the window' can be interpreted either way. What is the aspectual feature of each of these three verbs?

All the following sentences describe a distributed action that, depending on the verb, is repetitive or durative. Label each sentence Repetitive or Durative. Can any of them be interpreted both ways?

(a)   The tooth kept aching.
(b)   The wound kept bleeding.
(c)   She kept apologizing.
(d)   He kept asking for more.
(e)   The audience kept applauding.
(f)   The audience continued to clap.
(g)   Rudy and Ruby kept on arguing.
(h)   He kept blowing the horn.
(i)   She kept borrowing money from her parents.
(j)   She kept bouncing the ball.
(k)   Her health continued to deteriorate.
(l)   The cloth kept shrinking.
(m)   The band kept playing and the crowd kept on dancing.
(n)   Watson kept on digging in the cabbage patch.
(o)   Watson kept diving into the pool.
(p)   Alice kept falling and falling.
(q)   Alice kept falling in love.
(r)   We kept hoping things would get better.
(s)   Ruby kept hugging Rudy.
(t)   Rudy kept kissing Ruby.
(u)   He kept hitting the horse.
(v)   He kept beating the horse.

Why are these sentences unlikely – if not impossible?

??   She kept (on) owning a television set.
??   The television set kept belonging to her.

10.4 Telic and atelic

The actions and events that are designated by dynamic predicates may occur within a brief instant or may stretch out over a longer period of time, and the difference may be due to external circumstances or to the nature of the action itself; a single act of hitting or falling cannot take long but talking and walking are apt to continue for at least several minutes. Some acts such as breaking and arriving may take a certain amount of time but the act does not 'happen' until it is complete.

Vendler (1967) proposed a four-way classification of predicates as **stative**, **activity**, **achievement** and **accomplishment** predicates – a classification that derives essentially from Aristotle. Stative and activity predicates are **atelic**, and achievement predicates are **telic**. Later research by Dowty (1977), Dahl (1981), Brinton (1988), Shi (1990), Binnick (1991) and Smith (1991), among others, suggests that these terms should be applied to whole sentences because what a sentence expresses depends on more than the predicate alone.

Now, what do the terms 'atelic' and 'telic' mean? Examine these sentences.

14a	George was waiting.	Sandra was holding the baby.
14b	Sandra was swimming.	George was running.
14c	George was leaving.	Sandra was dying.
14d	Sandra was writing a letter.	George was cutting the rope.

The sentences in 14a are stative and those in 14b are activities. If it is true that George was waiting and Sandra was swimming, for example, then we can report that George waited and Sandra swam. The predicates do not have an end or a goal; they are atelic.

In contrast, 14c contains achievement sentences and the sentences in 14d are accomplishments. If George was leaving, he did not necessarily leave; Sandra might be dying for months and yet not die. These sentences do not report events, happenings, but processes moving towards events. *George left*, *Sandra died* report events that occur instantly, however long the process of moving toward that event may be. Since the events are instantaneous, we can ask "When did George leave?" or "When did Sandra die?" but not "How long did George leave or Sandra die?"

The sentences in 14d are also about processes moving toward completion. If Sandra was writing a letter but stopped, it would be true that Sandra wrote (an activity) but not that she wrote a letter (an accomplishment). Similarly, the fact that George was cutting a rope does not necessarily lead to the fact that he cut it.

Accomplishments (14d) are like achievements (14c) in having an end result, in being telic. Accomplishments differ from achievements in not having an instantaneous result. We can ask "How long does/did it take Sandra to write a letter?" and we can say, for example, "It took George several minutes to cut the rope."

To summarize:

States are non-dynamic, durative and atelic.
Activities are dynamic, durative and atelic.
Achievements are dynamic, instantaneous and telic.
Accomplishments are dynamic, durative and telic.

(Obviously, the terms 'achievement' and 'accomplishment' are used with a sense somewhat different from their everyday meanings.)

PRACTICE 10.3

The following are telic. Which are achievements and which are accomplishments?

(a) He awoke.
(b) I ran a race.
(c) We arrived at home.
(d) The child grew up.
(e) The child stood up.

Activities and accomplishments are both dynamic and durative, and duration means the passage of a period of time. But there is a difference: activities occur throughout a period of time, in English most commonly introduced by the preposition *for*.

15   Lucy wrote for half an hour/all afternoon.

Accomplishments require expenditure of effort during a period leading to the result accomplished. The period is most often introduced by the preposition *in*.

16   Lucy wrote a letter in half an hour.

Sentence 15 is indefinite about what Lucy wrote and sentence 16 is specific. Note that sentence 17 is indefinite like 15 and the sentences in 18 are specific like 16.

17   Lucy wrote letters for an hour/all afternoon.
18   Lucy wrote the letter/several letters/three letters in an hour.

If a sentence tells of an unbounded activity, either because the verb has no object, as in sentence 15, or because the object is itself an unbounded noun phrase, as in 17, the activity takes place throughout a measurable duration. When the object of a verb is a definite referring expression (*the letter*, *the letters*) or a quantified referring expression (*several letters*, *three letters*, for example), the sentence is an accomplishment and we can express how long it takes for this to be accomplished.

All telic events – achievements and accomplishments – are specific. In the following paired sentences note how a specific event (in the 'a' sentences) can be changed to a non-specific activity (the 'b' sentences).

19a   Bert arrived at noon and left at 3 o'clock.
19b   People arrived and left throughout the afternoon.
20a   Tim watched a wrestling match.
20b   Tim watched wrestling matches.
21a   Sally baked bread last Saturday.
21b   Sally baked bread every Saturday.

The (a) sentences have a punctual interpretation and the (b) sentences have a distributed sense. The distributed sense may be due to a plural indefinite subject (19b) or object (20b) – that is, a noun phrase which is unbounded – or to an adverbial phrase that expresses distribution, here by means of the proposition *throughout* (19b) or the specifier *every* (21b). But note that a plural subject or a plural object does not necessarily express distribution of what the predicate expresses:

22   People arrived at noon and left at three o'clock.
23   Tim enjoys wrestling matches.

One final note about atelic and telic predicates: a verb that is atelic by itself may become telic with the addition of a particle such as *up*, *down*, or out. Compare *The papers burned* and *The papers burned up*.

Read each sentence below and decide if it expresses a single act or a repeated activity, or can it be interpreted either way? If it can express a repeated act, it is 'distributed.' What shows that it is – or may be – distributed?

(a) He accepted the order gracefully.
(b) He accepted the orders gracefully.
(c) He accepted orders gracefully.
(d) I acknowledged my mistake.
(e) I always acknowledged my mistakes.
(f) She generally agreed with our decisions.
(g) She agreed with our decision.
(h) Rupert didn't allow anybody to see his butterfly collection.
(i) Rupert showed people his butterfly collection.
(j) Rupert gave away his butterfly collection.

10.5 Ingressive, continuative, egressive aspect

Some predicates express simple states; others express the beginning, the continuance or the ending of states. Some predicates have causative sense: they bring about, or maintain, or put an end to states that exist. We now examine such predicates in groups of common meaning.

10.5.1 Predicates of location

24a The lamp is on the table.
24b Some oranges are in that basket.
24c Donald is at the door.

In these sentences *on*, *in* and *at* are two-argument predicates. Other locative prepositions such as *above*, *beside*, *near*, *next-to*, and *under* are also two-argument predicates. (*Between* requires three arguments, of course.) They are all **locative predicates**.

When the subject noun phrase is an animate being like *Donald*, there are punctual verbs to express the beginning or **ingressive aspect** (25a), durative verbs that express the **continuative aspect** (25b), and punctual verbs which express the the end or **egressive aspect** (25c) of being in a location:

25a   Donald   gets to/arrives at/reaches the door.
25b   "   stays at/remains at   "
25c   "   leaves/departs from   "

Aspect differs but thematic structure is the same:

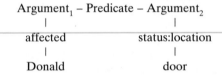

$$\text{Argument}_1 - \text{Predicate} - \text{Argument}_2$$

affected	status:location
Donald	door

Corresponding to these are causative verbs, expressing the action of an agent in causing some entity to be or not be in a place. Causative locative verbs have a valency of three.

26a   Someone   puts/ places   the lamp   on   the table.
26b   "   leaves/ keeps   "   "   "
26c   "   removes/ takes   "   from   "

Verbs like these have the meaning 'cause something to be, to remain, or not to be, in a place.'

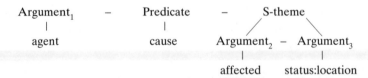

$$\text{Argument}_1 \quad - \quad \text{Predicate} \quad - \quad \text{S-theme}$$

agent		cause		

$$\text{Argument}_2 - \text{Argument}_3$$

affected	status:location

10.5.2 Predicates of possession

Similar to locative expressions are **expressions of possession**.

27   Eleanor   has/owns   a car.

We express the ingressive, continuative, and egressive aspects of the possessing with the verbs illustrated in the next group of sentences.

27a	Eleanor	gets/acquires	a car.	[inception]
27b	Eleanor	keeps	the car.	[duration]
27c	Eleanor	loses/gives up	the car.	[termination]

Some 3-argument predicates express a change of possession.

28a Someone gives/presents/awards/sells a car to Eleanor.
28b Someone takes/receives/buys the car from Eleanor.

The verbs in 28a have the meaning 'cause something to be in the possession of someone,' and those in 28b express 'cause something not to be in someone's possession.' There are no verbs equivalent to 'cause something to remain in someone's possession.'

Note the similarity of verbs that have to do with location and those that relate to possession: an agent causes something to be or not be in a place; an agent causes another person to have or not have some object. Some verbs are used both ways: We send something somewhere or to someone; we throw something to a place or to a person; we take something from a place or from a person.

10.5.3 Predicates of cognition

A third group of stative verbs expresses various aspects of knowing. They are **cognition predicates**.

29 Jeffrey knows/is-aware-of the answer.

Again there are ways of telling the beginning, middle and end of this situation.

29a	Jeffrey	learns/finds/gets	the answer.
29b	Jeffrey	remembers	the answer.
29c	Jeffrey	forgets	the answer.

And there are verbs that express the causing of Jeffrey's knowing.

30a Someone tells/ teaches/shows the answer to Jeffrey.

or, with a slightly different arrangement.

30b Someone informs Jeffrey of the answer.

Finally, we summarize some of these facts about locative, possessive and cognitive verbs. The paradigm below shows a few holes in the pattern.

TABLE 10.1 Locative, possessive, and cognitive predicates

State	Ingression	Continuation	Egression
LOCATION			
be at	arrive at	stay at	leave
	get to	remain at	depart from
	reach		
causative	put . . . at	leave . . . at	take . . . from
	place . . . at	keep . . . at	remove . . . from
POSSESSION			
have	get	keep	lose
own	acquire		give up
causative	give . . . to		take . . . from
	present . . . to		
	award . . . to		
COGNITION			
know	learn	remember	forget
be aware of	find out		
causative	inform		
	teach		

The basic predicates *be-at, have, own, know, be-aware-of* are stative – at least in the uses illustrated – and the corresponding durative predicates are also stative. They indicate some state of affairs going on over a period of time. In contrast the ingressive and terminative verbs are dynamic: they designate some kind of change – moving into or out of a situation or condition.

10.5.4 Event predicates

Just as concrete entities have location in space, events are located in time, as the next sentences illustrate.

31a   The meeting is at 2:00.
31b   The game was on Sunday.
31c   Our party is on Friday.
31d   The ceremony takes place this afternoon.

These sentences have the structure Event + Locative Predicate + Time. A time phrase can be added to almost any sentence, including most of those cited in the last chapter to illustrate valency. A time phrase is an argument in sentences like 31a–d. The noun in the subject is quite restricted; it must be an **event noun**. An event noun is one that refers to an activity, something that occupies time just as the referent of a concrete noun occupies space. The verb connecting the event argument with the time argument is a form of *be* or *happen*, *occur* or *take place*.

Sentences 31a–d are stative: each one simply locates an event in time. But an event must have a beginning, a middle and an end, as the next sentences illustrate.

32a The conference begins at 2.
32b Our party went on for hours.
32c The game ended on time.

Sentences 31a–c, which are stative, have a valency of two, and so do the dynamic sentences 32a, b and c. In the next group each verb has a valency of three.

33a The chairman began the lecture at 8 sharp.
33b The orchestra continued the performance until eleven.
33c We ended the show on time.

These sentences are causative; 33a, for example, means essentially, "The chairman caused the lecture to begin at 8 sharp."

The principal verbs that occur with event arguments are listed in Table 10.2.

TABLE 10.2 Event predicates

State	Initiation	Duration	Termination
EVENTS			
be at	start	go on	stop
occur	begin	continue	end
take place		last	finish
causative	start	continue	stop
	begin		end
			cease

10.5.5 Nouns and adjectives as predicates

A predication may consist of *be* and a noun phrase or adjective phrase, indicating some role, condition or status.

34a Phyllis is a physicist.
34b We were awfully tired.

There are lexical verbs that express the initiation and the continuance of such statuses, but none that express the termination.

35a Phyllis became a physicist.   [ingressive]
35b We got awfully tired.   "
35c Uncle Rufus remained a bachelor.   [continuative]
35d The vase stayed intact.   "

Causative verbs followed by noun phrases or adjective phrases are illustrated next.

36a Czar Peter made St Petersburg his capital.
36b We elected Albert the chairman.
36c Your decision makes me very, very happy.
36d You are driving us crazy.

Table 10.3 sets out the principal aspectual verbs that occur with adjectives and nouns.

TABLE 10.3 Adjectives and Nouns as Predicates

State	Initiation	Duration
adjectives		
be (dry)	get	stay
	become	remain
	turn	
CAUSATIVE	make	keep
	get	
nouns		
be (a lawyer)	become	remain
	turn	stay
CAUSATIVE	make	keep

(Instead of saying *The towels became dry* or *The towels got dry*, we can say *The towels dried*. And rather than *I made the knife sharp(er)*, we are likely to say *I sharpened the knife*. English has ingressive verbs and causative verbs derived from adjectives. An ingressive verb, like *dry* above, expresses the inception or attainment of the quality denoted by the adjective. A causative verb such as *sharpen* is about the same as 'cause to become [sharp].') There is more about causative/inchoative verbs derived from adjectives in Chapter 13.

10.5.6 Aspectual verbs

The four previous sections have dealt with predicates that express the initiation, continuance and termination of states. In English there are no predicates that express the beginning, maintenance or end of activities. Instead there are **aspectual verbs** (called **aspectualizers** by some scholars) which express some aspect of an event. An event, by definition, has duration.

> begin cease commence continue end finish go-on leave-off keep(-on) start stop

When an aspectual verb occurs in a sentence, the subject may be an event noun, in which case there is no other argument, though there is likely to be some expression of time:

> The meeting is beginning now.
> The game went on for hours.
> The dance ended promptly at midnight.

Or the subject may refer to a person or persons, in which case the object of the verb is an event noun or a reduced clause.

37a   The orchestra continued the performance.
37b   The orchestra continued to play until eleven.
37c   The boy kept on looking for the money he had lost.

Sometimes it is possible to consider sentences like the last ones in two ways, either:

Subject	Verb	Object
The orchestra	continued	the performance
The orchestra	continued	to play
The boy	kept on	looking for the money

or:

Subject	Predicate
The orchestra's performance	continued
The orchestra's playing	continued
The boy's looking for the money	kept on

What is the relation of the verb *keep on* (or *continue* or *start* or *stop*) to the rest of the sentence? Is it something the orchestra or the boy does, or something that their activities do?

Considering our sentence structures, we find the group as a whole occurring in four structures; the clause complement may be an infinitive clause with overt or tacit subject or a gerund clause with overt or tacit subject, but not all of the aspectual verbs appear in all four structures. The distribution is:

	Infinitive		Gerund	
	overt	tacit	overt	tacit
go-on finish keep-on leave-off				+
begin cease commence continue		+		+
start		+	+	+
keep stop			+	+

Note that *stop to [eat]* is quite different from *stop [eat]ing*. The latter is an aspectual verb; the former is not. On the contrary, *start to [eat]* and *start [eat]ing* are virtually equivalent. The chart shows that *start*, *keep* and *stop* are two-complement verbs as well as one-complement verbs. Note that there is a difference between *keep*, which is an aspectual verb, and *keep from*, which is not. There is a big difference between *keep the flag flying* and *keep the flag from flying*.

We have now discussed beginning, continuation and end of various states and happenings:

location in space
possession
knowing
location in time
qualities expressed by adjective phrases
roles expressed by noun phrases
actions expressed by verb phrases.

What do ingression, continuation, and egression mean? What they mean – and what everybody knows – can be described in terms of change or non-change from one state to another. Table 10.4 presents a summary. Explanation and discussion follow.

TABLE 10.4 The meaning of initiation, continuation and termination

| | Positive | | Negative | |
	before	after	before	after
Initiation	–	+	–	–
Continuation	+	+	+	–
Termination	+	–	+	+

A positive sentence that expresses initiation or ingression ("Alfred arrived at home," "I put the kettle on the stove," "The water froze," "Sally started sewing") tells us that a negative state existed before the time of this report (Alfred wasn't at home, the kettle was not on the stove, the water hadn't frozen, Sally wasn't sewing) but changed to a positive state (Alfred was at home, etc.). A statement of continuation tells us that there was no change (Alfred stayed at home, The general remained in charge, Sally kept sewing).

And a statement of terminative or egressive aspect (Alfred left home, I took the kettle off the stove, Sally stopped sewing) indicates that what existed before did not exist afterward.

Negative sentences often contain ambiguity. For instance, the sentences *Alfred didn't arrive home when we expected* or *Sally didn't start sewing at seven* are ambiguous because the little word *not* may negate the whole sentence or only the expression of time: it wasn't at seven (but at some other time) that Sally started sewing. If we ignore the second interpretation just now, we see that the sentence about Alfred implies that he was not at home before or after the time he was expected and Sally was not sewing either before or after the time mentioned. Similarly, *Kevin didn't keep whittling* implies that the whittling was going on before, but not after, whatever time is involved. And the negative of termination (*I didn't take the cover off the book*, *Kevin didn't stop whittling*) speaks of a situation existing before and after what is reported.

So the chart shows what anyone knows – that to continue doing something is the same as not to stop doing it, and to stop is not to continue. To state all of this in another way, any aspectual predicate carries a presupposition about the situation before and an implication about the following situation. Affirmative and negative have the same presupposition, as the chart indicates (Kevin kept whistling and Kevin didn't keep whistling, for example) and have opposite implications.

Some very common two-argument verbs that have to do with acquiring some object, or giving up the object, can be analyzed semantically in terms of possession previous and subsequent to the event of the verb, and whether the effect of the verb is intentional or not. The first two lines are completed. You can fill in the other three lines of the table:

	A has X before	A has X after	Intentional or not
A gets X	–	+	±
A finds X	–	+	–
A loses X			
A gets rid of X			
A keeps X			

(± means that it may be intentional or not)

PRACTICE 10.5

Any sentence that expresses iteration or a change in a state or activity carries a presupposition; for example, *Uncle Gustav left his office at five p.m.* presupposes that Uncle Gustav was in his office before five p.m. What is presupposed by each of the following sentences?

(a) Nancy has resigned her position on the Benevolence Fund Committee.
(b) My watch no longer keeps accurate time.
(c) Tommy wants another piece of cake.
(d) The ice is melting.
(e) Alexa closed the window.
(f) We're going to the market again.
(g) The three little kittens have lost their mittens.
(h) Desmond has recovered from his illness.

10.6 Prospective and retrospective

38a   Fred figured his friends had already started the trip.
38b   Fred figured his friends were starting the trip just then.
38c   Fred figured his friends would soon be starting the trip.

When a predicate such as *figure* is followed by a full clause, the verb in the full clause can have the complete range of tense and aspect modification. Consequently the clause can report an event that is prior to the time of the main clause verb (38a), or simultaneous with it (38b), or subsequent to it (38c). In these three sentences the friends' starting has different aspects in relation to Fred's figuring. However, when a predicate is associated with a reduced clause, the verb of that reduced clause is more limited in the range of times it can express. It may express an event that is simultaneous with the main clause verb, or one that is earlier or later. That depends on what predicate is in the main clause.

Let's start with these two sentences:

39a   We asked Ronald to drive slower.
39b   Jessica is thinking of visiting her grandmother.

In sentence 39a our asking has to do with Ronald's subsequent behavior. In sentence 39b Jessica's thinking obviously concerns something she may do later. We call such verbs as *ask* and *think-of* **prospective verbs**; they are oriented toward later happenings. Note that it is the orientation that is important; whether Ronald actually slows down or Jessica visits her grandmother is irrelevant.

Now consider these sentences:

40a   Edgar apologized for missing the meeting.
      (or, . . . for having missed the meeting)
40b   We denied seeing the report.
      (or, . . . having seen the report)

In both sentences the clause is about something that did or did not precede the apologizing and denying. Verbs like *apologize* and *deny* are **retrospective verbs**. The previous action to which the verb refers is expressed in a following clause, always a gerund clause, and the previousness can be emphasized by the use of the retrospective (or 'perfect') form of the gerund, having [missed]. If there is a preposition, it is most often *for*. Note the difference a preposition can make: *Mr Hawkins excused Jerry for missing the meeting* (or *for having missed the meeting*) necessarily reports an excuse being issued by Mr Hawkins after Jerry missed the meeting, whereas *Mr Hawkins excused Jerry from attending the meeting* is prospective, telling us that the excuse precedes Jerry's (probable) non-attendance at the meeting.

Not all verbs are prospective or retrospective. Some verbs indicate an action that goes on at the same time as whatever is reported in the following clause. The verb *help*, occurring with an infinitive clause, is seen, for example, in the following sentence:

41   I helped Josie (to) bring in the groceries.

The helping and the bringing-in must be simultaneous.

10.7 Some grammatical expressions of aspect

If an aspectual meaning can be expressed with all – or a significant number – of the predicates of a language, the expression is grammatical. To be sure, that aspectual meaning may be somewhat different with different predicates, depending on their intrinsic semantic nature. In this section we examine three aspects that are incorporated into the grammatical system of English, prospective, perfect (or perfective), and progressive.

10.7.1 The prospective

Sentences 7a–c illustrate a **prospective form**.

42a   They are to leave.
42b   You are not to worry
42c   Are we to wait here?

This form, be + *to* + verb expresses a 'looking forward'; it is not about the future but about present intentions regarding the future. There are other prospective forms – *be about to* [leave], *be going to* [leave], which are not discussed here. (And the simple present can be used in a prospective sense, e.g. *They leave next Wednesday*. See above, Section **9.3**.)

The past tense form of *be + to* combined with a verb makes the past prospective, *They were to leave*, expressing a looking forward from some point in the past.

10.7.2 The perfect or retrogressive

They have left illustrates a verb structure which is traditionally called 'present perfect.' A better term might be **present retrospective form**. Whatever the name, for any verb it consists of two parts, a form of *have* and the past participle of the verb. The present perfect, or present retrospective, form, in affirmative statements, refers to events that occurred in the past and situations that began in the past and which are seen as relevant 'now,' at the present time. Negative statements, of course, deny such events and situations; interrogative sentences question them.

There are two uses for the present retrospective. One is the description of present situations when we want to measure their duration from some point in the past. In the following paired sentences compare the simple present (a) and the present retrospective (b). The simple present sentences are about states (43a, 44a) or habitual activity (45a), which is a kind of state. The present retrospective sentences tell or ask about the duration of these states.

43a The house is empty now.
43b It has been empty for over a year.
44a Do you know the Robinsons?
44b Have you known them for long?
45a Jenkins works in the First City Bank.
45b He has worked there since 1985.

Second, the present retrospective is used for past events or states which are presented as relevant to the present. This time we want to compare the past tense (a) with the present retrospective (b).

46a I was here last Tuesday, last Friday and yesterday.
46b I have been here three times this month.
47a The Blakes lived in Singapore from 1980 to 1986.
47b The Blakes have lived in Singapore, but they don't live there now.
48a What did you see when you went to New York?
48b What have you seen since you came here?

The difference between past events which are relevant to the present moment and past events which lack such relevance is not a clear distinction, so in some cases there is divided usage among speakers of English. For events just accomplished, especially when the word just is used, British English (and the English of Australia, New Zealand, and South Africa) generally prefers the present retrospective, while North Americans often use the simple past. Thus coming upon the scene of an accident, an Englishman will ask "What's happened?," an American "What happened?" Similarly, in telling about the accident later the Englishman is apt to say "I've just seen the most amazing sight" and the American "I just saw the most amazing sight."

The past retrospective, as in *They had left*, presents a backward look from a time in the past. We can illustrate its uses by making changes in the sentences above: *In 1985 the house had been empty for a long time. I had been there three times in the previous month.*

10.7.3 The progressive

The syntactic form illustrated in 49a–b might appropriately be called the **bounded aspect**.

49a We're watching television.
49b Jack is smoking.

Sentences 49a–b illustrate a verb form composed of the present of *be* and the present participle, or *-ing* form, of the verb. It is called the present progressive, or the 'continuous' or 'durative' or 'ongoing.' A more appropriate name would be the temporary or bounded form. Sentences 49a and 49b have atelic predicates. The simple present tense form of these verbs (*We watch television, Jack smokes*) is **unbounded, general**; it includes more than the 'right now' and implies nothing about the beginning or end of the activity, watching television or smoking. The present bounded form, on the other hand, as in 49a–b, is specific. It is also about the present moment but calls attention to the fact that the activity is in process now and implies that the activity will end. The present bounded is part of the simple present, not vice versa. Thus we have

Jack smokes a pipe,
{ and he is smoking it now.
{ but he isn't smoking it now.

We cannot say

*Jack is smoking a pipe,
{ and he smokes.
{ but he doesn't smoke.

Thus *is smoking a pipe* expresses a situation with certain implied boundaries whereas *smokes a pipe* implies no time boundaries at all; it is habitual or generic. In the following paired sentences, also with atelic predicates, the two members of each pair may make the same kind of report about things; the difference is in aspect: the progressive form suggests boundaries; the phenomenon has not always been so and/or it may not continue to be so.

50a My watch is working very well now.
50b My watch works very well now.
51a They're living in Richmond.
51b They live in Richmond.

Since the simple present can express a general truth, something that is always or typically so, and the present progressive is used for what is temporarily true, temporariness can seem more dramatic, more interesting. Compare these sentences with stative verbs:

52a We admire the way you've arranged the furniture here.
52b We're admiring the way you've arranged the furniture here.
53a I wonder why the committee can't make a sensible decision.
53b I'm wondering why the committee can't make a sensible decision.
54a The doctor hopes that the new medicine will be effective.
54b The doctor is hoping that the new medicine will be effective.

The 'a' and 'b' sentences do not differ in what is predicated but in the intensity with which the predication is expressed.

The progressive form indicates that the activity predicated is distributed over a period of time with an implied endpoint, but it need not be distributed continuously over that time. Vlach (1981: 279) points out that one can stand beside an empty theater seat and ask, "Is anyone sitting here?" If the verb form is applied strictly to the time of asking, it would be nonsensical. The question more accurately means, "Is anyone sitting in this seat at some moments within a period of time that includes the present?"

One kind of distribution is a sequence of successive states which differ from one another by some small increments.

55   Jason is resembling his father more and more.

Achievement predicates cannot be distributed over time.

56   Our guests are leaving.
57   The plane is landing

Leave and *land*, as in 56 and 57, are achievement verbs. The act of leaving or of landing is momentary, and a momentary act cannot be in progress. So long as the guests are leaving, they have not yet left; if the plane is landing, it still has not landed. Thus the progressive or bounded aspect, with such verbs, emphasizes the incompleteness of the act. Furthermore, just as events planned for the future can be stated in the simple present (*They arrive tomorrow, The shop opens next week, Mr Edwards retires in May*), they can also be put into the progressive form: *They're arriving tomorrow, The shop is opening next week, Mr Edwards is retiring in May.* Here, too, the difference is not in the propositions communicated but in the dramatic nature of what is communicated.

The progressive can be used with atelic predicates to make a more dramatic statement of what is slated to happen in the near future. For instance, a tour guide leading a group of tourists on a walk around some historic monument might start with an announcement like this:

58   We'll be walking through several rooms and I'll be pointing out the interesting details and telling you the historic facts associated with them. You'll be seeing some valuable art objects and you'll be learning why the building has the form it has . . .

Omission of every *be* . . . -*ing* in this speech would have no effect on the content.

Summary

Aspect is the cover name for different ways in which the proposition contained in a sentence is viewed. Different aspects are fairly easy to recognize and understand, but any one aspect may be expressed in various ways. The semantic nature of a predicate often has something to do with the aspect it expresses, but it is also a fact that some predicates may occur in sentences with different aspects.

This chapter has drawn a distinction between states and activities, the former containing stative predicates and the latter dynamic predicates. Some states express generic propositions, essentially unchanging, and others express non-generic propositions which have come about through change and may change again. Relations between a present state and a previous one can be indicated with the aspectual modifiers *already*, *still*, *no longer* and *not yet*. States and activities are durative. They are also atelic, not expressing any definite endpoint.

Achievements and accomplishments are telic; the former are punctual, with the endpoint of the activity occurring instantaneously, whereas it takes some period of time for an accomplishment to reach its endpoint. Achievements and accomplishments are specific and require specific noun phrases as arguments.

Some predicates express the beginning (ingressive aspect), the continuation (continuative aspect), or the end (egressive aspect) of states. Some causative predicates express what happens when an agent brings a state into existence, maintains it, or ends it. Uneven matrixes of such predicates have been illustrated for the areas of physical location, possession, cognition, temporal location and sentences with adjectives and nouns as predicates.

Certain verbs followed by an infinitive clause are prospective: they express a meaning that is necessarily previous to the proposition in the infinitive clause. Other verbs, followed by a gerund clause, are retrospective and express a 'looking back' at the content of the gerund clause. English also has grammatical means of indicating prospective aspect. The most common form is composed of *be* plus the infinitive. The grammatical means of expressing retrospection has the traditional name 'perfect' and consists of forms of *have* plus the past participle. This grammatical form is used in telling the duration of states up to a present or past moment and in recounting events that are seen as relevant to such a moment. Finally, English has a progressive form consisting of *be* plus the present participle. The progressive expresses a temporary, or bounded, activity. With achievement predicates it expresses a process moving toward an occurrence. With stative predicates the progressive often adds intensity to what is said.

Suggested reading

Comrie (1976) is the best general account of aspect in a vast number of languages. Frawley (1992), Chapter 7, offers a more cogent overview of the same. Leech (1987) makes an Aktionsart classification of English verbs, which also appears in Quirk *et al.* (1984).

For more extensive study the following should be mentioned: Vendler (1967) is a milestone in modern investigation of this subject. Tedeschi and Zaenen (1981) is a collection of articles on aspect, including the Dahl and Vlach works mentioned in Section **10.3**. Smith (1991) seeks to develop a unified theory of aspect within Universal Grammar based on an explication of the quite different aspectual systems of five languages. Binnick (1991) surveys ancient and modern theories of tense and aspect and makes his own contribution. Brinton (1988) traces the historic development of the aspectual system of modern English.

Notes on the text

- A rather large number of terms have been used in this chapter to account for different kinds of aspect, but two terms commonly used in discussions of aspect have been omitted: **perfective** and **imperfective**. These seem unnecessary for the purpose here and their introduction might lead to confusion in a treatment of English. Whereas Slavic languages maintain a clear lexical distinction in two kinds of verbs, those that express what is done, completed, accomplished (perfective) and what is in progress, incomplete (imperfective), and Romance languages have such a distinction grammatically in past tenses, the 'preterite' (or 'past definite') versus the 'imperfect,' there is little need for drawing such a distinction in English. Telic predicates – achievements and accomplishments – are perfective, stative predicates are imperfective, but activities can be either. The English present perfect expresses imperfective aspect when it is applied to present states measured from a time in the past ("We have been here for an hour") and perfective aspect when predicating past events ("We have seen the reports") – but the past tense ("We saw the reports") is also perfective.

- Grammarians and semanticists describing the English language often insist, a priori, that the progressive aspect is incompatible with stative predicates – and then go on to classify the 'exceptions.' However, there would seem to be little reason for expecting correlation between aspects and their expression in a specific language. This viewpoint leads to a mis-classification of verbs like *remain* and *wait*, which can be progressive but which express no action, and fails to account for the difference between, for instance, *to wonder* and *to be wondering*. The verbs *stand*, *sit*, *kneel* and *lie* express bodily stance (stative) or the assumption of such a stance (dynamic), the latter often accompanied by a particle (*up* with *stand*, *down* with the others). In the absence of a particle the progressive forms (*He is standing*, *They were sitting*, etc.) are more likely to be interpreted as stative than as dynamic.

Factivity, implication and modality

In Chapter 1 we touched briefly on the notion of **presupposition**: the information in one sentence, for example, *Andy Murfee usually drives his Datsun to work*, presupposes the existence of a referent, Andy Murfee, and certain predications, the facts that he works, owns a Datsun, and knows how to drive it. The present chapter explores the notion of presupposition further, considering the notions of existence, possession and occurrence. One means of conveying such presuppositions is the factive predicate, the topic of Section **11.1**. Other predicates imply, rather than presuppose, the truth of some proposition; they are studied in Section **11.2**. Sentences often contain information about the necessity, possibility or probability of one or another proposition. This kind of information is called **modality**, the topic of Section **11.3**.

11.1 Factivity

1a   We forgot that the meeting was canceled.
1b   We didn't forget that the meeting was canceled.

These two sentences say opposite things about forgetting, but they are alike in communicating the information that a certain meeting was canceled. Kiparsky and Kiparsky (1970) first pointed out that certain predicates, among them the verb *forget*, are **factive**. A factive predicate has a predication as one of its arguments (a full clause, gerund clause or an abstract noun phrase) and, whether affirmative or negative, it presupposes the truth of that predication. Combining 1a and 1b, this can be stated in a formula in which '>>' stands for 'presupposes.'

> We forgot/didn't forget that the meeting was canceled.
> >> The meeting was canceled.

Other examples of factive predicates:

2   I regret/don't regret that smoking can cause cancer.
      >> Smoking can cause cancer.
3   I resent/don't resent John's decision.
      >> John decided something.
4   It's (not) surprising that the baby woke up.
      >> The baby woke up.

The predicates *regret, resent, forget, surprising* – and *amazing, remarkable* and others – are factive. Whether affirmative or negative, they present the following predication as true. Note that 'factive' is not the same as 'factual.' Whether the predication is true or not can only be determined by investigating events and situations outside language; 'factive' means that the predication is presented linguistically as being true.

In the examples above the factive predicates are followed by full clauses. Some factive predicates can be followed by gerund clauses or a deverbal noun like *decision*, with tacit or overt subjects.

5   Smedley regretted/didn't regret joining the club.
6   I blame/don't blame you for saying that.

PRACTICE 11.1

Here are other factive verbs that can be followed by a gerund clause. Make up a pair of sentences for each verb with a gerund clause following.

    forget/not forget -ing
    envy/not envy somebody for -ing
    excuse/not excuse somebody for -ing
    understand/not understand somebody's -ing

In contrast to all the sentences above, consider the following:

7   Andrea believes/doesn't believe that an apple a day keeps the doctor away. >> ?
8   We decided/didn't decide to stay for a while. >> ?
9   It's (not) likely that the bank will open again. >> ?

The predicates *believe, decide, likely, assert, hope, probable* and others are **nonfactive predicates**. They have a predication as one of their arguments but, whether affirmative or negative, they do not assert the truth of that predication.

One predicate is **counterfactive**: whether affirmative or negative, it carries the presupposition that the following predication is not true.

10   I (don't) wish I owned a villa on the Riviera.
     >> I don't own a villa on the Riviera.

Any verb can be counterfactive if used with the auxiliary verbs *would have*.

11a   I would have enjoyed seeing the play.
      >> I didn't see the play.
11b   I wouldn't have enjoyed seeing the play.
      >> I didn't see the play.

To summarize, where 'p' indicates an affirmative predicate, '~p' is a negative predicate, 'q' is a true proposition, and '~q' a proposition that is not true:

factive	p >> q	~p >> q
counterfactive	p >> ~q	~p >> ~q
nonfactive	p >> ?	~p >> ?

PRACTICE 11.2

Decide which of the following sentences have factive verbs and which do not.

(a)   Ms Jones acknowledged/didn't acknowledge that the money had been found.
(b)   Ms Jones conceded/didn't concede that the money had been found.
(c)   I dreamt/didn't dream that the money had been found.
(d)   Susie remembered/didn't remember that the money had been found.
(e)   Susie guessed/didn't guess that the money had been found.
(f)   Walter ignored/didn't ignore the fact that the money had been found.
(g)   We imagined/didn't imagine that the money had been found.
(h)   The students learned/didn't learn that the money had been found.

> (i) It occurred/didn't occur to us that the money had been found.
> (j) The treasurer reported/didn't report that the money had been found.
> (k) The treasurer revealed/didn't reveal that the money had been found.
> (l) The students sensed/didn't sense that the money had been found.

While there is only one counterfactive predicate in English, namely *wish*, the number of nonfactive predicates is large. Some examples:

> agree assume believe decide doubt dream feel
> fear hope imagine suppose think afraid sure

Most of us would accept that the following are factive:

> discover find-out forget hear know learn notice realize regret
> remember resent understand aware glad happy sorry

The following are also factive but differ from the group above in one small syntactic matter. They are followed not by a clause alone but by *the fact* and a clause: *I appreciate/don't appreciate the fact that you said exactly what you feel.*

> accept acknowledge appreciate deplore overlook tolerate

With some verbs the words *the fact* may or may not appear:

> I regret/don't regret (the fact) that the meeting was cancelled.

11.2 Implicative predicates

Some predicates do not presuppose the truth of a proposition that occurs as one of their arguments but carry some implication about the truth or non-truth of the proposition. We find an interesting variety of implications and can recognize different kinds of **implicative predicates**, first sketched by Karttunen (1971) and sometimes called 'conditional factives.' Consider first:

12a I managed to catch my bus, and I caught it.
12b I managed to catch my bus, but I didn't catch it.

Sentence 12a is as redundant as *I caught my bus, and I caught it.*
Sentence 12b is as contradictory as *I caught my bus, but I didn't catch
it.* If you hear someone say "I managed to catch my bus," you will no
doubt infer that the speaker did catch the bus in question. Hearing
the negative equivalent, "I didn't manage to catch my bus" you infer
that the speaker did not catch the bus.

The verb *manage*, like some other verbs followed by a reduced
clause, has a certain implicative value. Different predicates have
different implicative values, and we recognize six groups of predicates according to what they imply about the truth value of the
included clause. In our first group, which includes *manage*, if the
predicate is affirmative, it implies that the following proposition is
true, and if the predicate is negative, there is an implication that the
following proposition is false. (The symbol '→' below should be read
'implies.')

I managed to catch my bus. → I caught my bus.
I didn't manage to catch my bus. → I didn't catch my bus.

More examples:

13a We happened/chanced to see your brother.
    → We saw your brother.
14a He chose/condescended to wait for us. → He waited for us.
15a She remembered to stop at the post office.
    → She stopped at the post office.
13b We didn't happen/chance to see your brother.
    → We didn't see your brother.

Now it's your turn. Formulate sentences 14b and 15b with the
negative of *choose/condescend* and *remember*.

With these verbs, Group 1, affirmative implies affirmative and
negative implies negative.

+ → +   − → −

Group 2 verbs occur in these sentences:

16a We neglected/failed to make reservations.
    → We didn't make reservations.

16b　We didn't neglect/fail to make reservations.
　　　→ We made reservations.
17a　I avoided/missed/escaped attending that party.
　　　→ I didn't attend that party.
17b　I didn't avoid/miss/escape attending that party.
　　　→ I attended that party.

With these verbs affirmative implies negative – that the embedded proposition is not true – and negative has an affirmative implication – that the embedded proposition is true.

$$+ \rightarrow - \qquad - \rightarrow +$$

Both Group 1 and Group 2 verbs are followed only by clauses with tacit subject; the subject of the embedded proposition is the same as the subject of the main clause. Verbs in some of the groups discussed below are followed by clauses with tacit or overt subjects. When both kinds exist, both are illustrated here.
　　　Group 3:

18a　Henry acknowledged/admitted starting the fire.
　　　→ Henry started the fire.
18b　Henry didn't acknowledge/admit starting the fire. → ?
19a　Circumstances forced us to cancel our plans.
　　　→ We canceled our plans.
19b　Circumstances didn't force us to cancel our plans. → ?

We recognize that Henry's failure to admit starting the fire does not inform us whether he did or did not actually start the fire, and if we were not forced by circumstances to cancel our plans, we might have done so anyway. Note that we are concerned here with what is implied by a sentence, or the proposition expressed in the sentence. In utterances speakers can add their own implication through prosody. For example, if someone says

　　　Henry didn't ad ↓MIT starting the ↑ fire

with emphasis on *admit* and a fall-rise intonation, the speaker may be suggesting that admission or non-admission is quite apart from the relevant fact.
　　　So, for Group 3 implicative verbs, affirmative implies affirmative but negative has no implication.

$$+ \rightarrow + \qquad - \rightarrow 0$$

Group 4:

20a Mary pretended to be asleep. → Mary was not asleep.
20b Mary didn't pretend to be asleep. → ?
21a A sudden storm prevented the men from completing the job. →
    The men didn't complete the job.
21b A sudden storm didn't prevent the men from completing the job. → ?
22a We forgot to make reservations. → We didn't make reservations.
22b We didn't forget to make reservations. → ?

Here note that the contexts in which utterances occur can lead to one certainty or the other. With 20b, for example, first, "Mary didn't pretend to be asleep. Why should she bother to make such a pretense?," and on the other hand, "Miriam didn't pre ↓TEND to be asleep. She ↓WAS asleep." With 21b we might hear "A storm didn't prevent the men from completing the job; they completed it anyway" or, instead, "A storm didn't prevent the men from completing the job but something else did." The point is that *not pretend*, *not prevent* and *not forget*, in themselves, carry no implication about the status of the following clause.

In Group 4, then, affirmative implies negative but negative has no implication.

$$+ \to - \qquad - \to 0$$

Group 5:

23a We tried to answer. → ? (Did we answer?)
23b We didn't try to answer. → We didn't answer.
24a We risked their seeing us. → ?
24b We didn't risk their seeing us. → They didn't see us.

Affirmative has no implication, while the negative implies negative.

$$+ \to 0 \qquad - \to -$$

Group 6:

25a Joel denied drawing the caricature. → ? (Did he draw it?)
25b Joel didn't deny drawing the caricature. →
    Joel drew the caricature.
26a We hesitated to accept the offer. → ?
26b We didn't hesitate to accept the offer. → We accepted the offer.

Affirmative implies nothing, negative implies affirmative.

$$+ \rightarrow 0 \qquad - \rightarrow +$$

Here is a list of common implicative verbs in the six groups, with indication of the usual syntactic structure – that is, whether the included proposition is expressed in an infinitive or a gerund clause and whether it has a tacit or overt subject.

| | Tacit | | Overt | |
	infinitive	*gerund*	*infinitive*	*gerund*
1	chance happen choose condescend get manage remember	practice		
2	decline fail neglect refuse forget	avoid escape keep from miss refrain from		
3		acknowledge admit remember	cause compel force help lead oblige persuade	find leave remember
4	pretend			deter from dissuade from excuse from hinder from keep from prevent from
5	attempt endeavor try undertake venture	risk undertake	consider	risk
6	hesitate	deny		

Implications of the six groups are summarized in this table, with one example for each group:

		+	-
1	manage	+	-
2	neglect	-	+
3	compel	+	0
4	prevent	-	0
5	attempt	0	-
6	hesitate	0	+

PRACTICE 11.3

Verbs may have different implicative values when the embedded proposition is expressed as an infinitive clause or a gerund clause; they may also have different implications when these embedded propositions have tacit or overt subjects. For example, with a tacit subject in the clause *dare* belongs to Group 1: *We dared to speak out*; *We didn't dare to speak out*. But if there is an overt subject, *dare* is not implicative; *We dared Rudy to speak out* and *We didn't dare Rudy to speak out* lead to no inference about Rudy's speaking out. Similarly, *wait* with a tacit subject in the embedded clause belongs to Group 6: *We waited/didn't wait to reply*. But no implication exists when there is an overt subject in the embedded clause: *We waited/didn't wait for Rudy to reply*. Simply put, an activity which is under the subject's control is more predictable than an activity under another's control.

What are the implications of the following sentences, affirmative and negative?

(a)   I remembered/didn't remember to lock the door. [prospective]
(b)   I remembered/didn't remember locking the door. [retrospective]
(c)   We got/didn't get to watch the game.
(d)   We got/didn't get our friends to watch the game.
(e)   She kept/didn't keep from getting wet.
(f)   She kept/didn't keep the children from getting wet.

The discussion so far has been about propositions expressed as gerund or infinitive clauses. With some implicative verbs in English the embedded proposition may be expressed as an abstract noun or in a full clause. When the proposition appears as an abstract noun, implications are the same as for other reduced clauses. Thus *He neglected/didn't neglect his duty* carries the same implications as *He neglected/didn't neglect to do his duty*; *She admitted/didn't admit her error* is like *She admitted/didn't admit making an error*.

When an embedded proposition is expressed as a full clause, implication is less easy to state because the truth value of that clause (or its proposition) depends on a number of factors: whether the subject of the clause is the same as the subject of the main verb and whether the embedded clause has definite or indefinite NPs. The following verbs are like those of Group 3; an affirmative verb implies that the embedded proposition is true, while a negative verb leads to no certain conclusion.

> admit concede conclude discover learn realize
> recognize remember see

27a He admitted that the plan was a mistake.
→ The plan was a mistake.
27b He didn't admit that the plan was a mistake. → ?

11.3 Modality

People talk about factual matters – what is true and what is not true, what has happened and what has not happened – but we also talk about what may be true or not, what ought to be and what ought not to be, what certain individuals are capable of and what is impossible for them, what obligations we have to do or to refrain from doing. All these notions together constitute modality.

Two examples of modality:

28a It's your duty to visit your ailing parents.
28b You ought to visit your ailing parents.

These sentences are almost paraphrases. Both of them have a proposition 'you visit your ailing parents' and they make equivalent statements about that proposition: your duty = what you ought to do.

Two more examples of modality:

29a Jessica is possibly at home now.
29b Jessica may be at home now.

Here, too, there are nearly synonymous sentences containing the same proposition and making equivalent statements about the proposition: a possibility = what may be.

Sentences 28a and b are about obligation; sentences 29a and b are about possibility. All modality involves obligation or possibility of one sort or another. In 28a and b the obligation is centered on the subject, *you*; the sentences tell what is necessary for 'you' to do. But in 29a and b the possibility is not centered on the subject, *Jessica*; it applies to the whole proposition, Jessica's being at home now. So we recognize another distinction in modality: it may be centered on some entity or entities, typically denoted by the subject of the sentence, or centered on a proposition contained in the sentence.

Modality can be expressed in nouns like *duty*, *obligation*, *probability*, *likelihood*; in adjectives like *necessary*, *possible*, *likely*; in adverbs such as *obviously*, *probably*, *perhaps*; but for description of how modality is expressed in English we need to concentrate on **modal verbs** – verbs like *ought* and *may*. Semantically, the following are modal verbs:

> can could may might will would must should
> ought need have to have got to

Native speakers of English learn these verbs so early in life that they are unaware of having learned them. As Joos (1964: 147–8) points out, a child of four may ask the meaning of *duty* but is not likely to ask about the meaning of *must*. The child knows what *must* means, but neither a child nor an adult is capable of explaining the meaning.

It also has to be said that the modal verbs have numerous subtleties in what they express in different contexts. They have shifted semantically throughout the history of the language, and different speakers of the language differ somewhat in which modal verbs they prefer for what meanings.

What does *must* mean? It has two meanings, which we can first illustrate with two little dialogues. Suppose a young athlete plans to enter an important and difficult race and we say to him or her, "If you expect to win, you must train very hard," and he or she answers,

"I will." Suppose, on the other hand, this athlete is showing us trophies and medals that she or he has won in previous races. We might say, "If you have won so many races, you must train very hard," and the response might be, "I do."

In the first instance the verb *must* is about obligation, the obligation of the person denoted by *you*, and the statement is prospective, about actions yet to be accomplished, as shown by the answer "I will." The second dialogue has *must* expressing probability; the probability is not subject-centered – we are not talking about 'you' being probable but about the fact of 'your' training very hard; and the statement is not prospective: it takes into account a present phenomenon, the trophies and medals, and looks backward to account for it.

Just what is obligation? It is necessity that is centered on some person or persons. The utterance "You must train very hard" in the first dialogue can be paraphrased "It is necessary for you to train very hard." And what is probability? It is also necessity, the necessary truth or factuality of some proposition or propositions. The utterance "You must train very hard" in the second dialogue can be paraphrased as "It is necessarily the case that you train very hard." In the first dialogue *must* expresses **deontic modality**, the necessity of an individual to act or not act in a particular way. In the second dialogue *must* expresses **epistemic modality**, the possibility, probability or impossibility of a particular proposition.

Obligation is expressed in several English modal verbs. Examples:

30a We must leave immediately.
30b We have to leave immediately. We have got to leave immediately.
30c We need to leave immediately.
30d We ought to leave immediately.
30e We should leave immediately.

These verbs express different degrees of obligation, but probably different speakers of English do not agree on their relative rank. For this author, *must*, as in 30a, is the most forceful statement of obligation and is somewhat formal. *Have* and *have got* are more colloquial and not as strong as *must*. The others follow in order: *need* is nearly as strong as *have*; *ought* expresses a weaker obligation but is still stronger than *should*. Other speakers of English may well have a different ranking.

Negative obligations are illustrated next.

31a We mustn't stay here.
31b We don't have to stay here.
31c We needn't stay here. We don't need to stay here.
31d We oughtn't to stay here.
31e We shouldn't stay here.

There is a great difference between 31a and the rest of these. The first says that we are obliged not to stay; negativity is attached to the embedded proposition: not staying is our obligation. The others say that we are not obliged to stay; negativity applies to the modal verbs; staying is not an obligation. Schematically the difference can be represented this way:

must: not + stay here
not + have/need/ought/should: stay here

To express an obligation that existed in the past *have to* is the usual modal verb.

32a We had to complete the documents before 5 o'clock.
32b We didn't have to complete the documents that day.

Some speakers say *had got to* and *hadn't got to* instead of *had to* and *didn't have to*, respectively. *Must* is not used for past obligations except perhaps in reported speech: *The boss told us we must complete the documents before 5 o'clock.*

Turning now to the discussion of possibility and probability, we need to recognize first that probability presupposes possibility; nothing is likely to be true unless it can be true, nobody is likely to do something without being able to do it. And probability is a variable quantity: a given proposition may be highly probable, fairly likely, rather unlikely, or improbable (though still possible). These imprecise degrees of probability can be represented on a scale like this:

POSSIBLE					IMPOSSIBLE
apparently true	highly probable	fairly probable	slightly probable	improbable	

In English the degree of probability can be expressed with just the terms used here, *highly, very, fairly, rather, slightly, somewhat* combined with *probable, likely, improbable* and *unlikely*. Degrees of probability are also expressed with modal verbs.

Possibility that is subject-centered is expressed with the modal verbs *can* and *may*.

33 Edward can lift 250 pounds. (He has strength and training.)
34 Sally can speak four languages. (She has knowledge and experience.)
35 You may/can leave the room. (You have permission.)

If the potential for an act is entirely in the subject, *can* is used. If the potential rests in another person's authority, *may* is the preferred verb. However, this distinction has been declining for a long time, and *can* is often used to express permission, as in Sentence 35. The corresponding negative sentences are: *Edward can't . . .* , *Sally can't . . .* , *You may not/can't . . . .*

To express personal potential in the past *could* is used. It is thus the past tense form of *can*.

36 When I was younger, I could run a mile in four minutes, but I couldn't do better than that.

And *could* expresses a reduced potential – a lesser degree of possibility – at any time.

37 I could still run a mile in four minutes if I tried, but I couldn't do it easily.

The past tense form of *may* is *might*, which sometimes expresses permission at some time in the past, but usually only in reported speech: *Our teacher said we might leave the room for ten minutes*. We would not use *might* in place of *had permission to* in this sentence: *We had permission to leave the room for a while yesterday.*

We turn next to possibility, impossibility and degrees of probability that are centered on whole propositions. First, take a sentence that simply presents a proposition as fact:

38a Driving a car in a heavy rainstorm is dangerous.

Modal verbs modify this truth.

38b Driving in a heavy rainstorm can be dangerous.

38c   Driving in a heavy rainstorm may be dangerous.
38d   Driving in a heavy rainstorm might be dangerous.
38e   Driving in a heavy rainstorm must be dangerous.

Sentence 38b states a possible fact without comment on its probability. Sentences 38c and 38d are statements about the probability of the fact. Since they are vague regarding the probability, they are roughly equivalent, though *might* suggests less probability or more vagueness. Sentence 38e is an inference. From the knowledge available, it says, there is apparently a high probability of danger in driving during a heavy rainstorm.

To consider how negativity combines with modality, we start with a sentence that simply presents a proposition as non-fact:

39a   Stanley is not busy now.

Modal verbs can be added:

39b   Stanley may not be busy now.
39c   Stanley might not be busy now.
39d   Stanley must not be busy now.
39e   Stanley can't be busy now.

Compare 39b and 39e. Sentence 39b is about the possibility of Stanley not being busy, and 39e is about the impossibility of Stanley being busy. In 39b *not* applies to the proposition, in 39e to the modal verb *can*. (The fact that there is a common contraction for <u>can + not</u> but no such contraction for *may + not* is irrelevant.)

may:	not + be busy
not + can:	be busy

Sentence 39c is like 39b but is less forceful or more vague about the possibility. Sentence 39d presents high probability that Stanley is not busy. With *may*, *might* and *must* the embedded proposition, not the modal verb, is negated.

To describe possibility and probability at some time in the past we can say:

40a,b,c   Stanley may/might/could have been busy.
40d   Stanley must have been busy.

Sentences 40a–c all state the possibility of a certain phenomenon and express vague amounts of probability; 40d gives it a very high probability.

The negative correlates are these:

41a,b Stanley may/might not have been busy.
41c   Stanley could not have been busy.
41d   Stanley must not have been busy.

Ignoring the difference between *may* and *might*, match 41a, 41c and 41d with these three paraphrases:

It is apparently true that Stanley was not busy.
It is possible that Stanley was not busy.
It is not possible that Stanley was busy.

Earlier we had sentences in which the modal verb *can* stated possibility or potential attributed to single individuals (*Edward can lift 250 pounds*, *Sally can speak four languages*). This verb is also used to express the possibility of some general situation; for example:

42a   Summers can be miserably hot in this city.
43a   Duncan can be an awful nuisance sometimes.

Sentence 43a is not really about Duncan's ability, though that may seem to be the case; it is about the possibility of his being a nuisance just as, more transparently, 42a is about the possibility of miserable summers. To express such possibility in the past *could* replaces *can*.

42b   Summers could be miserable here when I was a child.
43b   Duncan could be an awful nuisance when he was younger.

The last modal verbs to discuss are *will* and *would*, which are not always modal verbs.

44   This summer is hot, and next summer will be hot, too.

The second clause in this sentence gives the proposition, next summer being hot, 100 percent probability, but since it is not yet a fact, as the first clause presumably is, it is a prediction.

Consider next:

45   Wood will float on water. (Wood floats on water.)
46   Accidents will happen. (Accidents happen.)

When *will* is used in general statements like 45 and 46, it denotes such a high probability that the sentences are almost equivalent to statements of fact, with no modality expressed.

Since *will* expresses a prediction, it can also express an intention:

47   I'll phone you first thing in the morning.
48   You will proceed to Fort Darcy and report to the commanding officer upon arrival. [spoken by someone in authority]

In 47 the speaker takes on an obligation; in 48 the speaker imposes an obligation on another person.

What is highly probable is predictable in a general sense, hence characteristic of some entity:

49a   Stephanie will spend hours on end practicing her music.

The past equivalent is *would*.

49b   She would spend hours at the piano every day.

However, this use of *will* and *would* is better described as a kind of aspect rather than a kind of modality.

PRACTICE 11.5

The following sentences are grouped in sets of two or more. In each group explain how the sentences differ in the modality they express.

a-1   I may have misunderstood you.
a-2   I must have misunderstood you.
b-1   You may smoke in the visitors' lounge, if you want to smoke.
b-2   You must smoke in the visitors' lounge, if you want to smoke.
c-1   Even experts can make mistakes.

c-2   Even experts will make mistakes.
d-1   They could do that easily, if they tried.
d-2   They would do that easily, if they tried.
e-1   Herbert could have explained the problem to us.
e-2   Herbert might have explained the problem to us.
e-3   Herbert should have explained the problem to us.
e-4   Herbert ought to have explained the problem to us.

Summary

A predicate that has a clause, an embedded proposition, as one of its arguments may be factive, counterfactive or nonfactive. Whether the proposition appears as a full clause, an infinitive clause or a gerund clause is a grammatical matter; the factivity of the predicate is semantic, an element of its meaning. A factive predicate, whether affirmative or negative, presents the embedded proposition as established truth; a nonfactive predicate gives no indication whether the proposition is true or not; and a counterfactive predicate, the verb *wish*, presents the embedded proposition as not true.

Other predicates accompanied by embedded sentences, always in reduced form, are implicative predicates. They imply the truth or non-truth of what is stated in the embedded sentence. Six groups of implicative predicates are recognized, differing from one another in what can be inferred about the content of the embedded sentence from affirmative and negative values of the main predicate.

Modality has to do with two kinds of necessity, obligation or possibility/probability. Modality may be expressed in various ways, but our presentation has concentrated on the modal verbs of English. Deontic modality has to do with obligation (the necessity of action or non-action); epistemic modality is concerned with possibility (the necessity of existence or non-existence). Deontic modality is typically centered on some entity, generally expressed in the subject of the sentence; epistemic modality is centered on the whole predication. Obligation is prospective, while possibility may involve looking backward or forward in time. The set of modal verbs express different degrees of obligation and different degrees of possibility or probability. Occurrence of *not* with a modal verb may negate the modal verb itself or the content of the following proposition.

Suggested reading

Leech (1987) is the best succinct account of English modal verbs. Joos (1964) and Palmer (1988) offer more extensive treatments. Palmer (1986) treats modality in language generally. A shorter, valuable exposition of modality in general is Frawley (1992), Chapter 9.

Notes on the text

• Section **11.3** is a discussion of modality as it is expressed in English, with emphasis on modal verbs. It is by no means a complete account of modal verbs – among other omissions, nothing is said here about *shall*. We should distinguish between the syntactic category of **auxiliary verbs** and the semantic category of **modal verbs** in English. The two overlap but are not identical. An auxiliary verb can occur before another verb, is negated by *not* immediately following, with which it may form a contraction, and can occur before its subject, as in a question. Thus the following illustrate auxiliary verbs which are not modal verbs.

She *is*n't playing, *is* she?
They *have*n't gone, *have* they?
You *do*n't believe me, *do* you?

A verb which is not an auxiliary requires the insertion of the auxiliary *do* for negation and question-formation.

He *plays*. He doesn't *play*, does he?

The verbs *must, may, might, can, could, shall, should, will* and *would* are auxiliary verbs because they follow the syntactic criteria regarding negation and inversion with the subject. They are modal verbs because they express necessity and/or possibility – semantic criteria – though, as indicated above, some uses of *will* and *would* are not truly modal.

The verbs *have to, ought to* and *need (to)* are modal verbs. The first of these is not an auxiliary verb in the usage of most speakers of English today (*We don't have to go, Do we have to go?*, for instance, rather than *We haven't to go, Have we to go?*). The syntactic status of the other two verbs is marginal. *We oughtn't to go* and *Ought we to go?* are typical of constructions used by some speakers but simply avoided by others; neither **We don't ought* nor **Do we ought?* is possible. Need follows the criteria for auxiliary verbs (*We needn't go, Need we go?*) or for non-auxiliaries (*We don't need to go, Do we need to go?*). There is no semantic difference.

A variety of predicates

This chapter is an examination of three groups of predicates (mostly verbs, but some adjectives as well). The first, rather amorphous group we call **attitudinal predicates**; these express mental states that people have about their past experiences and possible future ones and general feelings about likes, dislikes and preferences. The second group expresses actions that cause something to be done, enables someone to act, or prevents someone from acting. The third group of predicates are perceptual ones, expressing the experiences that we have through sight, hearing, taste, smell and feeling.

12.1 Attitudinal predicates

We frequently use language to talk about the way human beings think about other humans, various physical phenomena, and the states and activities they observe and the states and activities they experience, or have experienced, or expect to experience. These mental processes we call attitudes, and here we'll try to explore some of the predicates that express different attitudes. An **attitudinal predicate** is a verb or adjective that expresses the feelings of the subject: *I hate this music*; *I'm fond of swimming*

We start with prospective attitudes, mental states regarding what may come to be. In the first six types (A–F) the subject of the sentences is the Affected and what affects is a specific predication, a potential act.

A Intent regarding one's own possible performance

1   Jenkins intends to withdraw from the race.
     verbs: aim, mean, intend

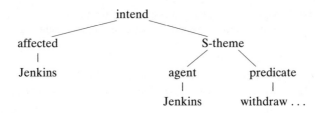

Aspect: prospective

B Mental rehearsing of possible performance

2   Jenkins considered withdrawing from the race.
    verbs: consider, contemplate

Note that the role structure is the same as that for sentence 1.

C Conclusion regarding possible performance

3   Jenkins decided to withdraw from the race.
    verbs: decide, determine
          choose, elect
          prefer

Again, the role structure is the same as 1.

D Getting ready for performance

4a   Jenkins planned to withdraw from the race.
4b   Jenkins planned for his supporters to withdraw his name.
     verbs: arrange, plan, prepare

(*Plan* is more precise than *arrange*; *prepare* signifies physical activity, which the others do not necessarily indicate.) The role structure is again the same except that the agent in the included clause need not be the same as the agent of the main clause.

E Proceeding to perform

5a   We tried to start the motor (but we couldn't).

5b   We tried running the motor for a while.
       verbs: attempt, endeavor, seek, strive, try, undertake, venture

Role structure: same as 1.

Only *try* and *attempt* occur in both structures, with the infinitive clause or the gerund clause; the other verbs occur only with the infinitive. For *try* and *attempt* the gerund, but not the infinitive, suggests some degree of success, as Sentences 5a and 5b illustrate (Dixon 1992: 179–82).

F Readiness for a possible act or event

6a   I'm afraid to look at my test marks.
6b   I dread looking at my test marks.
      predicates:
(a)   aspire, desire, hope, long, want, wish, yearn
      expect
      disposed, eager, impatient, inclined, keen, ready, willing
      afraid, dread, fear
      disinclined, reluctant
      anxious
(b)   feel-like
      anticipate
      dread, fear

The distinction between groups (a) and (b) is syntactic; the former are followed by an infinitive clause, the latter by a gerund clause – *dread* and *fear* belonging to both groups. There seems to be no semantic difference.

The next group of attitudinal predicates has to do with someone else's input or contribution to a potential act.

G Attitude regarding another's input

7   I'm counting on you to help us.
     verbs: count-on, depend-on, rely-on, trust

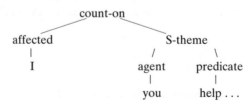

If a prospective verb occurs in the present tense ("Jenkins intends to withdraw from the race," "I'm afraid to look at my test marks"), what presupposition does the sentence have? If the verb is past tense, is there a presupposition?

Next we take up a group of attitudes about what has happened.

H Retrospective attitudes

8   I regret wasting time on that lecture.
     verbs: miss   regret   resent

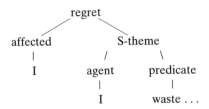

Aspect: retrospective
     This is a factive predicate.

I Predicates of liking and disliking

These are neutral in aspect and are accompanied by generic predications.

9   I like swimming.
     verbs:
     positive: like love (infinitive, gerund)
                    enjoy relish (gerund)
     negative: dislike detest hate loathe (infinitive, gerund)
                    afraid reluctant unwilling (infinitive)
     comparative: prefer (infinitive, gerund) favor (gerund)

Role structure: same as 8. Aspect: neutral

J Attitudinal predicates

We shall call this next group 'evaluation of others.'

10   I admire you for your courage,
11   but I pity you for your stubbornness.
      verbs:
      positive: admire approve-of cherish honor prize respect value
      negative: pity resent scorn

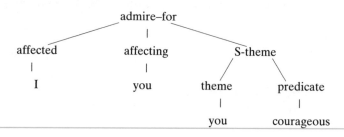

Aspect: neutral

Table 12.1 recapitulates the ten kinds of attitudinal predicates just surveyed.

TABLE 12.1 Attitudinal predicates

Prospective (regarding future action)

A Intent	aim, intend
B Mental rehearsing	consider, contemplate
C Decision	choose, decide
D Preparation	plan, prepare
E Attempt	attempt, try
F Reliance on another	count on, depend on
G Desire or lack of desire	afraid, want

Retrospective (regarding past action)

H Mental review	regret, resent

Aspect-neutral

I Liking and disliking	enjoy, hate
J Evaluation	admire, pity

12.2 Enabling and preventing

An **enabling predicate** is a verb or adjective which tells that the following predication is made possible: *We allowed the car to pass.* A **preventing predicate** is a verb which states that an agent causes the non-occurrence of the predication that follows: *I kept the ball from rolling away.*

Some predicates, followed by an infinitive clause, express the fact that one person makes it possible for another person or persons to do something. Stated another way, Person$_1$, with power or knowledge, causes Person$_2$ to have power or knowledge to perform an act.

Three types of such predicates can be recognized.

A Enabling by use of authority:

12   Henry's teacher allowed him to come late to class.
      verbs: allow authorize permit

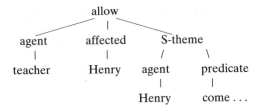

B Enabling by effort or action:

13   Henry helped his teacher (to) distribute books.
      verbs: assist help

The role structure is the same as for 12, as are the ones below.

C Enabling by instruction:

14   Henry taught his dog to roll over and play dead.
      verbs: instruct teach train

The opposite of enabling is preventing, 'disenabling.' Here again three types can be recognized. Person$_1$ acts so that Person$_2$ does not act as Person$_2$ wants to act.

A Preventing by use of authority:

15   Henry's teacher forbade him to leave the room.
      verbs: forbid prohibit

B Preventing through effort:

16 Henry's teacher kept him from leaving the room.
    verbs: bar block curb deter hinder keep
    prevent restrain stop turn-away (*from* + gerund clause)

C Preventing through speech:

17 Henry's teacher discouraged him from entering the contest.
    verbs: discourage inhibit (*from* + gerund clause)

One form of prevention, viewed in a different way, is protection. Prevention and protection may be different aspects of the same action: We prevent the dog from trampling on the flower bed. We protect the flower bed from the dog/ We protect the flower bed from being trampled on (by the dog).

18 The regiment defended the fort from attack.

Agent₁ acts so that Agent₂ cannot affect Theme.

conceal defend guard hide protect safeguard save shelter
shield

The affecting, in this case, is a potential attack, and that may be viewed as a predication: Somebody attacks/will attack/may attack the fort.

Finally, we may consider that one form of 'disenabling' is what we do to ourselves. The verbs in the foregoing group can be used reflexively, as in:

19 The regiment defended itself from attack.

Some verbs have a reflexive meaning without requiring a reflexive pronoun.

20   Sharon is abstaining from drinking, these days.
21   She's refraining from boasting about it, however.

Here a person acts so as not to perform the action denoted by the
gerund clause.

Verbs: abstain-from avoid evade refrain-from shrink-from
shy-away-from

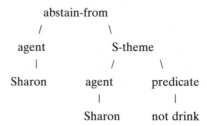

```
                    abstain-from
                   /            \
               agent           S-theme
                 |             /      \
              Sharon       agent     predicate
                             |           |
                          Sharon      not drink
```

The enabling/preventing predicates are summarized in Table 12.2.

TABLE 12.2 Predicates of enabling and preventing

Enabling
A by authority   allow, permit
B by effort   assist, help
C by instruction   teach, train

Preventing
D by authority   forbid, prohibit
E by effort   deter, keep
F by use of language   discourage, dissuade
G protecting   defend, protect
H self-preventing   abstain, refrain

PRACTICE 12.2

Show the role structures of these sentences:

(a)   Fatima expects Ahmed to help her.
(b)   Fatima convinces Ahmed to help her.
(c)   Leila prevented Ahmed from helping Fatima.

12.3 Perceptual predicates

Perceptual verbs, also called 'sensory verbs,' express the sensations that we receive from outside stimuli through our five senses. Most of the basic English ones are illustrated in these fifteen key sentences (Viberg 1983: 123–6).

22a   We saw some penguins.
22b   We looked at the penguins (with considerable interest).
22c   The penguins looked strange (to us).
23a   Alice heard a funny song.
23b   Alice listened (intently) to the song.
23c   The song sounded awful (to Alice).
24a   Ted tasted onion in the soup.
24b   Ted tasted the soup (cautiously).
24c   The soup tasted good (to Ted).
25a   I felt a sharp pain.
25b   I felt the table top (carefully).
25c   The table felt rough (to me).
26a   Mama smelled smoke.
26b   Mama smelled the soup (suspiciously).
26c   The soup smelled rather odd (to Mama).

Our perceptions are reactions to stimuli: reflected light strikes our retinas, vibrations impinge on our eardrums, other sensations affect the nerves in our tongue, skin or nose. The five groups of sentences are about visual, auditory, gustatory, tactile and olfactory experiences, respectively. In the (a) sentences here (22a–26a) the verb expresses the particular sense through which the experience comes; the subject of the verb names the affected, the animate being affected by a stimulus, and the object of the verb names the stimulus that affects. Sentences 22a–26a have the same role structure, shown here for the first two sentences.

affected	predicate	affecting
|	|	|
we	see	penguins
Alice	hear	song

While the acts of seeing, hearing, tasting, feeling and smelling do not require conscious effort, we often do make a conscious effort. The (b) sentences express an animate being's dynamic involvement in the experience. The subject of these verbs names an entity that is both agent and affected. English has separate verbs to express the visual and auditory efforts, *look-at* and *listen-to*, respectively, but *taste*, *feel* and *smell* do double duty for effortless and for intentional sensations. (Consequently, some readers may need a little while to recognize the distinction. Note that a manner adverbial can occur with the (b) sentences but not with the (a) sentences. *Alice listened intently to the song*, *Ted tasted the soup cautiously*, but not **Alice heard a song intently*, **Ted tasted onion in the soup cautiously*.)

The role structure of 22b–26b can be represented this way, illustrating with just 22b and 23b.

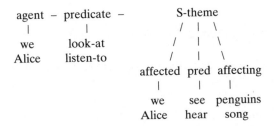

The (b) sentences are then the 'involved' equivalents of the (a) sentences. Where the (a) sentences tell only of reception of stimuli, voluntary or involuntary, the (b) sentences indicate a process of conscious attention to stimuli.

We can look at something for an instant or for a long time, so Sentence 22b can be expanded with various expressions of duration, e.g.:

We looked at the penguins for a second/for 30 minutes.

The verbs *glance-at* and *watch* are different:

22d   We glanced at the penguins for a second/for 30 minutes.
22e   We watched the penguins for 30 minutes/? for a second.

So *glance-at* is momentary, and when it occurs with an expression of duration ('for 30 minutes'), the only interpretation is that the act was repeated – over and over – during that length of time. *Watch* is durative, and *look-at* is neutral in aspect. *Listen-to* is like *look-at*; there are no corresponding momentary or durative verbs for auditory experiences.

There are two more perceptual verbs to consider before we

discuss sentences 22c–26c: *notice* and *observe*. These two verbs are noncommittal with respect to the sense of perception. Which of the five senses would you take to be most likely when one of these verbs is used?

27   We noticed/observed the music/the soup/the table top/the smoke.

How do *notice* and *observe* differ in aspect?

PRACTICE 12.3

Consider the complex predicate *catch sight of*, as in

Suddenly we caught sight of a woodpecker on the branch of a pine tree in front of us.

How does *catch sight of* differ from *see*? Is there an analogous predicate corresponding to *hear*? to *feel*? *smell*? *taste*?

Sentence 22c, *The penguins looked strange to us*, contains a predication about penguins, as it affects "us." Whereas *We saw some penguins* states that we experienced a physical response to an outside stimulus, 22c says that we had an attitudinal reaction to the stimulus. Sentences 23c–26c contain similar predications, telling how different stimuli affect some animate being – and the affected being does not have to be expressed.

```
            S-theme    –   predicate   –   (affected)
            /      \            |               |
        theme      pred       look             us
          |         |         sound           Alice
      penguins    strange
        song      funny
```

Two other verbs, *seem* and *appear*, also express sensory impressions. They are not related to any specific sensory field, but most of us would probably connect them to visual experiences first.

All these English verbs can be charted this way:

A	b	B b'	b''	C
see	look at	glance at	watch	look
hear		listen to		sound
		taste		
		feel		
		smell		
notice		observe		seem, appear

Where there is more than one verb on a line, the verb in Column A indicates the mere perception of a stimulus, the verb in Column B expresses conscious involvement in the perceptual act, and the verb in Column C indicates an impression by the perceiver. For visual experiences English distinguishes neutral (b), momentary (b') and durative (b'') aspects; no such distinctions are expressed for auditory, gustatory, tactile or olfactory sensations. The sixth line has verbs which are not specifically tied to any of the five senses.

28a I often see Mr Haynes leave home in a big rush.
28b I see him leaving now.
29a The campers heard someone approach their tent.
29b The campers heard someone approaching their tent.
30a A night watchman observed a strange figure run out of the warehouse.
30b A night watchman observed a strange figure running out of the warehouse.

We can perceive some entity, and we can also perceive some event. In English the event is expressed as an infinitive clause, without *to*, (sentences 28a, 29a, 30a) or as a gerund clause (sentences 28b, 29b, 30b). Whether expressed by an infinitive or a gerund clause, the event perceived is, at least roughly, simultaneous with the perception. The difference between gerund clause and infinitive clause is clear with perceptual verbs (but not necessarily with other kinds of verbs). The gerund clause emphasizes the duration of what is perceived (though there is no necessary difference in the event perceived):

31 We watched the moon coming up/We watched the moon come up.
32 I felt a bug running across my back/ I felt a bug run across my back.

The difference is especially clear when the verb of the clause indicates a repeatable act:

33 I saw a light flash/I saw a light flashing.
34 I heard a dog bark/I heard a dog barking.

The infinitive clause can be interpreted as information that the light flashed just once and there was a single bark from the dog; the gerund clause tells of repetitive events. When a predicate expresses a change of status, the infinitive clause expresses that the change has occurred while the gerund indicates that the change is in progress:

35a I saw her drown.
35b I saw her drowning (but I rescued her). (Kirsner and Thompson 1976: 215)

Only a dynamic verb can occur in a gerund or infinitive clause. We can say *I saw him wash(ing) a car*, but not **I saw him own(ing) a car*.

36 Hector felt that the decision was a mistake.
37 I've heard that you're going to France next month.
38 Graciela saw that her words were having no effect.

Some of our perceptual verbs can be followed by a full clause, as in sentences 36–38. When a verb is followed by a full clause, it indicates cognition – mental reaction – more than sensory reaction to a stimulus. Note that in such sentences the person affected – named by the subject – is not affected by the perception of an entity nor of a simultaneous event but by a mental reaction to what has been observed (Kirsner and Thompson 1976: 205–8).

The possible structures are indicated below:

	full	*gerund*	*infinitive*
feel hear see	+	+	+
notice observe	+	+	+
listen-to look-at watch		+	+
perceive	+	+	
smell taste		+	

This table suggests another division: *listen-to, look-at, watch, smell* and *taste* are purely sensory; *feel, hear, see, notice, observe* and *perceive* involve mental activity or reaction.

The preposition *for* following perceptual verbs introduces a goal not yet reached.

39 We looked for tools.

40   We listened for footsteps.
41   We tasted the food for flavor.
42   We felt the surface for lumps /I felt for the wall.
43   We smelled the food for aroma /We smelled [sniffed] for smoke.

Summary

Attitudinal predicates have the structure of affected and an S-theme. They express the way some situation or event, actual or potential, indicated in the S-theme, impinges on some entity, the affected. The aspect may be prospective, retrospective or neutral. Attitudinal predicates are further distinguished by favorable or unfavorable reactions to the event or situation.

Enabling and preventing generally require an agent who enables or prevents, an entity affected by this action, and an event (S-theme) that is made possible or impossible.

Perceptual predicates express our intake of knowledge through the five senses. The person who sees, hears, etc., is affected, the source of the stimulus affects. There may be a lexical difference between merely being affected (e.g. *see*) and being actively involved in the perception (*look at*). Verbs differ in expressing momentary or enduring perception. English – and perhaps not just English – makes more distinctions regarding vision than hearing, and more about hearing than feeling, tasting, or smelling.

Suggested reading

The predicates treated here as 'attitudinal' overlap with the verbs which, in a different framework, Dixon 1991 treats under the heading 'Primary B verb types,' (124–67). Our predicates of enabling and preventing are similar to Dixon's 'Secondary C types' (192–208).

Readers can find treatments of these and other predicate types in Talmy (1975) and (1985). Jackendoff (1990) has more elaborate analyses of certain argument structures; the theoretical foundations of his work are best expressed in Jackendoff (1985). Ravin (1990) is valuable for exploration of event structures within a time frame.

Note on the text

- The treatment of perceptual verbs here has been borrowed from Kirsner and Thompson (1976) and especially from Viberg (1983).

The semantics of morphological relations

The adjective *long*, the noun *length* and the verb *lengthen* are partly alike and partly different in form (the way they sound and the way they are written) and partly alike and partly different in meaning. If we take *long* as the one that has the simplest form, we can say that the noun and the verb are derived from the adjective by certain processes. The noun *length* is derived from the adjective *long* by the addition of *-th* and a change, or mutation, of *o* to *e*. The verb *lengthen* is formed by another addition, namely *-en*. These formal processes are fairly easy to describe. Semantic relations are more subtle. The noun *length* is an abstract term, roughly 'the amount or extent by which something is considered long' (the length of a room, the length of a day) or a concrete term for a piece of something that is measured linearly (a length of rope). The verb *lengthen* is approximately 'to make longer' (to lengthen a skirt) or 'to become longer' ("Days lengthen after the vernal equinox"). In form the verb *lengthen* seems to be derived from the noun *length*, but when we consider meanings, the sense of *lengthen* is derived directly from that of the adjective *long*.

The words *strong-strength-strengthen* show the same formal relationships as *long-length-lengthen* and similar semantic relationships. However, in English there is generally no regular correspondence between formal processes of derivation and the semantic relationships that result from these processes; compare, for example, the adjective-noun-verb sets *deep/depth/deepen*, *beautiful/beauty/beautify* and *silent/silence/silence*; for the adjective *happy* there is a noun *happiness* but no formally related verb that means 'to make or become happy.' The remainder of this chapter explores, first, the formal ways of derivation and then, at greater length, the semantic relations that exist when verbs are derived from nouns, nouns from adjectives, adjectives from verbs, and so on.

13.1 Formal processes of derivation

There are four different types of derivational relationship between words: addition, mutation, conversion and subtraction.

addition: Some lexemes are formed by combining morphemes: those like *armchair* and *busybody*, which consist entirely of free morphemes; words like *violinist*, *disarm* and *blue-eyed*, which have partly free and partly bound morphemes; and the type represented by *astronaut* and *biology*, composed entirely of bound morphemes.

mutation: The words *proud* and *pride* are semantically related and are related formally as well, but it is impossible to say that one is formed by adding something to the other. Rather, derivation is accomplished here by a change of vowel; in other pairs of words the change may be in consonants, as in *believe* and *belief*; or both vowel and consonant, as with *choose* and *choice*; or by change of stress: e.g. verbs *extráct*, *insúlt*, *progréss* in contrast to nouns *éxtract*, *ínsult*, *prógress*.

conversion or **zero change**: This is the simple change of a word of one class to a word of another class with no formal alteration. Thus *clean*, *dry* and *equal* are adjectives and also verbs; the relation of the adjective *clean* to the verb *clean* is the same as that of the adjective *long* to the verb *lengthen*. *Fan*, *grasp* and *hammer* are verbs and also nouns; *capital*, *initial* and *periodical* are nouns and adjectives.

subtraction (or **reduction**): By removing parts of certain lexemes new lexemes are formed. One kind of shortening is called an **acronym**; another is called a **clipping**. An acronym is a word derived from the written form of a construction; a construction is a sequence of words that together have a meaning. Some acronyms are pronounced as a sequence of letters: *UK* for 'United Kingdom,' *USA* for 'United States of America.' In other acronyms the letters combine to produce something pronounceable: *AIDS* for 'Acquired Immune Deficiency Syndrome,' *UNESCO* for 'United Nations Educational, Scientific, and Cultural Organization.' As these examples show, the acronym is typically but not always formed from the first letter of each written word. The acronym may be formed from parts of a single word: *ID* for *identification*, *TB* for *tuberculosis*, *TV* for *television*; or it may include more than initial letters: *Nabisco* (*Na*tional *Bis*cuit *Co*mpany), *Sunoco* (*Sun O*il *Co*mpany). With a few exceptions, acronyms are essentially names (Kreidler 1979).

Another process applied to existing words is clipping, the use of part of a word to stand for the whole word. *Laboratory* is abbreviated to *lab*, *telephone* to *phone*, *refrigerator* to *fridge*. Sometimes a vowel is added when other material is cut away, as in *Chevy* for *Chevrolet*, *divvy* for *dividend*, *ammo* for *ammunition*. In these examples and many others we see only new, shorter ways of designating what was previously designated by a longer term, but sometimes clipped forms come to have meanings that are distinct from the original sources. The part of speech may change (a kind of conversion): *divvy*, just cited, is used as a verb whereas *dividend* is a noun. Without a change in part of speech the clipped form may have a connotation different from the source word: *hankie*, *undies*, *nightie* are 'cuter' than *handkerchief*, *underwear*, *nightgown*, respectively.

When one word is formed by adding to another, like *paint-er*, or by subtracting from another, as in the case of *prep* from *preparation*, the direction of derivation is clear. But the direction is not clear when the process is mutation or conversion. In some cases there may be a problem in deciding what is derived from what: which comes first, the noun *hammer* or the verb *to hammer*, the noun *kiss* or the verb *to kiss*? We look for ways to decide such questions consistently. In general, here, we go from the concrete to the abstract. The noun *hammer* names a concrete object, the verb *hammer* means to use that object; we say that the verb is derived from the noun. On the other hand, the verb *kiss* names a physical, observable action; the noun *kiss* is the result of the action; we say that the noun is derived from the verb. In numerous instances, however, we may have to be arbitrary in saying which is the primary or basic word and which is the derived word.

13.2 Semantic processes in derivation

Determining in which direction the derivation goes is part of a bigger, more important matter, describing the meanings that are added when a verb becomes a noun, a noun becomes an adjective, an adjective becomes a verb. In general we can recognize the following facts.

Nouns represent entities, verbs represent activities or states, and adjectives represent qualities or characteristics. Thus when a verb is converted to a noun, the noun may refer to a concrete entity – a person, object or place associated with what the verb signifies. Or the noun may be a way of treating the activity or status as an entity, a 'thing,' that can be quantified. In the simple sentence *He kicked it*, with a verb *kick*, there is no indication of how many times he kicked it; the information can be added to the sentence, but not to the verb itself. (Conceivably there could be a verb that meant to make one contact with the foot, another to mean between two and ten such contacts, another to mean more than ten – but this would be quite different from what actually exists in the semantic system of English. Quantity is not a semantic feature of verbs.) In contrast, if we use the count noun *kick* to fill this blank, *He gave it _____*, we are forced to choose *a kick* or *a couple of kicks*, *several kicks*, or some other expression that, precisely or loosely, indicates the number. The verb *kick* cannot be quantified; the noun *kick* must be. Similarly, from adjectives like *hard* and *stingy* nouns *hardness* and *stinginess* can be formed; the adjectives can be preceded by little words, **qualifiers**, that intensify or lessen the meanings they convey (*very hard*, *rather stingy*); the nouns cannot be modified this way. Most such nouns are abstractions – *heat*, *stinginess*, for example – a way of reifying the qualities expressed by *hot* and *stingy*, treating them as 'things.'

When a verb is derived from a noun, an entity becomes a predicate – an activity or status – losing its quantifiable nature but becoming part of a tense–aspect system. Whatever *soldier*, for instance, might mean as a verb, it yields the possibilities of *soldiered*, *is soldiering*, *would have been soldiering*, and so on. Similarly, when an adjective like *rich* is converted to a verb *enrich*, there is no longer the possibility of quantifying modifiers like *very*, *somewhat*, or *too* associated with the quality 'rich'; instead, temporal modification is required. Furthermore, the adjective, a stative predicate, is converted to a causative predicate.

A noun or verb converted to an adjective gives a word that names a quality associated with some entity (e.g. *milky*) or act (e.g. *congratulatory*). Many such adjectives, however, are simply linguistic conversions: an adjective like *periodic* does not really mean something different from *period*; it has only a different use in sentences.

13.3 Verbs formed from nouns

Verbs derived from nouns fall into several fairly well defined types. We present a classification with a few illustrations of each type and then discuss the classes with more examples. Here 'N' stands for the noun from which the verb 'V' is derived and 'X' means the object of the verb, if there is one.

13.3.1 Transfer meanings

1a   Roger painted the wall.

The noun *paint* names an entity, a concrete substance. The verb phrase *paint the wall* can be paraphrased as 'put paint on the wall,' 'apply paint to the wall,' 'provide the wall with paint,' or 'cause paint to be on the wall,' that is, cause the inception of a new location. The verb denotes the transfer of an entity named by the underlying noun, *paint* and the object of the verb, *the wall*, is a location, the goal of the transfer. *Roger* names the agent who causes the new location.

We might represent the thematic structure this way:

$$
\begin{array}{ccc}
 & \text{verb} & \\
 & \uparrow & \\
\text{agent} - \text{theme} - & \text{goal} \\
| & | & | \\
\text{Roger} & \text{paint} & \text{wall}
\end{array}
$$

But the notion of 'goal' is, more explicitly, a combination of causation plus location. So a more explicit representation of 1a would be this:

$$
\begin{array}{ccc}
\text{agent} & - & \text{predicate} \\
| & / & \quad \backslash \\
\text{Roger} & \text{inceptive} & \text{S-theme} \\
 & \text{cause} & / \quad \backslash \\
 & & \text{theme} \quad \text{place} \\
 & & | \qquad | \\
 & & \text{paint} \quad \text{wall}
\end{array}
$$

Other such verbs are: *water* (the flowers), *oil* (a hinge), *comfort* (a friend) – in the last example the underlying noun is abstract rather than concrete.

1b   Susan peeled an apple.

The underlying noun *peel* names a concrete entity and the verb phrase is equivalent to 'remove the peel from an apple,' 'separate the peel from an apple,' 'affect an apple by removal of the peel.' The verb *peel* denotes transfer and its object, *an apple*, names a sort of location, the source of transfer. Again we can show this in two ways:

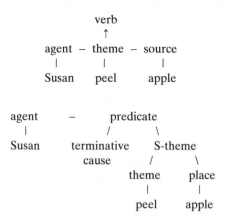

Similar verbs are *dust* (the furniture), *milk* (a cow), *skin* (a rabbit).

1c   We're bottling wine.

The verb phrase *bottling wine* is equivalent to 'putting wine in bottles,' 'causing wine to be in bottles.' Like 1a, this sentence expresses the causing of a new location, but in 1c it is the place, not the object, that is converted to a verb. The underlying noun *bottle* names an object that can also be a container, a location for its contents; the verb *bottle* names the goal of transfer, and the entity that is transferred is indicated by the object of the verb, *wine*. The noun *bottle* can be singular or plural, but of course the verb has no such variation. To save space we give only the simpler thematic description.

```
                verb
                 ↑
    agent  –  theme  –  goal
      |         |        |
      we       wine    bottle(s)
```

Other goal-transfer verbs are: *shelve* (the provisions), *imprison* (criminals).

1d   They're mining coal.

The verb phrase *mining coal* is roughly equivalent to 'removing coal from a mine.' Like 1b, 1d is about causing the termination of a location, but here the source becomes a verb rather than the theme. The noun *mine* names the source of transfer, the verb *mine* designates the transfer, and *coal*, the object of the verb, tells the entity transferred. A simple representation of thematic structure:

$$
\begin{array}{ccc}
 & & \text{verb} \\
 & & \uparrow \\
\text{agent} - & \text{theme} - & \text{source} \\
| & | & | \\
\text{they} & \text{coal} & \text{mine}
\end{array}
$$

Other examples of this type seem to be rare.

   To recapitulate, transfer verbs, with their objects, tell about the movement of some thing to a goal or from a source – that is, causing the inception of a new location or the termination of a previous one. The noun from which the verb is derived may name the thing moved, the new location (goal), or the previous one (source). (A table appears on page 279.)

PRACTICE 13.1

Verbs that designate the removal of an object from a location are infrequent, but verbs which tell about causation of a new location are fairly common, either derived from the theme, like *paint*, or from the goal, like *bottle*. Sort out the verb phrases below; which verbs are like *paint* and which like *bottle*? Draw a thematic structure tree for one phrase of each type.

(a)   box the provisions
(b)   brand cattle
(c)   grease the wheel
(d)   land a fish

(e)   market a new product
(f)   powder one's face
(g)   saddle a horse
(h)   salt the meat
(i)   seat a spectator
(j)   splint a broken arm
(k)   thread a needle
(l)   wax the skis

13.3.2 Effective meanings

Some nouns name a status. Verbs derived from such nouns express causation, the inception of that status.

2a   The accident crippled my friend.

This sentence can be paraphrased as 'The accident made my friend a cripple, caused him to be/become a cripple.' A shorter and a longer display of the thematic structure is as follows:

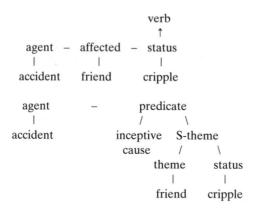

Similar verb phrases are *group the papers, cash a check*. Other verbs:

arch branch cake curve halve parade peak picture slice

2b   She babies her husband. (makes him [like] a baby)

This sentence tells of a pseudo-effect. To baby someone is to treat the person like a baby, give the person a status similar to that of a baby. The thematic structure is the same as in 2a. Similar verb phrases are *scrap the papers, befriend a stranger*.

Some nouns that name a status are converted to verbs that have a meaning something like 'cause oneself to have the status (with regard to another entity).' Two examples:

2c-i   Eddy is always clowning.
2c-ii Mr and Mrs Blake chaperoned the party.

Compare 2c-i with the sentence "Eddy is a clown," which links a theme, *Eddy*, and a status, *clown*. Sentence 2c-i tells us that Eddy takes on this status, makes himself (like) a clown. Similarly, 2c-ii says that the Blakes become or make themselves chaperons with respect to a party.

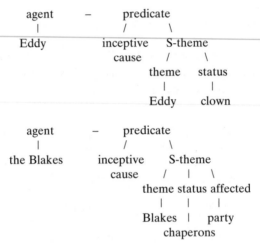

Similar to 2c-i: *The road branches, Flowers blossom, The stream flooded, The plot boomerangs*. Like 2c-ii: *Frieda cooked a meal, Paddy pilots a plane* and similar sentences with *guide the expedition, head the department, judge a case, patrol the area, referee a game*.

Some nouns name an entity and the corresponding verbs can be interpreted as meaning 'produce [the entity], cause [the entity] to exist.'

2d-i   Ruth gardens.
2d-ii This tree shades the garden.

If we interpret the proposition embodied in 2d-i as something like 'Ruth creates/produces/makes a garden' and 2d-ii as 'The tree produces shade with reference to the garden,' the structures are:

```
                        verb
                         ↑
           agent  –  effect  –  (affected)
             |         |
     (i)    Ruth     garden         |
     (ii)   tree     shade        garden
```

If we go a step farther and consider the meanings to be "Ruth causes a garden to exist," "The tree causes shade to exist and affect the garden" we have:

```
           agent      –      predicate
             |             /         \
     (i)    Ruth        cause        effect
                                       |
                                     garden
           agent      –      predicate
             |             /     |     \
     (ii)   tree        cause  effect (affected)
                                 |        |
                               shade    garden
```

Similar verbs:

blossom copy crowd encircle knot ruin shame

13.3.3 Instrumental meanings

3a   Harry locked the door.

The noun *lock* names a kind of useful object or instrument; a verb derived from such a noun indicates the use of that object with respect to some entity named by the object of the verb. Thus *lock the door* means 'use the lock with respect to the door,' 'affect the door by means of the lock.'

```
                        verb
                         ↑
           agent  –  affected  –  means
             |          |          |
           Harry       door       lock
```

277

Similar verbs appear in such phrases as *button a coat*, *comb and brush one's hair*, *hammer a nail*, and so on. To bring out more clearly the notion of causation – 'Harry caused the door to be affected by the lock' – the structure is:

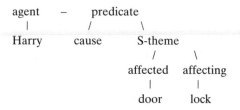

Similar verbs:

> brake button comb drain flag hook lock nail pin
> pipe plow sponge whip whistle

3b   Lucy penned a note.

The noun *pen* names a useful object, and the verb *pen* means 'use N to produce, effect, cause X' or 'effect X by-means-of N.'

```
                                          verb
                                           ↑
              agent   –   effect   –    means
                |           |             |
              Lucy        note          pen
```

The type does not seem to be common. Perhaps *voice* (an opinion) is another example.

13.3.4 Vehicular meanings (instrument + transfer)

A special kind of instrument is a vehicle, a means for going and coming and for moving some entity from one place to another.

4a   Sandra is skating from here to the corner.
4b   The company is trucking ore from the mine to the factory.

The verb *skate* is more or less equivalent to 'move (oneself) on skates,' and *truck* can mean 'move (something) by truck.' Other verbs that are derived from nouns which name instruments of moving are *bicycle, bus, canoe, parachute, ski*. The sentences express transfer, causing an entity (Sandra, ore) to change from one location to another.

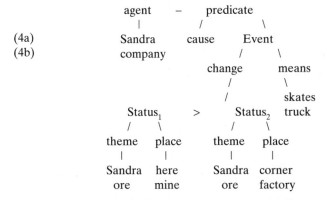

(4a)
(4b)

The various types of verbs derived from nouns are recapitulated in Table 13.1.

TABLE 13.1 Classification of verbs derived from nouns

		Verb names	*Object names*
1	*Transfer*		
(a)	paint	the thing transferred	the goal
(b)	peel	the thing transferred	the source
(c)	bottle	the goal	the thing transferred
(d)	mine	the source	the thing transferred
2	*Effect*		
(a)	cripple	a status effect	the entity affected
(b)	baby	a pseudo-effect	the entity affected
(c-i)	clown	an assumed role status	–
(c-ii)	chaperon	" "	the entity affected
(d-i)	garden	the thing produced	–
(d-ii)	shade	" "	the entity affected
3	*Means*		
(a)	lock	the instrument	the affected
(b)	pen	the instrument	the effect
4	*Vehicle*		
(a)	skate	the vehicle	(subject moves self)
(b)	truck	the vehicle	the thing moved

A word may fit more than one category because it has more than one sense. To *bone* means 'to stiffen by inserting bone' (1-a) and also 'to remove bones from' (1-b); similarly, to *dust* is 'to apply dust to' (1-a) and 'to remove dust from' (1-b).

But a word may fit more than one of the categories because there is more than one way of considering the meaning. To *hammer a nail* or to *pump water* mean using the objects named (1-a), or they may mean to do something as if using [a hammer, a pump]: 'to hammer with a rock.'

PRACTICE 13.2

Creating a verb from a noun by conversion – that is, without any formal change – is a productive process that speakers can use with a fair degree of freedom. We might, for instance say "We *jeeped* into town" or "She *scissored* the pattern from the catalogue" and be understood. What might the following mean if used as verbs?

toboggan
window
cupboard
thorn
plumber

13.4 Verbs from adjectives

5a   Ella dried the dishes.
5b   The towels dried (in the sun).
5c   The highway department is widening the road.
5d   The path widens in one place (and narrows in another).

Adjectives are typically stative predicates: *The dishes/towels are dry*. Verbs derived from adjectives are either causative, as in 5a ('Ella caused the dishes to be/become dry'), or inchoative, as in 5b ('The towels became dry'). Both sentences report the inception of a status named by the adjective. 5a has an agent, 5b does not. For some adjectives – *dry* and *sterile* are examples – the causative verb, *dry* or *sterilize*, means 'make, cause to be [dry, sterile],' 'affect X so that it becomes [dry, sterile].' For other adjectives, such as *wide* and *narrow*, the derived verbs, *widen* and *narrow* in these examples, mean 'make [wide]r,' 'cause to become more [narrow].' The verbs *dry*, *widen* and *narrow* are also inchoative 'become dry, become wider, more narrow': We widen the road here and narrow it there; the road widens in one place and narrows in another.

Thus:

Verb	Effect of verb
dry (intr.)	subject attains quality
dry (tr.)	object attains quality
widen (intr.)	subject increases quality
widen (tr.)	object increases quality

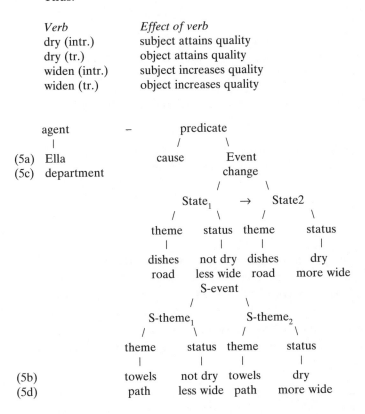

In English there are causative verbs which are also inchoative, like *dry* ('make dry' and 'become dry') and causative verbs that are not usually inchoative, like *sterilize* ('make sterile' but not 'become sterile'). There are no verbs that are inchoative but not causative. Examples of causative verbs follow. Those marked '(i)' also have a common inchoative use, but there is no rigid separation between inchoative and non-inchoative.

THE SEMANTICS OF MORPHOLOGICAL RELATIONS

blacken broaden (i) cheapen deepen (i) redden (i) sadden sharpen
stiffen (i) widen (i) – lengthen (i) strengthen (i)
purify simplify – beautify
enrich
fertilize modernize sterilize
cleanse
fill (i) heat (i)

The largest group is composed of verbs that are identical with the adjectives:

brown cool (i) clean (i) clear (i) complete dirty dry (i)
free hollow narrow (i) open (i) parallel (i) quiet ready
round slim (i) slow (i) smooth thin (i) warm (i) wet yellow (i)

A number of such causative (inchoative) verbs add a particle. Examples:

clear away (i); calm down (i) quiet down (i); cool off (i)
dry off (i); dry out (i) empty out (i) thin out (i)

PRACTICE 13.3

The sentences below contain causative or inchoative verbs, each derived from an adjective. Some of the verbs are like *dry*, with a meaning 'make or become [dry], change from a state of being not [dry] to a state of being [dry].' Others are like *widen*, with a meaning 'make or become [wide]r, change from less [wide] to more [wide].' Which are which? Is any of them ambiguous in this regard?

(a)   After it was taken from the oven, the cake cooled quickly.
(b)   We'll fill these barrels with water.
(c)   The welder heated the pipe with an acetylene torch.
(d)   This charcoal filter helps to purify the water.
(e)   The teachers readied the young children for their field trip.
(f)   See how the sunset reddens those clouds.
(g)   The unpleasant experience saddened us all.
(h)   Would you sharpen these pencils, please?
(i)   Your solution to the first problem simplifies the second problem.
(j)   The damage done by the storm weakened the wall considerably.

13.5 Verbs from verbs

Chapter 4 dealt with verbs of variable valency like *break* and *roll*. It is possible to consider each such verb as a pair of homonyms, one derived from the other, but in this section we turn our attention to verbs not previously discussed. In English nearly all other verbs derived from verbs have prefixes. One type has the repetitive prefix *re-* : *re-write, re-capture, re-tell*. (Numerous verbs begin with *re-*: *reduce, refrain, reject* and others. This may or may not be considered a prefix, but it is not the repetitive prefix.) Another type of prefix has a reversive or 'undoing' prefix, namely *un-, de-* or *dis-* . Compare:

6a   Kathleen folded the tablecloth.
6b   Kathleen unfolded the tablecloth.

Both *fold* and *unfold* have a causative sense, here 'cause the table-cloth to be folded/unfolded,' where *folded* and *unfolded* indicate a **resultative status**. The thematic structure is identical; only the resultant status is different.

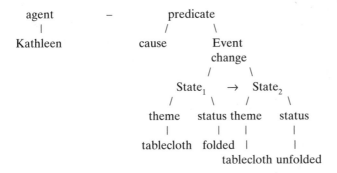

Other examples are found in Table 13.2.

TABLE 13.2 Reversive verbs

accelerate, decelerate	furl, unfurl
appear, disappear	hook, unhook
attach, detach	lace, unlace
bolt, unbolt	leash, unleash
button, unbutton	lock, unlock
clasp, unclasp	pack, unpack
classify, declassify	pin, unpin

continued

TABLE 13.2 continued

clog, unclog	reel, unreel
coil, uncoil	roll, unroll
couple, uncouple	screw, unscrew
compress, decompress	seal, unseal
curl, uncurl	settle, unsettle
do, undo	snarl, unsnarl
embark, disembark	tangle, untangle
encode, decode	tie, untie
entangle, disentangle	twist, untwist
fasten, unfasten	wind, unwind
fold, unfold	zip, unzip

Disappear and *disembark* are the reversive of *appear* and *embark*, respectively (intransitives from intransitives). *Disinherit* and *dispossess* appear to be the reversive of *inherit* and *possess*, respectively, but are not; the former means 'deprive of the right to inherit, cause to not-inherit' and the latter 'deprive of possessions, cause to not-possess.' *Disappoint* has no relation to *appoint*.

In the following pairs the first verb is a transfer verb derived from a noun – in fact, in each case identical with a noun – and has the meaning 'apply or attach N to.' The second verb, with prefix, is a *privative verb* with the meaning 'remove or detach N from' (Marchand 1973). Compare these to such transfer verbs as *paint* and *peel*, discussed in Section **13.3**.

TABLE 13.3 Privative verbs

arm, disarm
cork, uncork
cover, uncover
harness, unharness
load, unload
mask, unmask
muzzle, unmuzzle
saddle, unsaddle
veil, unveil
wrap, unwrap
yoke, unyoke

PRACTICE 13.4

Draw thematic structure trees for these sentences:
Brendan covered the birdcage.
Brendan uncovered the birdcage.

13.6 Adjectives derived from verbs

Adjectives derived from verbs are either **active-subjective** or **passive-objective** (Magnusson and Persson 1986: 195–8). An *envious* person is one who envies, an *enviable* person is one that we envy, one to be envied. *Envious* is active-subjective, *enviable* is passive-objective. A verb has two participles; the present participle with *-ing* is often an active-subjective adjective: *amusing, charming, interesting*; the past participle, with *-ed, -en* or something else, is often a passive-objective adjective: *amused, broken, interested*.

This book bores me.
```
affecting  –  predicate  –  affected
    |             |             |
   book          bore           I
```

This book is boring (to me).
```
affecting  –  predicate  –  (affected)
    |             |             |
   book         boring          I
```

I am bored (with/by this book).
```
affected  –  predicate  –  (affecting)
    |            |             |
    I          bored          book
```

Thus the verb *bore* has a causative sense; the adjective *boring* presents this causative sense as a status; *bored* expresses a resultative status, telling what has been affected by the action of the verb.

In English the construction of *be* + the past participle has two functions, the resultative status just discussed and the passive voice. Compare:

Resultative: The road was closed (all day). [a status]
Passive: The road was closed (by the police at ten o'clock). [an event]

So *The road was closed* is ambiguous by itself. German and Spanish, among other languages, keep these expressions separate.

German
Resultative: Der Weg war (den ganzen Tag) geschlossen.
Passive: Der Weg wurde (um zehn Uhr von der Polizei) geschlossen.
Spanish
Resultative: El camino estaba cerrado (todo el día).
Passive: El camino fue cerrado (por la policía a las diez).

Some deverbal adjectives with the negative prefixes *un-* and *in-* (*im-, il-, ir-*), such as *undaunted* and *incessant* 'not ceasing,' are more common than the corresponding adjectives without the prefixes. Of course, it is the positive adjectives that are derived from verbs; there are no such negative verbs as **undaunt* or **incease*.

Examples of active-subjective adjectives from verbs are:

calculating inspiring stimulating thriving unrelenting dependent
incessant (in)coherent repentant (in)tolerant
appreciative argumentative deceptive impressive informative
offensive productive protective provocative (un)obtrusive
(dis)respectful thoughtful/thoughtless
continuous studious
discriminatory
leaky
sympathetic

Some passive-objective adjectives are equivalent to past participles or archaic past participles; for example:

bent broken chosen cut mixed molten past shrunken slain
stolen stricken swollen tired

The majority of passive-objective adjectives have the suffix -ible/-able. A is refillable = A can be refilled; A is accessible to B = A can be accessed by B:

conceivable contemptible impassable impenetrable interminable
reasonable

Among words of Latin origin there is often a verb, a noun and an adjective with the same base and different suffixes, as *compel, compulsion, compulsive*. Often, as in this case, the adjective resembles the noun more than the verb in form, but its meaning is better seen as derived from the verb. Thus *compulsive* has the sense of 'being compelled.' As with the set *long, length, lengthen*, presented at the beginning of this chapter, formal and semantic derivation do not coincide.

13.7 Adjectives derived from nouns

Most English adjectives derived from nouns are descriptive; they predicate some characteristic associated with the underlying noun. Several distinct kinds of relationship with the underlying noun are seen:

1 The adjective means 'like N'; *childish = like a child*

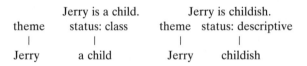

```
         Jerry is a child.        Jerry is childish.
  theme     status: class      theme   status: descriptive
    |           |                |           |
  Jerry       a child         Jerry       childish
```

Other examples:

foolish devilish motherly brotherly foxy piggish golden
wooden leathery cylindrical pyramidal spherical

2 The adjective means 'having (some quantity of) N,' 'affected by N,' 'displaying N'; *muddy = having mud*

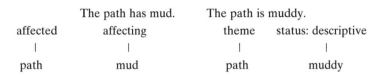

```
          The path has mud.      The path is muddy.
  affected         affecting        theme    status: descriptive
    |                 |               |              |
  path               mud            path          muddy
```

Other examples:

bushy feathery foggy sandy shady colorful shapely barbed
healthy

3 Some adjectives mean 'leading to N, likely to produce N'; *healthful* = *leading to (good) health*

<table>
<tr><td colspan="2">This diet produces good health.</td><td colspan="2">This diet is healthful.</td></tr>
<tr><td>affecting</td><td>affected</td><td>theme</td><td>status: descriptive</td></tr>
<tr><td>|</td><td>|</td><td>|</td><td>|</td></tr>
<tr><td>diet</td><td>health</td><td>diet</td><td>healthful</td></tr>
</table>

The distinction between *healthy*, 'having good health,' and *healthful*, 'producing good health,' is clear though some speakers use *healthy* in both the 'having' and 'producing' senses: *Arthur is healthy*; *This diet is healthy*. However, for various other adjectives the relation to underlying nouns is ambiguous: does *This plan is dangerous* tell us that the plan has danger(s) or that it is apt to lead to danger? Similar adjectives are the following:

disastrous hazardous harmful shameful

4 Numerous English adjectives do not really add a meaning to that of the noun; they merely convert the occurrence of that meaning to a different syntactic function. Compare *ceremonious* and *ceremonial*, both clearly from *ceremony*. A ceremonious act is an act characterized by ceremony, displaying ceremony – Group 2. A ceremonial act is an act that is a ceremony – Group 4. Adjectives of this sort are more often used attributively than predicatively.
Examples:

daily hourly weekly monthly yearly biological geographical
residential partial medicinal peninsular cinematic

PRACTICE 13.5

Comment on each of the following adjectives, trying to assign it to one or more of the four classes discussed above.

graceful
malicious
opinionated
original
timely

13.8 Adjectives derived from adjectives

There are two kinds of adjectives formed from other adjectives. The less common type has a suffix *-ish* with the meaning 'partially, tending toward':

bluish oldish yellowish

The other type has a prefix to indicate the negative of the plain adjective or changes the suffix *-ful* to *-less*.

unbiased unfinished unparalleled untutored
undaunted uneasy
dissatisfied
illegal impatient indecent irregular
harmless painless

13.9 Nouns derived from verbs

When a noun is derived from a verb, the verb is one that can predicate some action. This predication is turned into a name that designates the act; the product or result of the act; the agent or means of carrying out the act; the entity affected by the act; or the place where the act occurs.

1 action nouns

V refers to a physical action and N means the event or act of the V.

The bus arrived promptly.   the prompt <u>arrival</u> of the bus

2 effect nouns

V refers to a (basically) physical action and N means the result, product, effect of the V.

George replied to our letter   George's <u>reply</u> to our letter

3 agent/instrument nouns

V refers to some activity and N means the (habitual, usual) agent or instrument of the V.

Harry drives. Harry is a <u>driver</u>.
This compound lubricates. This compound is a <u>lubricant</u>.

4 affected nouns

V refers to some activity and N means the entity affected by the action of the V.

Somebody employs Harry. Harry is an <u>employee</u>.

5 place nouns

V refers to some activity and N means the place where the action of V occurs.

The ships anchor here. This is an <u>anchorage</u>.

Quite often a noun indicates both the event or activity signalled by the verb (Group 1) and the result or product of that action (Group 2), the former an abstract noun, the latter abstract or concrete depending on whether the verb is abstract or concrete. Thus *laughter* is the act of laughing and also the product of the act. The following nouns indicate the event only:

attack delay departure renewal revival robbery

Flight is another such noun, corresponding to both *flee* and *fly*. *Disappearance* is an event noun, 'the act of going out of someone's sight'; *appearance* is likewise an event noun related to the intransitive *appear* 'come into view' (*We were greatly relieved by the appearance of the train*) but it has a product meaning related to the pre-clause verb *appear* 'seem, look' (*We were surprised by Amelia's appearance* [ambiguous]).

In the common Anglo-Saxon part of the vocabulary there are numerous verb-noun pairs in which V is a concrete action, and N refers to a brief instance of that action, something seen, heard or both. The N is both the event and the result of the event (Groups 1 and 2):

> bark belch blush cough flash frown glance groan jerk jump kick kiss knock leap nod plunge pull push shiver shriek shrug sigh smack splash wink

But the same double value occurs in other instances where the event is not brief:

> leak look swim talk work

Breath can be a short-duration movement but also 'the air stream' (as in 'catch one's breath') and the odor carried by the air stream (as in 'bad breath').

For verbs of communication (Chapter 9) the corresponding nouns are often event and product, the act of saying and what is said:

> agreement announcement boast challenge command complaint demand denial excuse promise protest publication remark warning welcome

More examples of nouns from verbs follow:

Group 1 (count nouns)

> approach arrest attack attempt delay departure fight renewal revival risk robbery triumph

(noncountable nouns)

> absorption defiance

Group 2 (countable nouns)

> break bruise crease cut gesture mistake slice spill

(plural nouns, but not countable nouns)

> earnings savings shavings

(noncountable nouns, concrete)

> breakage arrangement inheritance lather leakage sweat

(noncountable nouns, abstract)

> applause damage grief laughter

Some are more abstract than others:

> belief choice desire doubt mixture possession supply
> (the act of believing, choosing, etc. and what is believed, chosen, etc.)

Group 3 There are numerous agent/instrument nouns with the suffix *-er* (sometimes spelled *-ar* or *-or*). It is a productive suffix: it is constantly being used to form new nouns from verbs. Examples:

> announcer borrower dancer invader manager publisher
> raider rescuer robber singer teacher trader traveler
> upholsterer waiter wholesaler; collector navigator sailor

Other examples of instrument Ns with the same suffix:

> container divider freezer heater knocker plunger recorder
> reminder zipper; incubator

Another common ending is found in these words:

> disinfectant intoxicant lubricant stimulant

Amusement and *hindrance* refer, respectively, to 'that which amuses' and 'that which hinders.'

Not many nouns belong to Group 4, entity affected by the action of the verb. Most of them refer to persons:

> acquaintance addressee amputee nominee

One at least indicates a concrete object: *projectile*. The word *reject* (stressed on the first syllable) can refer to a human or an object that is rejected.

Examples of nouns that indicate the place of action (Group 5):

> anchorage bakery brewery distillery laundry refinery

Frequently we find nouns that indicate the event, the result of the event and the place involved. Thus an *exit* can be the act of going out and the result of the act ('to make one's exit'), and it can also be the place marked EXIT. Similar are these:

> drive stand step tread walk

The noun *arrival* belongs in Group 1, the act of arriving, and also in Group 3, one who arrives/has arrived/will arrive. The latter only occurs in limited contexts: *an early/late/recent arrival. Exile* belongs to both Group 2, the result of being exiled, and Group 4, the person affected by the action. A *reader* is both 'one who reads,' Group 3, and 'that which is read,' Group 4.

13.10 Nouns derived from adjectives

There are just two common types of de-adjectival nouns:

Abstract nouns

These are simply the reification of the adjectives from which they are derived, a way of treating the quality as a thing.

depth warmth width (length strength)
fanaticism liberalism pessimism skepticism
boredom freedom wisdom
indecision
certainty equality loyalty modesty sanity validity
costliness darkness kindness
accuracy dependency hesitancy literacy

Characterized nouns

Such nouns denote people, individuals who have the quality named by the adjective, or places characterized by what the adjective represents.

absentee youngster
rapids shallows

These examples, representative though few, show that the most common de-adjectival nouns are abstract nouns, the meaning of an adjective treated as an entity.

13.11 Nouns derived from nouns

Nouns that are both count and non-count like *paper* and nouns like *character*, which can be both concrete and abstract, may be viewed as pairs of homonyms, one derived from the other. This section is concerned with nouns not yet discussed.

Denominal nouns are numerous but mostly belong to just two types: they name either places or persons associated with whatever is denoted by the simple noun.

Place nouns

These name localities where the referent of the basic noun is to be found.

fishery hermitage orphanage

Person nouns

are labels for humans associated with whatever the basic noun signifies. The basic noun may name a place or kind of place, and the derived noun names an inhabitant.

mountaineer islander New Yorker Vietnamese

Or the derived nouns provide labels for people by what they do for a living, the occupation having something to do with what is named in the basic noun.

auctioneer engineer; jeweler; custodian librarian
electrician obstetrician; columnist machinist violinist

Then there are pairs in which one noun is an abstract condition or system and the other noun names a person who is affected by the condition or is an adherent of the system. It is impossible to say which of these is primary.

pyromania, pyromaniac; Communism, Communist

Summary

In many languages, including English, lexical items of different classes show formal and semantic relationships, and we say that the forms which are more complex, formally and/or semantically, are derived from the simpler forms. Formal processes of derivation include addition, mutation, conversion and subtraction.

In exploring semantic relationships that arise through derivation we have dealt with three large classes of words (or parts of speech), verbs, adjectives and nouns, as simple lexemes and as derived lexemes. The nine large categories of derived words are recapitulated below with their subdivisions.

1   Verbs from nouns
        transfer; effect; means; vehicle
2   Verbs from adjectives
        causative; inchoative
3   Verbs from verbs
        repetitive; reversive; privative
4   Adjectives from verbs
        active-subjective; passive-objective
5   Adjectives from nouns
        class-descriptive; affecting-descriptive; affected-descriptive
6   Adjectives from adjectives
        tendency; negative
7   Nouns from verbs
        action; effect; agent/instrument; affected; place
8   Nouns from adjectives
        abstract; characterized
9   Nouns from nouns
        place; person

Thematic structure trees show the function of the simple word in a predication and the function of the derived word in a different, but obviously related predication.

Suggested reading

Standard works on English word-formation are Marchand (1969), Adams (1973), and Bauer (1983). Magnusson and Persson (1986) provide a framework for inter-class derivations that is different from the presentation here but which has influenced this account in many ways.

Glossary of technical terms

abstract/concrete nouns An abstract noun denotes one or more entities that do not have physical existence: *idea, problem*; a concrete noun denotes one or more physical entities: *chair, food*.

accent The heaviest stress on one syllable in a phrase or sentence, giving the word in which the syllable occurs greatest emphasis.

accomplishment verb A verb that takes an object and denotes a change in the status or condition of what that object refers to: *I broke the window*.

achievement verb A verb that indicates a change in the status or condition of the referent of the subject: *We moved away*.

acronym A word made from the initial letters of the words of a phrase: North Atlantic Treaty Organization → *NATO*.

action noun An abstract noun, often derived from a verb, that expresses something that somebody does: *discovery, swimming*.

active-subjective/passive-objective adjectives An active-subjective adjective is derived from a verb and describes what its subject does: *She is very attractive*; a passive-objective adjective is derived from a verb and describes what may be true of the object of such a verb: *breakable*.

active voice see **voice**

activity verb A verb that expresses action without expressing an end to the action: *They ran*.

actor role see Table 4.2.

addition The process of creating words by putting meaningful elements together: *mean-ing-ful*.

adjective A word that expresses some attribute of a noun and is modified by *very, more* and other qualifiers: *a very nice day*.

297

adjective phrase An adjective along with any modifiers it may have: *very nice*; *five feet tall*.

affected noun A noun derived from a verb which names an entity that receives the action of the verb: *advisee*.

affected role, affecting role see Table 4.2.

affirmative see **polarity**

affix A meaningful form that is attached to another form; it may be a **prefix** as *un-* in *unkind* or a **suffix** like *-ness* in *kindness*.

agent noun A noun, usually derived from a verb, which names a person who performs the action of the verb: *painter, cook*.

agent role see Table 4.2.

ambiguity The condition whereby any linguistic form has two or more interpretations: *club* = a heavy stick; a social group.

animate Said of a word, especially a noun, that denotes some living thing(s): *dog, boy*; an inanimate noun denotes some non-living thing(s): *stone, happiness*.

anomalous sentence A meaningless sequence of words which deviates from the rules for sentence formation.

antonym A word that is opposite in meaning to another word; *good* and *bad* are antonyms.

arbitrariness The characteristic of language such that there is no natural relation between a word, for example *cat*, and what it stands for.

aspect The expression of some temporal characteristic of a predicate; includes **ingressive, durative, egressive, prospective**, and **retrospective**.

aspectual verb A verb such as *start* or *continue* which tells the aspect of the main verb that follows.

attitudinal predicate A verb or adjective that expresses the feelings of the subject: *I hate this music*; *I'm fond of swimming*.

auxiliary verb A verb used with a lexical verb to make grammatical modifications, as in *are working, have seen, will go*.

binary antonyms Two lexemes such that, if used as predicate for the same subject, only one can be true: *dead, alive*.

blend The result of two clipped forms put together to make a compound: *smog = smoke + fog*.

causative verb A verb that expresses an action which results in the status or activity of some entity: *insert* X *in* Y = cause X to be in Y.

characteristic adjective An adjective derived from a noun and which expresses the quality of that noun: gold → *golden*.

characterized noun A noun derived from an adjective and which expresses an entity of whom the adjective can be predicated: young → *youngster*.

clause A construction of words that expresses a proposition but forms part of a sentence rather than being a sentence in itself: *She told us she will wait*.

clipping A process of word formation in which a new word is made by shortening an existing word: *laboratory* → *lab*.

co-hyponyms Two or more lexemes that have the same superordinate: *collie, dachshund* and *poodle* (among others) are co-hyponyms.

collective noun A noun that refers to a group of entities; *army, furniture, luggage*.

collocation Words occurring together in a phrase or sentence.

command A type of sentence in which someone is told to do or not do something: *Wait. Don't go*.

commissive predicate A verb that expresses the commitment of the subject to the performance or non-performance *of an action*: *I pledge to carry out all orders given to me.*

common noun A noun that refers to one or more of a class of objects or concepts: *cat, idea.* Cf. **proper noun**.

complement Any form that follows a predicate and completes its meaning: *I made a mistake; She looks nice; They're afraid of the dark.*

compound A word made of two or more independent words: *armchair.*

compound verb (as used here) A combination of verb + particle or verb + preposition, which acts as a single semantic unit: *stand up, listen to.*

concrete noun see **abstract/concrete nouns**

conjunction A word that connects two linguistic expressions: *John and Mary; now or at five o'clock.*

connotation The personal associations produced by words; cf. **denotation**.

containing adjective An adjective derived from a noun and which expresses the presence of some quantity of what is expressed by the noun: *color → colorful.*

context The linguistic environment of a form in a sentence; the social, spatial, temporal situation in which a form is produced.

contradiction The relation between two propositions such that if one is true, the other must be false: of the two propositions represented by *John is here* and *John is not here*, each is the contradiction of the other.

converse antonyms Two lexemes so related that either one presupposes the other: If A *gives* X to B, B *receives* X from A.

conversion A type of word formation in which, without change, a word of one class becomes also a word of another class: *hammer* is both noun and verb.

coreferents Two expressions that denote the same entity.

countable noun A noun that has singular and plural forms and which denotes separable entities: *child(ren), house(s).* See **non-countable noun**.

counterfactive predicate A verb that, whether affirmative or negative, communicates that the following predication is untrue: *pretend.*

creativity The characteristic of language which makes it possible for us to produce and understand utterances we have never heard or produced before.

declarative sentence see **statement**

definite Said of a noun phrase that refers to an entity or group of entities whose identity is presumably known to the addressee.

deletion The omission of some language element.

demonstrative Applied to forms that have the function of identifying by proximity to the speaker: *this, that.*

denotation The objective relationship between a linguistic form and its referent.

derivation Any process whereby one word is formed from another: *writer* from *write.*

determiner A word that occurs before a noun to express number, quantity, or (in)definiteness: *a, the, some, all.*

directive An utterance intended to get the addressee(s) to do or not do something: *Wait, I wish you'd wait.*

directive predicate A predicate that can occur in an overt directive utterance: *I ask you to wait.*

discourse A continuous stretch of spoken or written language, consisting of at least one sentence and usually more than one.

displacement The ability of language to refer to contexts which differ from the time and place of an utterance.

distribution The total set of linguistic contexts in which a lexeme can occur.

durative aspect The expression of continuance of an action or permanence of a status: *He kept running*; *They stayed at home*.

dynamic verb A type of verb that expresses activity or change of state: *They're moving*. Cf. **stative verb**.

effect noun A noun derived from a verb and which expresses the product or outcome of the action expressed by the verb: *song ← sing*.

ellipsis The omission of part of a sentence, where the missing part is understood from context: *Where are you going? Out*.

embedding Inserting one sentence into another sentence: *I believe you're right*.

enabling predicate A verb or adjective which tells that the following predicate is made possible: *We allowed the car to pass*.

environment The parts of an utterance that are adjacent to a lexeme; in *The dog is barking* the environment of *bark* is *The dog is _____ing*.

euphemism An expression used in place of one considered unpleasant: *pass away* instead of *die*.

extension The class of entities which a lexeme denotes; the extension of *Albert Einstein* is a single individual, while the extension of *scientist* is a large number of individuals.

extralinguistic Said of anything outside of language to which language can refer.

focus Special attention to one element in a sentence: *Henry* in *Henry is the one I told what you said*; in speech focus it is often accomplished through accent: *I told Hénry what you said*.

function The role played by a word in a sentence; in *George saw me* and *I saw George* the word *George* has different functions.

generic Used to refer to a whole class of entities: *A child can do that* (= any child, all children); *The Child from Three to Six* (= children in general).

gerund The form of a verb ending in *-ing* used as (part of) a noun phrase: *I enjoy swimming, She accused me of telling lies*.

goal The role that expresses what is affected by the action of a predicate: *Roger gave Ellen a present. Ellen received a present*.

gradable Said of an adjective that can be compared or intensified: *hot → hotter, very hot*.

grammar The rules by which a language operates, and therefore the implicit knowledge that speakers of that language have which makes them competent to use the language; also, an account of the rules.

habitual Said of a form, especially a verb, that expresses customary, repeated activity: *He smokes a pipe*.

head The main word in a phrase on which other elements depend and which controls the function of the phrase: *all those dirty clothes in the corner*.

homonyms Words with the same pronunciation but different meanings: *club* 'a heavy stick' and club 'a social organization.'

homophones = homonyms that sound the same but have different spellings.

hyponym A word whose referent is included in the referent of a more general word, called the **superordinate**: *rose* is a hyponym of *flower*, and *flower* is a superordinate of *rose*.

implicative verb A verb that expresses something about the truth of the predication that follows in the sentence: *We didn't hesitate to accept the offer* implies that we accepted the offer.

implicature A meaning derived not from what is said but deduced from the necessary way of interpreting what is said.

inanimate see **animate**

inceptive Said of a form that expresses the beginning of a status or action: *arrive*; *begin running*.

indefinite see **definite**

infinitive A non-finite form of a verb; in English often, but not always, consisting of *to* + the verb: *I want them to go, I let them go*.

information The content of a message.

inhabitant noun A noun like *New Yorker* which names the inhabitant of a particular place.

instrument noun A noun that refers to an inanimate object by which the action of some verb is accomplished: *brush, projector*.

intention What a speaker or writer wants to communicate in producing an utterance.

interpretation The message that a hearer or reader gets from an utterance.

intonation The system of melodies with which utterances are spoken and which can make differences of meaning.

lexeme A minimal form that conveys one meaning and can be used in reference or predication: the word *cat*, and the 'idiom' *put up with* are both lexemes.

lexicon The vocabulary of a language, together with information about the pronunciation, use, and meaning of each item in it.

linguistic meaning The meaning conveyed by linguistic forms, as distinct from meanings conveyed by the circumstances of an utterance, which is speaker meaning.

locution An utterance, that is, what is said as distinct from the intention of the speaker (**illocution**) or the interpretation of the hearer (**perlocution**).

metalanguage The language used in talking about language.

metaphor A figurative expression in which a notion is described in terms usually used for a different kind of notion.

metonymy A way of denoting an entity by using some characteristic of that entity, e.g. blue eyes as a way of referring to a person with blue eyes.

modal verb An auxiliary verb that expresses permission, probability or necessity: *can, must*.

modality The expression of necessity, possibility and probability, often through modal verbs.

morpheme The smallest contrastive unit of meaning: a single word like *cat* or an affix such as *un-* and *-ness* in *unhappiness*.

negation A process that expresses the denial or contradiction of some part, or all, of a sentence.

non-binary antonyms Two lexemes that have opposite meanings but for which there are intermediate degrees of the same quality: *hot* and *cold*.

non-countable noun A noun that has no plural form: *mud, misery*.

nonverbal Said of communication that does not use words.

noun A class of words with a naming function, showing contrasts of countability and number.

noun phrase A phrase with a noun as head; hence, a noun alone may be a noun phrase.

number The grammatical category that expresses the distinction of singular and plural.

object The noun phrase that names the entity which receives the action of the verb: John hit *Bill.*

paradigmatic The relation of items that can substitute for one another at the same place in a sentence. Cf. **syntagmatic**.

paralanguage Characteristics of the voice, apart from the words spoken, which can communicate something about the speaker's attitude.

paraphrase An alternative way of expressing the content of a sentence.

participle A non-finite form of a verb, either present (*amusing*) or past (*amused*).

particles Words that combine with verbs to make compound verbs: *in, out, on, off, up, down, over, away, through.*

passive voice see **voice**

perceptual predicate A verb that expresses the activity of any of the five senses.

performative verb A verb that may be used to state the actual performance of an action; *declare.*

period adjective An adjective derived from a noun that expresses some period of time: *monthly* ← month.

person A grammatical category of reference, in English expressed with pronouns, referring to the speaker and perhaps others (1st person: *I, we*), the addressee(s) (2nd person: *you*), or others (3rd person: *he, she, it, they*).

phatic Said of utterances used mainly to establish social contact.

phoneme A unit in the sound system of a language, which combines with other such units to form syllables and words; English *cash* and *shack* have the same three phonemes differently arranged.

phrase A group of words smaller than a clause, forming a grammatical unit.

plural see **number**

polarity The contrast of affirmative and negative.

possessive A language category that indicates possession: *my, your.*

pragmatics The study of language in use, including the ways in which we derive meanings from the context and from knowledge of speakers apart from the linguistic meanings of what is said.

preposition One of a class of function words that ties a following noun phrase to the rest of the sentence: *at, for, with.*

presupposition The information that must be assumed in order for a sentence to be meaningful; *Have you stopped beating your wife?* presupposes that the addressee has been beating his wife, which presupposes that the addressee is married and that the addressee is an adult male.

preventing predicate A verb which states that its subject is the agent causing the non-occurrence of the predication that follows: *I kept the ball from rolling away.*

privative verb A verb that expresses removal of something: *undress.*

productive process A means of making new words which is frequently used at the present time: adding *-er* to verbs to make nouns like *driver*.

productivity The ability of humans to produce and understand constantly new utterances.

progressive The extended verb form composed of forms of *be* and the present participle, expressing the duration or incompleteness of what the verb signifies: *He is running, They were waiting*.

pronoun One of a small class of words that can substitute for a noun phrase: *he, somebody, who*.

proper noun A noun or noun phrase that labels some specific person, place, building, historic event, etc. and which lacks the grammatical forms of a common noun.

proposition The meaning of any sentence that is asserted to be true or false.

prospective verb A verb that expresses some action or attitude oriented toward a later time: *We expect to go*.

qualifier A word or phrase that modifies another word, thereby limiting the reference of that word: *very nice, big enough*.

quantifier/quantifying determiner A word or phrase that expresses the amount of what is expressed by another word: *all, several, a dozen*.

reciprocal A relationship that can be expressed by *each other* or *one another*.

redundant Said of any item that is more than necessary in a message for conveying the meaning.

reference The relation between a language form and some physical entity, which is the **referent** of that sign.

reflexive A verb or a construction in which the subject and the object have the same referent: *She hurt herself*.

retrospective verb A verb that expresses an action or attitude oriented toward a previous time: *We regretted having gone there*.

reversive verb A verb that expresses the reversing or undoing of what is expressed by another verb: *disconnect* is the reversive verb that corresponds to *connect*.

rhetorical question A question for which no answer is expected.

semantic field/set A group of lexemes that are defined with respect to one another: kinship, colors, etc.

semantics The study of meaning expressed by language.

sense relations The relations of meaning between words, as expressed in synonymy, hyponymy, antonymy, etc.

sentence A grammatical construction that is complete in itself.

sign Any formal item that conveys meaning, especially a conventional piece of a system.

simple sentence A sentence that contains only one clause.

simple verb A finite verb that has no auxiliary and so consists of just one word.

singular see **number**

speacher meaning see **linguistic meaning**.

speech act An utterance defined in terms of the speaker's intention and the effect on the audience.

statement A sentence that tells something.

stative verb A verb that expresses some state of affairs, rather than an action or event.

structural semantics The study of the sense relations between words.

structure A system of interrelated elements that have repeatable relations to one another and which are defined by their relations to one another.

subject The noun phrase about which something is stated; _John and I are ready_.

synonym A word that is equivalent in sense to another word (in a particular context or contexts); _select_ is a synonym of _choose_ in "Will you help me choose a new suit?" (but not in "I don't choose to wait.").

syntagmatic The relation of words to one another when they form a construction.

syntax The study of how words go together to form sentences.

tense The expression of time in a verb; in English a verb has two tenses, **present** (_play_) and **past** (_played_).

utterance A stretch of speech by one person; it may consist of a single word, a single sentence, or numerous sentences.

valency The number of arguments (noun phrases) that a predicate may have in one sentence.

verdictive predicate A verb that occurs in a sentence which expresses the speaker's judgement of some presumed action by the addressee: _I blame you for what happened_.

voice the relation of the action of the verb to its subject; either **active**, as in _She loves me_, or **passive**, as in _She is loved by me_.

weather predicate An adjective like _rainy_ or a verb such as _snow_ which occurs with the empty subject _it_.

Bibliography

Adams, Valerie. 1973. *An Introduction to Modern English Word Formation*. London: Longman.

Allan, Keith. 1986. *Linguistic Meaning*. 2 vols. London: Routledge & Kegan Paul.

Allerton, D. J. 1975. *Valency and the English Verb*. London: Academic Press.

Anderson, John M. 1985. *Case Grammar and the Lexicon*. Ulster: University of Ulster.

Anderson, Steven R. and Keenan, Edward. 1985. "Deixis," in Shopen 1985: 259–308.

Austin, J. L. 1962. *How to Do Things with Words*. Oxford: Clarendon Press.

Barwise, J. and Cooper, R. 1981. "Generalized quantifiers and natural language," *Linguistics and Philosophy* 4: 159–219.

Bauer, Lauri. 1983. *English Word-formation*. Cambridge: Cambridge University Press.

Berlin, Brent and Kay, Paul. 1969. *Basic Color Terms*. Berkeley, CA: University of California Press.

Bickerton, Derek. 1990. *Language and Species*. Chicago: University of Chicago Press.

Bierwisch, Manfred. 1970. "Semantics," in J. Lyons, ed., *New Horizons in Linguistics* (Harmondsworth: Penguin), 166–84.

Binnick, R. I. 1991. *Time and the Verb: A Guide to Tense and Aspect*. Oxford: Oxford University Press.

Bolinger, Dwight. 1980. *Language, the Loaded Weapon: The Use and Abuse of Language Today*. London: Longman.

Brinton, Laurel J. 1988. *The Development of English Aspectual Systems: Aspectualizers and Post-verbal Particles*. Cambridge: Cambridge University Press.

Cann, Ronnie. 1993. *Formal Semantics: An Introduction*. Cambridge: Cambridge University Press.

Chafe, Wallace L. 1994. *Discourse, Consciousness, and Time*. Chicago: University of Chicago Press.

Chierchia, Gennaro and McConnell-Ginet, Sally. 1990. *Meaning and Grammar: An Introduction to Semantics*. Cambridge: Cambridge University Press.

Chomsky, Noam and Halle, Morris. 1968. *The Sound Pattern of English*. New York: Harper and Row.

Clark, Eva V. and Clark, Herbert H. 1979. "When nouns surface as verbs," *Language* 55: 430–77.

Clark, Herbert H. 1973. "Space, time, semantics, and the child," in T. Moore, ed., *Cognitive Development and the Acquisition of Language* (New York: Academic Press), 28–64.

—— 1996. *Using Language*. Cambridge: Cambridge University Press.

Clark, Herbert H. and Clark, Eva V. 1977. *Psychology and Language: An Introduction to Psycholinguistics*. New York: Harcourt Brace Jovanovich.

Comrie, Bernard. 1976. *Aspect: An Introduction to the Study of Verbal Aspect and Related Problems*. Cambridge: Cambridge University Press.

—— 1985. *Tense*. Cambridge: Cambridge University Press.

Cook, Walter J., SJ. 1976. "Durative aspect: The process of no change," *Georgetown University Papers in Languages and Linguistics* 12: 1–23.

Coseriu, Eugene. 1975. "Vers une typologie des champs lexicaux," *Cahiers de Lexicologie*, 27: 30–51.

Couper-Kuhlen, Elisabeth. 1986. *An Introduction to English Prosody*. London: Edward Arnold.

Cruse, D. A. 1986. *Lexical Semantics*. Cambridge: Cambridge University Press.

Cruttenden, Alan. 1986. *Intonation*. Cambridge: Cambridge University Press.

Crystal, David. 1969. *Prosodic Systems and Intonation in English*. Cambridge: Cambridge University Press.

—— 1991. *A Dictionary of Linguistics and Phonetics*. 3rd edn. Oxford: Blackwell.

—— 1995. *The Cambridge Encyclopedia of the English Language*. Cambridge: Cambridge University Press.

Dahl, Östen. 1981. On the definition of the telic-atelic (bounded-non-bounded) distinction, in Tedeschi & Zaenen 1981: 79–90.

—— 1985. *Tense and Aspect Systems*. Oxford: Blackwell.

Declerck, Renat. 1979. "Aspect and the bounded/unbounded (telic/atelic) distinction," *Linguistics* 17: 761–94.

Dillon, George. 1977. *Introduction to Contemporary Linguistic Semantics*. Englewood Clffs, NJ: Prentice-Hall.

Dixon, R. M. W. 1991. *A New Appproach to English Grammar on Semantic Principles*. Oxford: Clarendon Press.

Dowty, David R. 1977. "Toward a semantic analysis of verb aspect and the English 'imperfective' progressive," *Linguistics and Philosophy* 1: 45–77.

Fillmore, Charles J. 1966. "Deictic categories in the semantics of *come*," *Foundations of Language* 2: 219–27.

—— 1968. "The case for case," in E. Bach and R. Harms, eds, *Universals in Linguistic Theory* (New York: Holt, Rinehart and Winston), 1–88.

—— 1971. "Verbs of judging; Exercises in semantic description," in Fillmore and Langendoen 1971, 273–91.

—— 1973. "May we come in?," *Semiotica* 9: 97–116.

—— 1975. "Santa Cruz lectures on deixis." Bloomington, IN: Indiana University Linguistics Club.

—— 1979. "Topics in lexical semantics," in R. W. Cole, ed., *Current Issues in Linguistic Theory* (Bloomington: Indiana University Press), 76–158.

Fillmore, C. J. and Langendoen, D. T., eds. 1971. *Studies in Linguistic Semantics.* New York: Holt, Rinehart & Winston.

Fodor, Janet Dean. 1977. *Semantics: Theories of Meaning in Generative Grammar.* Cambridge, MA: MIT Press.

Frawley, William. 1992. *Linguistic Semantics.* Hillsdale, NJ: Lawrence Erlbaum Associates.

Frege, Gottlob. 1980. *Translations for the Philosophical Writing of Gottlob Frege.* Oxford: Blackwell.

Geckeler, Horst. 1971. *Strukturelle Semantik und Wortfeldtheorie.* Munich: Fink.

Givon, Talmy. 1979. *On Understanding Syntax.* New York: Academic Press.

Grice, H. Paul. 1975. "Logic and conversation," in Cole, Peter, and Morgan, Jerry L., eds, *Syntax and Semantics 3: Speech Acts* (New York: Academic Press), 41–58.

—— 1978. "Further notes on logic and conversation," in Cole, Peter, ed., *Syntax and Semantics 9: Pragmatics* (New York: Academic Press), 113–28.

—— 1981. "Presupposition and conversational implicature," in Cole, Peter, ed., *Radical Pragmatics* (New York: Academic Press), 183–98.

Gundel, J. K., Hedberg, N. and Zacharski, R. 1993. "Cognitive status and the form of referring," *Language* 69: 274–307.

Hall, Robert B. 1949. *Pidgin and Creole Languages.* Ithaca, NY: Cornell University Press.

Halliday, M. A. K. and Hasan, Ruqaiya. 1976. *Cohesion in English.* London: Longman.

Hancher, Michael. 1979. "The classification of cooperative illocutionary acts," *Language in Society* 8: 1–14.

Hipkiss, Robert A. 1995. *Semantics: Defining the Discipline.* Mahwah, NJ: Lawrence Erlbaum.

Hjelmslev, Louis. 1971. "Pour une sémantique structurelle," *Essais Linguistiques.* Paris: Minuit.

Hockett, Charles F. 1957. *A Course in Modern Linguistics.* New York: Macmillan.

Hofmann, Theodore R. 1993. *Realms of Meaning: An Introduction to Semantics.* London: Longman.

Huddleston, R. 1969. "Some observations on tense and deixis in English," *Language,* 45: 777–806.

Hurford, J. R. and Brendan Heasley. 1983. *Semantics: A Coursebook.* Cambridge: Cambridge University Press.

Jackendoff, Ray. 1985. *Semantics and Cognition.* Cambridge, MA: MIT Press.

—— 1990. *Semantic Structures.* Cambridge, MA: MIT Press.

Joos, Martin. 1964. *The English Verb.* Madison: University of Wisconsin Press.

Karttunen, Laurie. 1971. "Implicative verbs," *Language* 47: 340–58.

Kay, Paul and McDaniel, C. K. 1978. "The linguistic significance of the meanings of the basic color terms," *Language* 54: 610–46.

Kempson, Ruth M. 1977. *Semantic Theory*. Cambridge: Cambridge University Press.

Kiparsky, Paul and Kiparsky, Carol. 1970. "Fact," in Steinberg and Jakobovits 1971: 345–69.

Kirsner, Robert S. and Thompson, Sandra A. 1976. "The role of pragmatic inference in semantics: A study of sensory verb complements in English," *Glossa* 10: 200–40.

Kreidler, Charles W. 1979. "Creating new words by shortening," *Journal of English Linguistics* 13: 24–36.

—— 1997. *Describing Spoken English*. London: Routledge.

Lakoff, George and Johnson, Mark. 1980. *Metaphors We Live By*. Chicago: University of Chicago Press.

Larson, Richard K. 1990. "Semantics," in Osherson and Lasnik, 1990, 23–42.

Lebeaux, David. 1988. "The feature [+ affected] and the formation of the passive," in Wilkins, W., ed., *Thematic Relations (Syntax and Semantics 21)* (New York: Academic Press), 243–61.

Leech, Geoffrey N. 1969. *Toward a Semantic Description of English*. London: Longman.

—— 1981. *Semantics*. 2nd edn. Harmondsworth: Penguin Books.

—— 1987. *Meaning and the English Verb*. 2nd edn. London: Longman.

Lehrer, Adrienne J. 1969. "Semantic cuisine," *Journal of Linguistics* 5: 39–55.

—— 1970. "Indeterminacies in semantic description," *Glossa* 4: 87–110.

—— 1974. *Semantic Fields and Lexical Structure*. Amsterdam: North Holland.

—— 1985. "Markedness and antonymy," *Journal of Linguistics* 21: 397–429.

Lehrer, Adrienne and Lehrer, Keith. 1982. "Antonymy," *Linguistics and Philosophy* 5: 483–501.

Lenneberg, Eric. 1967. *Biological Foundations of Language*. New York: Wiley & Sons.

Levin, Beth. 1993. *English verb classes and alternations*. Chicago: University of Chicago Press.

Levinson, Stephen C. 1983. *Pragmatics*. Cambridge: Cambridge University Press.

Lyons, John. 1977. Semantics. 2 vols. Cambridge: Cambridge University Press.

—— 1981. *Language, Meaning and Context*. London: Fontana.

—— 1995. *Linguistic Semantics: An Introduction*. Cambridge: Cambridge University Press.

Magnusson, Ulf and Persson, Gunnar. 1986. *Facets, Phases and Foci: Studies in Lexical Relations in English*. Umeå: Almqvist & Wiksell.

Marchand, Hans. 1969. *The Categories and Types of Present-Day English Word-Formation*. 2nd edn. Munich: Beck.

—— 1973. "Reversive, ablative, and privative verbs in English, French, and German," in Kachru, Braj B. *et al.*, eds, *Issues in Linguistics: Papers in Honor of Henry and Renee Kahane* (Urbana: University of Illinois Press), 636–43.

Matisoff, James A. 1979. *Blessings, Curses, Hopes and Fears: Psychoostensive Expressions in Yiddish*. Philadelphia: Institute for the Study of Human Issues.

McCawley, James D. 1988. *The Syntactic Phenomena of English*. 2 vols. Chicago: University of Chicago Press.

Mettinger, Arthur. 1994. *Aspects of Semantic Opposition in English*. Oxford: Clarendon Press.

Mey, Jacob L. 1993. *Pragmatics: An introduction*. Oxford: Blackwell.

Newmeyer, Frederick J. 1975. *English Aspectual Verbs*. The Hague: Mouton.

Nida, Eugene A. 1975. *Componential Analysis of Meaning: An Introduction to Semantic Structures*. The Hague: Mouton.

—— 1979. *Exploring Semantic Structures*. Munich: Fink.

Nilsen, Don L. F. and Nilsen, Aileen P. 1975. *Semantic Theory: A Linguistic Perspective*. Rowley, MA: Newbury House.

Ogden, Charles W. and Richards, Ian. 1965 (first published 1923). *The Meaning of Meaning*. 10th edn. London: Routledge & Kegan Paul.

Osherson, Daniel N. and Lasnik, Howard. 1990. *Language* (vol. 1 of *An Invitation to Cognitive Science*). Cambridge, MA: MIT Press.

Palmer, Frank R. 1981. Semantics. 2nd edn. Cambridge: Cambridge University Press.

—— 1986. *Mood and Modality*. Cambridge: Cambridge University Press

—— 1988. *The English Verb*. 2nd edn. London: Longman.

—— 1990. *Modality and the English Modals*. 2nd edn. London: Longman.

Parsons, Terence. 1990. *Events in the Semantics of English: A Study in Subatomic Semantics*. Cambridge, MA: MIT Press.

Pinker, Steven. 1994. *The Language Instinct: How the Mind Creates Language*. New York: William Morrow & Co.

Pustejovsky, James and Boguraev, Branimir, eds. 1996. *Lexical Semantics: The Problem of Polysemy*. Oxford: Clarendon Press.

Quirk, Randolph, Greenbaum, Sydney, Leech, Geoffrey and Svartvik, Jan. 1984. *A Comprehensive Grammar of English*. London: Longman.

Ravin, Yael. 1990. *Lexical Semantics without Thematic Roles*. Oxford: Clarendon Press.

Ruhl, Charles. 1989. *On Monosemy: A Study in Linguistic Semantics*. Albany, NY: State University of New York Press.

Sadock, J. M. 1974. *Toward a Linguistic Theory of Speech Acts*. New York: Academic Press.

Saeed, John I. 1997. *Semantics*. Oxford: Blackwell.

Schiffrin, Deborah. 1994. *Approaches to discourse*. Oxford: Blackwell.

Searle, John R. 1969. *Speech Acts*. Cambridge: Cambridge University Press.

—— 1976. "The classification of illocutionary acts," *Language in Society* 5: 1–24.

Shi, Ziqiang. 1990. "On the inherent aspectual properties of NPs, verbs, sentences and the decomposition of perfectivity and inchoativity," *Word* 41: 47–67.

Shopen, Timothy, ed. 1985. *Language Typology and Linguistic Description*. 3 vols. Cambridge: Cambridge University Press.

Smith, Carlota S. 1986. "A speaker-based approach to aspect," *Linguistics and Philosophy* 9: 97–115.

—— 1991. *The Parameter of Aspect (Studies in Linguistics and Philosophy, 43)*. Dordrecht: Kluwer.

Sperber, Dan and Wilson, Deirdre. 1986. *Relevance: Communication and cognition*. Cambridge: Cambridge University Press.

Steinberg, Danny and Jakobovits, Leon, eds, *Semantics: An Interdisciplinary*

Reader in Philosophy, Linguistics, and Psychology. Cambridge: Cambridge University Press.

Talmy, Leonard. 1975. "Semantics and the syntax of motion," in Kimball, J. P., ed., *Syntax and Semantics 4* (New York: Academic Press), 181–238.

—— 1985. "Lexicalization patterns: Semantic structure in lexical forms," in Shopen 1985, 57–149.

Tedeschi, Philip and Zaenen, Annie, eds. 1981. *Tense and Aspect (Syntax and Semantics, 14)*. New York: Academic Press.

Tench, Paul. 1990. *The Roles of Intonation in English Discourse*. Frankfurt am Main: Peter Lang.

Tesnière, Lucien. 1959. *Éléments de Syntaxe Structurale*. Paris: Klincksieck.

Trier, Jost. 1934. Das sprachliche Feld: Eine Auseinandersetzung, *Neue Jahrbücher für Wissenschaft und Jugendbildung* 10: 428–49.

Vendler, Zeno. 1967. *Linguistics in Philosophy*. Ithaca, NY: Cornell University Press.

Viberg, Ake. 1983. "The verbs of perception: A typological study," *Linguistics* 21: 123–62.

Vlach, Frank. 1981. "The semantics of the progressive," in Tedeschi and Zaenen 1981: 271–90.

Wardhaugh, Ronald. 1993. *Investigating Language: Central Problems in Linguistics*. Oxford: Blackwell.

Wierzbicka, Anna. 1987. *English Speech Act Verbs*. Canberra: Academic Press.

Index of lexemes

Index of names

Index of technical terms